What to Expect and How to Respond

What to Expect and How to Respond

Distress and Success in Academia

Earl Wright II and Thomas C. Calhoun

ROWMAN & LITTLEFIELD
Lanham • Boulder • New York • London

Published by Rowman & Littlefield
A wholly owned subsidiary of The Rowman & Littlefield Publishing Group, Inc.
4501 Forbes Boulevard, Suite 200, Lanham, Maryland 20706
www.rowman.com

Unit A, Whitacre Mews, 26-34 Stannary Street, London SE11 4AB

British Library Cataloguing in Publication Information Available

Library of Congress Cataloging-in-Publication Data

ISBN 978-1-4758-2744-6 (cloth : alk. paper) -- ISBN 978-1-4758-2745-3 (pbk. : alk. paper) -- ISBN 978-1-4758-2746-0 (electronic)

∞ ™ The paper used in this publication meets the minimum requirements of American National Standard for Information Sciences Permanence of Paper for Printed Library Materials, ANSI/NISO Z39.48-1992.

Printed in the United States of America

This book is dedicated to Thomas C. Calhoun. Over your career you unhesitatingly and enthusiastically mentored scores of undergraduate and graduate students, including me. Without your excellent guidance and friendship it is quite possible that I may have experienced academic horror stories similar to those portrayed in this volume. Thank you for your selflessness in serving as a mentor to me and many, many others.
With love and respect, Earl Wright II

Contents

Preface

While attending a sociology conference a few years back, the editors of this book became engaged in conversation with colleagues while having cocktails. The conversation began with general summaries of each person's semester to that point and their thoughts on the research paper presentations and talks they had heard on that day. After these topics were exhausted, the real conversations began.

Our colleagues, ranging from newly minted junior faculty to senior administrators, began to discuss their current or past challenges and obstacles in academia. We listened carefully and thoughtfully to each account expressed. The experiences recounted in these conversations included, but were not limited to, workplace sexual harassment, administrative retaliation, and the challenges of attempting to obtain tenure and promotion. Each account was even more difficult to listen to and fully comprehend than the previous. At one point, a contributor of this volume proclaimed, "These are really some horror stories! My God, how could one possibly survive such hostile environments such as those?"

After the group conversation ended, we debriefed one another to more fully grasp what we had just experienced. We both agreed the experiences shared with us were traumatic. We were also in agreement that those experiences were not the singular province of the members of that specific group of people. We both have experienced, witnessed, and/or been told similar accounts of academic horror stories.

What crystalized at that moment was the idea that there existed no book in the academic literature that directly articulated the challenges experienced in academia while offering solutions to address the obstacles presented. What we had conceived was an edited collection that academics across disciplines could use as a resource to learn about potential challenges they may experience as well as techniques to overcome the obstacles placed before them. It was at this point that we decided to gather the experiences of junior and senior faculty, as well as administrators, into this volume.

In part I, emphasis is centered on the challenges experienced by graduate students, caused by chilly departmental climates, cultural obstacles for international students, and the job-search process. Graduate students, and those soon to be, will find this section beneficial as they are offered tools with which to address situations that could easily be placed before them.

In "*Cuentos* and *Testimonios*: Professional Socialization into Academia," Alma L. Zaragoza-Petty examines the challenges of Hispanic students through the voice of a Latina doctoral student who articulates the importance of community, institutional *buy-in* on diversity, and departmental collegiality. The chilly classroom and departmental climate is a real challenge for many Latino/a students, and this chapter includes several recommendations to overcome the specific set of challenges this Latina experienced. The graduate school experience is difficult for the vast majority of students. However, for international students, the challenges are uniquely different from their domestic peers.

In "Hanging by a Thread: International Students Reaching for the American Dream," Cristina S. Stephens and Elena Gheorghiu outline the ways that the experiences of international students differ from their peers. From obtaining the proper visa to enter the country, to selecting a place to live sight unseen, to negotiating where one will live when university residences are closed during holiday and break seasons, this chapter provides insight into the challenges experienced by this group of students that can be useful in helping their fellow graduate students, faculty, and administrators better understand their unique situation and, hopefully, construct policy to alleviate some of the challenges experienced by this group of students.

The concluding chapter in part I examines the job-search process. In "Gritty Tales of Tenure-Track Job Seekers in Academia," Thomas Hochschild outlines the process of obtaining a job in academia. From completing the online application, to conducting Skype interviews, to negotiating and managing the varied personalities that one meets at an on-campus interview, the author offers a guide of what to expect and how to (and how not to) respond for job seekers as well as faculty and administrators participating in the job-search process.

Part II builds on the previous section and offers those already working in academia a glimpse into what they may experience once they have secured a job. The authors in this section offer unique insights into the service demands within academia and how to embrace the beauty of the word *no* when appropriate. They also offer insights into the challenges of entering and maintaining a long-distance relationship with a significant other who is also an academic and how to negotiate the expectations of working in a *publish-or-perish* academic environment.

Deborah L. Smith and Brian J. Smith, in their chapter titled "Paperwork, Meetings, and Program Review: The Challenges of University Teaching in the 21st Century," expound on the notion that, generally speaking, the working conditions of academics relative to those in more physical-labor intensive professions are largely positive and that they understand how fortunate they are to be professors. However, they ultimately conclude that if academics do not learn to say no to excessive paperwork, meetings, and program review and assessment requests, they may find themselves in the starring role of an academic horror story where the climax of the film is their denial of tenure.

Another potential academic horror story is one's attempt to maintain a long-distance relationship with a significant other who is also an academic. In the chapter "Honeymooning Alone: On the Challenges of Dual-Career Long-Distance Academic Couples," Breanne Fahs discusses the challenges of dual-career academic couples engaged in long-distance relationships. Fahs weaves existing investigations on academic couples into her analysis of the challenges of maintaining long-distance marriages and, ultimately, offers several policy recommendations that institutions could embrace in order to better support academic couples, maximize research productivity, and boost faculty morale.

The final chapter in this section emphasizes "what to do after you have the job" and examines the stratified and sometimes complicated process of publishing in top peer-reviewed journal outlets within a publish-or-perish culture. In "Who Publishes in Leading Sociology Journals (1965–2010)?" by Robert Perrucci, Mangala Subramaniam, and Carolyn C. Perrucci, the authors review the top-ranked sociology journals between 1965 and 2010 to ascertain if there is a correlation between one's publishing in a top-tier journal and their graduation from a top-tier doctoral program. The authors conclude that there are very high rates of publication in the leading sociology journals by those from elite or hidden elite programs, and they explore the role of competitive social closure and knowledge social closure on the high rates of publication for the authors identified.

Part III centers on some of the potential pitfalls and challenges that exist at a variety of institutions. The authors in this section address divisions within departments based on intellectual hegemony, religion, ethnicity, and race. In so doing, the authors offer strategies and solutions promoting resilience and determination.

For example, in "The Tyranny of the Majority: A Case Study of Intellectual Exclusion in Sociology," Joseph Michalski examines how, under certain conditions, academic departments exercise intellectual hegemony through a dominant culture that helps ensure the perpetuation of particular paradigms, to the detriment and possible exclusion of other perspectives. Grounded in the work of Alexis de Tocqueville, the author discusses how the exultation of one paradigm, whether theoretical or methodological, can have a detrimental impact on a department. He ultimately concludes that a plurality of paradigms better serves students, faculty, and institutions.

In "Two Professors and Their Stories from a Tiny College," the authors construct a narrative that examines the ethnic and religious challenges experienced by faculty at a small southern liberal arts institution. They conclude that, despite the racial and religious challenges that some academics experience, their presence is needed at institutions like theirs to provide sound recommendations for a variety of relevant areas so that students will have faculty allies.

Using a critical-race-theory lens, "Down the Rabbit Hole: Racism and Microaggressions at a Public New England University" by Shanette M. Harris and Donald Cunnigen argue that the majority of faculty of color who choose employment at predominately white institutions will eventually come face-to-face with their powerlessness in an environment where their realities are seldom confirmed and often challenged by those who hold power and privilege. Ultimately, the microaggressions experienced by faculty of color, according to the authors, will wake them from their *Alice in Wonderland*–like slumber and into action against the forces of negativity.

Part IV focuses on the strategies that one can employ to overcome personal and professional tragedy in academia. Whether dealing with the trauma of a mass school shooting, developing supportive friendship/collegial networks to navigate life in academia, or understanding the best practices in successfully traversing the tenure and promotion process, the authors in this section emphasize agency and one's ability to be successful in academia once given the right tools and environmental conditions.

Bobbi A. Knapp, in the chapter titled "We Are All Huskies: Constructing a Collective Memory after the Tragedy at Northern Illinois University," offers an account of the Valentine's Day 2008 shooting at Northern Illinois University where, in less than two minutes, six students (including the gunman) were killed and eighteen wounded. Knapp examines how university administrators attempted to construct an institutional collective memory including the gunman and designed to simultaneously understand the events of that fateful day and provide guidelines on how to move forward. While such a goal may never come to fruition, Knapp concludes that all faculty members should become familiar with their university's procedures for when there is an active shooter on campus as well as for all other emergency situations.

In the chapter "Horror Stories from the Hallowed Halls of Academia: How Six Women Lived to Tell the Tale," Claire H. Procopio, Helen Tate, Kristina Horn Sheeler, Krista Hoffmann-Longtin, Sarah Feldner and Karrin Vasby Anderson report on the importance of community among friends within academia working at separate institutions. They suggest that the development of strong bonds among friends, or the *girlfriends*, within small groups can help those in academia process situations experienced and to more effectively respond to the many strange encounters that manifest in life in the academic world. Ultimately, they offer examples of the importance of community and friendship, in the hopes that this survival technique may help others overcome whatever obstacle is in their path.

The final chapter in this book offers the perspectives of administrators on the tenure and promotion process. In "Turning Nightmares into Victories: Handling Promotion and Tenure Horrors," Lin Huff-Corzine and Melvin Rogers draw on their more than twenty years of collective administrative experience to craft three case studies of promotion and tenure horror stories. Each case study concludes with suggestions on how a faculty member might decide to handle some of the challenges on the road to tenure and/or promotion as well as how they may look to supporters of fair practices that may be codified in the university's policies.

As a collective, the chapters in this volume are a useful tool for undergraduate students as the volume offers a glimpse into the profession they are seriously considering entering; for graduate students as it may help allay some concerns over whether the uneasiness that often accompanies the graduate school experience is unique to them; for junior faculty as it provides concrete recommendations on how to address obstacles and challenges they will face; for senior faculty as it offers a possible glimpse into their role, overtly or covertly, in creating, or not, a warm and welcoming departmental and university climate; and for administrators as it offers solid recommendations on how to proactively address problems that are certain to arise in areas including tenure and promotion and spousal hires.

It is without question that this book can potentially save current and future academics from experiencing the full brunt of horror stories and, instead, help them pass safely (or as safely as possible) through the obstacles and challenges within academia and onto the path of a successful career in academia.

I

Navigating the Academic Pipeline

Chapter One

Cuentos and *Testimonios*

Professional Socialization into Academia

Alma L. Zaragoza-Petty

Jenkins (2000) once argued that we can resist how we are racialized and that groups can strive for autonomy and self-identification. In academia, Latinx[1] scholars have accomplished this by accepting their experiential knowledge as legitimate, appropriate, and critical to understanding, analyzing, and teaching about racial subordination within the academy (Delgado Bernal 2002). Through *cuentos* and *testimonios* (stories and testimonies), presented here as a distinct form of autoethnography advanced by Latinx scholars, the experience of one Latina and how others categorized and marginalized her experiences is discussed.

Scholars in the academy have long sought to document the struggles of Latinx undergraduate and graduate students and junior and senior faculty members as a way to resist racial subordination from the margins and to challenge White racial framing in the academy (Watford et al. 2006; Feagin 2010). In examining social interactions and discourses through cuentos and testimonios, this chapter adds to the type of knowledge that is produced in doctoral training by examining what forms of power and authority are enacted via White logic and methods (Zuberi and Bonilla-Silva 2008) to shape what Latinx scholars learn and from whose perspective.

Researchers have shown how racialized communities have struggled to enter and graduate from educational systems based on white culture and values. For example, Latinx and African Americans have historically been excluded from equal educational access and opportunity (Feagin, Vera, and Imani 1996; Gloria and Castellanos 2003) through white privilege and the construction of colorblind stories about race in a higher education that upholds White racial framing (Feagin 2010; Yosso, Parker, Solórzano, and Lynn 2004).

LITERATURE REVIEW

Race in Academia

In the 1920s, social scientists, led by Robert E. Park from the Chicago school of sociology, developed the first modern analysis of race (Omi and Winant 1994). Park's seminal, although Eurocentric, work led to assumptions that continue to pervade the sociological field. Specifically, these assumptions have led to what Zuberi and Bonilla-Silva (2008) call "white logic and methods," that is, how racial considerations within the field of sociology have shaped both epistemological and methodological analyses of race. Zuberi and Bonilla-Silva suggest instead a multicultural and pluralistic approach to the sociological imagination.

In an effort to turn the gaze of the sociological imagination on itself, the once *separate but equal* contributions of scholars of color have been reexamined, and the merits of these works increasingly place them within the contested canon (Rabaka 2010). Numerous authors (Wright 2005; Zuberi and Bonilla-Silva 2008; Rabaka 2009, 2010; Wyse 2010) claim that a boundary-making mechanism constitutes what has been claimed as *real* sociological knowledge in academia through racially gendered classed power relations that have structured history, knowledge, and American sociology's historical memory and disciplinary knowledge production (Wyse 2010).

Historical and Contemporary Implications of Race

White racial framing in the United States has led to discriminatory practices against racialized communities in many sectors of society. Oliver and Shapiro (2007) illustrate how the Fair Housing Association utilized redlining practices to prevent African Americans from purchasing homes. They also presented evidence on the lack of opportunities for African Americans to take an economic detour from poverty, citing the discrimination and racist practices that impeded African Americans from opportunities in self-employment.

Pivotal in understanding how the United States has afforded white privilege on the basis of racial exclusion is the intensification of racial inequalities in wealth accumulation. This is due to many socio-historical factors, including the inability of some African Americans to obtain mortgage loans due to redlining practices, for example. Unequal practices and policies, conversely, help Whites gain significant financial advantages (Lipsitz 1995; Brown et al. 2003; Oliver and Shapiro 2007). Latino/as in the United States have also been relegated to underprivileged statuses in different but related ways to those of African Americans.

Latinxs Racialized in U.S. Context

Although much of the historical formation of racial categories has been understood from the Black/White binary, Almaguer (1994) argues that the U.S. Southwest offers a counterexample of racial understandings due to the presence of Mexicans, indigenous people, and Asians. The presence of Mexicans and other Latinxs in California offer a particularly unique contribution in the formation of racial hierarchies for several reasons.

First, some Latinxs possess physical attributes that resemble White Americans'. Second, Almaguer argues that historical realities point to a social hierarchy wherein most other ethnic groups were ranked between Mexicans and Indians with the status of Whites above all else. By making an argument for the regional differences in racial hierarchies, Almaguer argues that California's ethnic makeup problematizes previous Black/White national and historical understandings of race. Immigrant replenishment (Jiménez 2008) accounts for the continuing importance of the Latinx population in the Southwest.

Seminal local cases and U.S. Supreme Court cases since the 1930s have substantially impacted the current standing of Latinxs in educational settings (Castellanos, Gloria, and Kamimura 2006). Latinxs fought against segregation and for the right to equal education through several court cases, including: *Alvarez v. Lemon Grove School District* (1931), *Mendez v. Westminster School District* (1946, 1947), and *Delgado et al. v. Bastrop Independent School District of Bastrop County et al.* (1948) (for a complete discussion of these see Almaguer 1994). These cases point to the exclusion and unique racialization processes of Latinxs, Mexicans specifically.

Through White racial framing, Latinxs have been excluded from equal educational opportunities, thus exacerbating racial and class inequalities. Many researchers have been able to differentiate the varying experiences of Latinxs based on language, phenotype, immigration status, educational attainment, and color, among other variables (Bonilla-Silva 2003; Alba 2005; Feliciano, Lee, and Robnett 2011; Lee and Bean 2007; Jiménez 2008; Roth 2010). This differentiation is pivotal in understanding the varied experiences of Latinxs in academia.

Colorblind ideology promotes an unequal racial status quo and race-neutral policies that maintain the myth of meritocracy and Whites' investment in a racial frame that affords them an unearned advantage and dominance; the reality that people are treated differently because of their color is negated, and instead the claim is made that any person of any color can pull themselves up by their bootstraps (McIntosh 1998; Omi and Winant 1994; Brown et al. 2003). This is true in university contexts as well. Students of color continue to experience marginalization in academia as a result of colorblind ideology (Solórzano, Ceja and Yosso 2000).

THEORETICAL FRAMEWORK

The ethos of colorblind meritocracy that pervades higher educational settings and practices as well as the role it plays in racializing the experiences of underrepresented communities is challenged and repositioned in the following sections. Castellanos, Gloria and Kamimura's (2006) Latinx doctoral-student narrative analysis is used here to examine Maya's (pseudonym) experiences in a majority White doctoral program. What is taught as *appropriate* methods and *classic* theories is critiqued as White racial framing (Zuberi and Bonilla-Silva 2008).

METHODS: CUENTOS AND TESTIMONIOS

Maya is a first-generation Latinx from a working-class background. She's a doctoral student in education in Southern California where she grew up. She earned a master's degree prior to beginning her doctoral training. In the past, she balanced graduate school, being a single mother, and working part-time. Now she has received various fellowships from West Coast University that motivated her to continue her studies. She recently married and is balancing the demands of being a wife, mother, and full-time student again, after taking off a few years in a career as a college outreach counselor.

Maya's professional socialization into the academy mostly happens in informal spaces and via informal conversations with both colleagues and faculty members. In analyzing Latinx doctoral student narratives, Castellanos, Gloria, and Kamimura (2006) found six consistent patterns in Latinx doctoral experiences; while four of them are especially relevant to Maya's experiences, all six are explained first, and then the four that relate to Maya's experiences are discussed. The six student narrative analyses are:

1. *Negotiation and Context of the Training Environment* refers to the importance of navigating the educational environment during doctoral training;
2. *Discrimination Based on Gender Stereotypes* is the marginalization and exclusion from projects, based on gender stereotypes, by department peers, which limits the scholarship of Latinxs while in academia;
3. *Management of Resulting Effect* is the ways that students cope with the feelings and symptoms of working in a hostile environment and their uprooting to join doctoral programs;

4. *Solidification of Ethnic Identity* refers to the relearning and reinforcement of students' culture and cultural practices as a result of the self-questioning, marginalization, and cultural conflict prompted by adjustment to a new environment with different values and norms;

5. *Family Comes in Different Forms and Fashions* describes the university families that Latinx and other students of color establish to validate their realities and create a support system for navigating their doctoral programs;

6. *Taking Care of Business-Self-Care* is the balance between personal and professional roles that students achieve despite the racism, prejudice, cultural incongruity, and social adjustment challenges that they face in universities.

In the following sections, Maya's cuentos and testimonios are presented and are based on four patterns of the Latinx doctoral-student narrative analysis that were most relevant to the first two years of her doctoral training.

NEGOTIATION AND CONTEXT OF THE TRAINING ENVIRONMENT

During Maya's graduate application phase, some of her concerns revolved around low GRE scores and her ability to perform well in a graduate program, despite successfully earning her bachelor's and master's degrees. Because Maya is a single mother, the West Coast was her only geographical option because of her need to live near family and friends. Dealing with these doubts made the full-tuition scholarship her current graduate program offered very attractive. At the time, no other financial support for students of color was available.

During recruitment weekend, the administration in Maya's department asked other Latina graduate students in the program to organize as a group to help welcome and recruit her as well as other students of color. At first, this group seemed genuinely friendly and was one of the reasons Maya chose to commit to her department. Since then, however, these Latinas have left the program. In fact, before Maya began her program and during the few weeks into the start of the program, she heard stories about the four Latinas who had left the department.

Maya met with two of them, one currently at West Coast University and the other in another department within the same institution. It was during these conversations that her professional socialization into the academy first began. Maya learned about the hostile environment and lack of diversity in the department. Once she began her graduate studies, she learned that a faculty member she wanted to work with (also Latina) had accepted a position at another institution and was no longer in the department. Since then, another Latino faculty member has also left the department and accepted a position in another institution.

Attrition itself does not characterize a hostile environment for students of color, but primarily Latinxs leaving the department does. Maya was worried but resolved to succeed and decided to stay. Her first term was challenging, as it is for all first-time graduate students. Maya was the only Latina in her cohort. In one of her first classes, a White faculty member mentioned how Latinx peers teased her as she was growing up. Apparently, she was one of the only White students in her school.

At first Maya took this comment as normal—lots of people get teased as kids, Maya thought. The faculty member later mentioned, however, how this type of discrimination shaped her research interests. As the only Latina in class Maya felt uncomfortable by this statement. Maya was unsure whether the faculty member wanted to empathize with her or confront her for what other Latinxs had done to her. Possibly, the faculty member did not even consider Maya's feelings when making the comment. Why would she make that comment the first day of class? Maya decided to give her the benefit of the doubt.

Later in the term, a White cohort member made a comment about Latino/as. She wondered why Latino/as ate unhealthful foods. She described her experience as a tutor in an inner-city school, and could not understand why their parents let them eat Cheetos and soda and why they purposely packed these foods for them. Maya was appalled by this comment. That was not Maya's experience growing up and the statement about all Latinxs eating this way offended her.

Thankfully, the professor informed Maya's colleague that people from impoverished backgrounds sometimes need to negotiate whether to buy non-perishable long-lasting food or healthy but more expensive and perishable food—not to mention the lack of grocery stores in these neighborhoods and transportation issues related to making it to the nearest ones. Maya's colleague was not satisfied with this explanation, and despite the efforts of the class to help her understand, it was a foreign concept to this West Coast city–raised, winery-owning colleague.

Toward the end of the first term, Maya was looking ahead to the methods courses. She knew that her first-year project would require qualitative methodology; however, she was surprised by the lack of courses with philosophical grounding in interpretive research. She was also surprised by the refusal of her methods professor to teach critical epistemologies, or nonpositivist ones, despite the mid-quarter feedback she solicited on what we wanted to learn.

In fact, Maya quickly learned that senior faculty interested in similar issues to hers possessed a deficit paradigm. They sought to learn what would make students of color or those from low socioeconomic backgrounds motivated or smarter. She was also surprised by the lack of required courses in which she and her colleagues learned and acknowledged different paradigms and questioned their own paradigms because these would ultimately inform their studies.

Instead, the department upheld a view of knowledge that perpetuated exploitation and privilege by denying *othered* knowledge, situating educational inequality within a humanity as historically developed into a racially gendered, classed, capitalist world system (Cabral 1970). Maya now understood why Latino/as before had left the department; without acknowledgment of various types of knowledge their very existence was invalidated.

DISCRIMINATION BASED ON RACIAL AND GENDER STEREOTYPES

Rather than leave and uproot her family, Maya decided to stay and become more involved. She thought that by doing so, she could help bring more awareness and different perspectives to the current practices in the department. She became a student representative, and in this role she was excited at the prospect of attending faculty meetings and voicing student concerns. This is what Maya thought she would be able to do, but this was not the case.

The first year Maya served as a student representative she was expected to remain silent during meetings. As a Latino/a student, she did what Achor and Morales (1990) refer to as *resistance with accommodation*. She wanted to challenge and reject dominant discourses but also embrace institutional means of academic attainment, and that meant she had to follow protocol.

OVERT MARGINALITY

Universities have policies against blatant discrimination, but research has shown that Latinas continue to experience overt marginality within higher education (Nieves-Squires 1991; Watford et al. 2006). By the end of Maya's second term, the only other remaining Latina in the program drafted a letter to express her concerns to the chancellor regarding the hiring practices of the department, retention of faculty of color, and the racial climate that may have led to many students of color leaving the program. She invited others into the e-mail conversation and asked that they provide input into the letter-drafting process.

Maya attended a job talk by a Latina professor in a different department and, after contacting her directly to feel out whether she was accepting the position she had been offered, found out that she had asked for her spouse to also get hired. He would have had to be considered by our department, yet there had been no announcements of a job talk in our department. Maya really wanted to work with this Latina professor because their interests aligned very well. She did not understand why a spousal hire wasn't being pursued. She knew that the department had openings so she decided to join in drafting a letter to voice this concern.

Before receiving any feedback on the letter, a barrage of e-mails, intended to both intimidate and silence their experiences, were sent to them. In the e-mails, Maya and her colleagues were told to stop "making accusations that were only one part of the story" (i.e., their part). It was clear that what they had to say as Latinas was not considered the real story but a partial and, by implication, unimportant one. Another student told them that "some attrition is expected in every program," and that they "should get the facts straight before forwarding such a document." What was clear in that statement was that "their thoughts, beliefs and feelings were not 'facts.'"

This language invalidated Maya's experiences and overtly marginalized her. Others were told "when this hit the open, there was going to be a lot of taking sides and hostility between students, faculty, and others. . . . That's not something you want to see and we hope that's not something anyone else here wants to see." This type of language was used to intimidate Maya and her colleagues, and it worked. They decided not to voice their concerns.

Days later, Maya found out that a White colleague, who had not been invited to view the letter, had been shown the letter and talked to a faculty member about it. This made Maya feel further marginalized and upset because she had abandoned her desire to help draft the letter, yet someone else who did not take part in writing those concerns decided to present them to faculty anyway. She mentioned this to some of her cohort members during a finals week study session and days later she was cornered and confronted by two White colleagues.

They wanted to know why Maya told everyone that she knew they had shown the letter to a faculty member. One of them waited outside Maya's classroom while she took a three-hour final exam to let her know what she had done was *slander*. This colleague was once a lawyer and Maya was afraid she would be taken to court. Maya decided to apologize in the hopes that she would not be sued.

The colleague was not satisfied with the apology and instead told Maya that she was concerned about her choices. She then offered her tips on how to be professional and how she should act. She told Maya that she should never voice her personal concerns. If Maya was struggling in the department or did not like the options within it, she was advised to be proactive and not complain. Maya was in awe. She sat through it, agreed with the statements and went home.

COVERT MARGINALITY

Most of the marginality that Maya experienced was covert, as evidenced by the lack of varying epistemological perspectives represented by both course offerings and faculty member paradigms. Course curriculum that presents race through historical relationships between African Americans and Whites is biased because it ignores how issues of race are also constructed through issues of immigration, language, and culture for Latinxs (Solórzano and Yosso 2002).

Maya was interested in studying college access issues within Latinxs, (i.e., gender differences), but when she mentioned her research interests to the White faculty she was redirected to more privileged research topics that included working with national data sets and more psychological and developmental (read as individual) understandings of school failure. She was consistently reminded to think about her future employment opportunities when she did not heed this advice. This discouraged her from pursuing both research and a life in the academy in general.

Although she was not directly told so, she felt that if she decided to have more kids, she would be seen as not taking her studies and career seriously. In general, the stories she heard from female faculty members suggested that waiting to have kids was better for one's career and employability. The lack of a nursing room made it clear that women with young babies were not welcome in her department.

MANAGEMENT OF RESULTING EFFECT

After Maya's first two terms, she felt the best thing to do was to isolate herself and no longer be involved with her department community. She did not feel supported, and the marginalization she experienced reminded her that she could not trust anyone. If she was to survive in graduate school, she would need to protect herself. She withdrew from everyone except her faculty advisor, who had now become her mentor. Besides her advisor, family, and close friends, she spoke to no one else in the department. She began to feel alienated and displaced.

She could not turn to close friends and family for comfort or understanding because they had no idea or suggestions on how to deal with these professional socialization issues. In fact, most of her close friends and family were unaware of what she was experiencing in the department. As a first-generation high school and college graduate, Maya's family became her source of support and encouragement, and she was reminded of how proud they were for her to have come so far in her schooling. However, they did not have the knowledge or experience in these environments to guide her.

SOLIDIFICATION OF ETHNIC IDENTITY

As recruitment season for the department was getting closer, Maya's cohort was assigned to assist in organizing the event. When she first saw the Spanish surnames in some of the admitted students she became excited again and hopeful that more Latinas in the program would mean more support and camaraderie. She decided to seek out the new scholars of color. It regenerated and reenergized her and provided a sense of hope to see more people who looked like her in this setting. Maya would no longer be one of the only Latinas in the program.

Similarly to how she was professionally socialized by the two Latinas prior to entering her program, she felt it her duty to warn prospective students using as few details as possible about the climate of the department. She did not want to scare them away, but she also wanted to prepare them for what might hit them when they finally started the program. Maya also extended her support to them and continued to mentor them. She has since sought out more opportunities to create counterspaces in which she is supported as a scholar with valid research interests.

She negotiated being able to speak in faculty meetings at the beginning of her second year and can now report back to students what was discussed. Although what she reports is edited by administration, being privy to the process allowed her to gain professional socialization into the academy. She could either be upset and leave the systemic marginalization she experienced behind or learn how to work within the system and continue to challenge dominant discourses and paradigms. On some days, Maya feels like leaving, but on other days, she feels renewed and excited again about how her research could be used as a tool to challenge the status quo.

FINAL THOUGHTS

The methodology of cuentos and testimonios may not be understood as knowledge, due to White racial framing and the resulting White logic and methods prevalent in academia, but Maya's experiences and feelings of marginalization are real. When students of color voice their concerns, silencing them or telling them to stop whining or complaining further marginalizes them. Telling them to use more *appropriate* methods and *classic* theories upholds White racial framing.

In educational settings and practices, there is an ethos of colorblind meritocracy. When people challenge that paradigm, those invested in their Whiteness will experience discomfort. Open and transparent dialogue in decision-making processes can help students of color feel included and help inform other students of their privilege. Even at the graduate level and in academia,

Latinx and other racialized communities continue to struggle against hegemonic and privileged beliefs, norms, and discourses.

Currently, diversity and colorblind rationales inform admission and retention policies and practices in academia. But researchers have shown these rationales only benefit White students (Solórzano and Yosso 2002). Drawing on Maya's experiences as a racialized minority scholar, one can better understand her perspective in an institution that privileges Whites. This challenges Eurocentric and patriarchal paradigms as well as institutions that claim to value diversity, but do little to create or maintain environments that are welcoming for students of color (Watford et al. 2006).

The experiential knowledge of people of color is legitimate, appropriate, and critical to understanding, analyzing, and teaching about racial subordination. Cuentos and testimonios (stories and testimonies) helped to define Maya's professional socialization into academia as a Latina scholar and refute how others categorize and marginalize her experiences and the experiences of those like her.

NOTE

1. Latinx is used to acknowledge gender neutrality.

REFERENCES

Achor, Shirley, and Aida Morales. 1990. "Chicanas Holding Doctoral Degrees: Social Reproduction and Cultural Ecological Approaches." *Anthropology & Education Quarterly 21*(3), 269–87.

Alba, Richard. 2005. "Bright vs. Blurred Boundaries: Second-Generation Assimilation and Exclusion in France, Germany, and the United States." *Ethnic and Racial Studies 28*(1), 20-49.

Almaguer, Tomas. 1994. *Racial Fault Lines: The Historical Origins of White Supremacy in California.* Berkeley and Los Angeles: University of California Press.

Bonilla-Silva, Eduardo. 2003. "New Racism, Color Blind Racism, and the Future of Whiteness in America." In Ashley W. Doane and Eduardo Bonilla-Silva (Eds.), *White Out: The Continuing Significance of Racism* (271–84). New York: Routledge.

Brown, Michael K., Martin Carnoy, Elliot Currie, Troy Duster, David B. Oppenheimer, Marjorie. M. Shultz, and David Wellman. 2003. "Of Fish and Water: Perspectives on Racism and Privilege." In Michael K. Brown, Martin Carnoy, Elliot Currie, Troy Duster, David B. Oppenheimer, Marjorie M. Shultz, and David Wellman (Eds.), *Whitewashing Race: The Myth of a Color-Blind Society.* (34–65). Berkeley and Los Angeles: University of California Press.

Cabral, Amilcar. 1970. "National Liberation and Culture." In J. Ayo Langley (Ed.), *Ideologies of Liberation in Black Africa, 1856–1970: Documents on Modern African Political Thought from Colonial Times to the Present* (703–21). London: R. Collings.

Castellanos, Jeanett, Alberta M. Gloria, and Mark Kamimura (Eds.). 2006. *The Latina/o Pathway to the Ph.D.: Abriendo.* Sterling, VA: Stylus.

Delgado Bernal, Dolores. 2002. "Critical Race Theory, Latino Critical Theory, and Critical Raced-Gendered Epistemologies: Recognizing Students of Color as Holders and Creators of Knowledge." *Qualitative Inquiry 8*(1), 105–26.

Feagin, Joe R. 2010. *The White Racial Frame: Centuries of Racial Framing and Counter-Framing.* New York: Routledge.

Feagin, Joe R., Hernan Vera, and Nikitah Imani. 1996. *The Agony of Education. Black Students at White Colleges and Universities.* New York: Routledge.

Feliciano, Cynthia, Rennie Lee, and Belinda Robnett. 2011. "Racial Boundaries among Latinos: Evidence from Internet Daters' Racial Preferences." *Social Problems 58*(2), 189–212.

Gloria, Alberta M. and Jeanett Castellanos. 2003. "Latino/a and African American Students at Predominantly White Institutions: A Psychosociocultural Perspective of Educational Interactions and Academic Persistence." In Jeanett Castellanos and Lee Jones (Eds.), *The Majority in the Minority: Retaining Latina/o Faculty, Administrators, and Students* (71–92). Sterling, VA: Stylus.

Jenkins, Richard. 2000. "Categorization: Identity, Social Process, and Epistemology." *Current Sociology 48*(3), 7–25.

Jiménez, Tomas. R. 2008. "Mexican Immigrant Replenishment and the Continuing Significance of Ethnicity and Race." *American Journal of Sociology 113*(6), 1527–67.

Lee, Jennifer, and Frank D. Bean. 2007. "America's Changing Color Lines: Immigration and America's New Racial/Ethnic Divide." *Social Forces 86*(2), 561–86.

Lipsitz, George. 1995. "The Possessive Investment in Whiteness: Racialized Social Democracy and the 'White' Problem in American Studies." *American Quarterly 47*(3), 369–87.

McIntosh, Peggy. 1998. White Privilege: "Unpacking the Invisible Knapsack." In Paula S. Rothenberg (Ed.), *Race, Class, and Gender in the United States* (165–69). New York: Worth Publishers.

Nieves-Squires, Sarah. 1991. Hispanic Women: Making Their Presence on Campus Les Tenuous. Washington, DC: Association of American Colleges. (ED 334 907).

Oliver, Melvin L., and Thomas M. Shapiro. 2007. "A Sociology of Wealth and Racial Inequality." In Michael T. Martin and Marilyn Yaquinto (Eds.), *Redress for Historical Injustices in the United States: On Reparations for Slavery, Jim Crow, and the Legacies,* (91–115). Durham, NC: Duke University Press.

Omi, Michael, and Howard Winant. 1994. *Racial Formation in the United States.* New York: Routledge.

Rabaka, Reiland. 2010. *Against Epistemic Apartheid: W. E. B. Du Bois and the Disciplinary Decadence of Sociology.* Lanham, MD: Lexington Books.

Roth, Wendy D. 2010. "Racial Mismatch: The Divergence between Form and Function in Data for Monitoring Racial Discrimination of Hispanics." *Social Science Quarterly 91*(5), 1288–1311.

Solórzano, Daniel G., and Tara J. Yosso 2002. "Critical Race Methodology: Counter-Storytelling as an Analytical Framework for Education Research." *Qualitative Inquiry 8*(1), 23–44.

Solórzano, Daniel G., Miguel Ceja, and Tara Yosso. 2000. "Critical Race Theory, Racial Microaggressions, and Campus Racial Climate: The Experiences of African American College Students." *Journal of Negro Education 69*(1–2), 60–73.

Wacquant, Loic. 2002. "From Slavery to Mass Incarceration: Rethinking the 'Race Question.'" In Michael H. Tonry (Ed.), *Why Punish? How Much?: A Reader on Punishment,* (41–60). New York: Oxford University Press.

Watford, Tara, Martha A. Rivas, Rebecca Burciaga, and Daniel G. Solórzano. 2006. "Latinas and the Doctorate: The 'Status' of Attainment and Experiences from the Margin." In Jeanett Castellanos, Alberta M. Gloria, and Mark Kamimura. (Eds.), *The Latina/o Pathway to the Ph.D.: Abriendo Caminos,* (113–33). Sterling, VA: Stylus.

Wright, Earl II. 2005. "W. E. B. Du Bois and the Atlanta Sociological Laboratory." *Sociation-Today 3*(1). Retrieved Oct. 1 2015 (http://www.ncsociology.org/sociationtoday/v31/outline5.htm)

Wyse, Jennifer P. 2013. "American Sociology: History and Racially Gendered Classed Knowledge Reproduction." *Journal of Historical Sociology 27*(1), 49–74.

Yosso, Tara J., Laurence Parker, Daniel G. Solórzano, and Marvin Lynn. 2004. "From Jim Crow to Affirmative Action and Back Again: A Critical Race Discussion of Racialized Rationales and Access to Higher Education." *Review of Research in Education 28*, 1–25.

Zuberi, Tufuku, and Eduardo Bonilla-Silva (Eds.). 2008. *White Logic, White Methods: Racism and Methodology*. Lanham, MD: Rowman & Littlefield.

Chapter Two

Hanging by a Thread

International Students Reaching for the American Dream

Cristina S. Stephens and Elena Gheorghiu

When Anna was accepted in a PhD program in the United States she knew "she had made it." She was finally going to study in a "civilized place" and had won the ticket to a better life! "Academic civilization" meant access to libraries with hundreds of thousands of books, databases replete with cutting-edge research articles, labs with plenty of computers, shiny campus facilities, and pristine landscapes where carefree students played Frisbee on lushly green grass.

These were images she had seen on American university websites. She walked on clouds from the moment she received the acceptance letter in Bucharest, Romania, until the day she arrived at her graduate program in the American Southwest in August 2009.

INTERNATIONAL STUDENTS IN THE UNITED STATES

Anna, whose confessions appear intermittently throughout the text, is one of the tens of thousands of international students who have entered the United States in recent years and whose numbers have increased steadily over the past two decades. Driven by the imperatives of a rapidly rising global economy, cross-national student mobility has become a pervasive phenomenon.

With a share of 21% of all students studying abroad, the United States remains the top destination for international students globally (Ruiz 2013). The most talented and driven of them target leading research universities holding promises of dizzying social mobility. The academic year 2012–2013 registered a record high of 900,000 international students enrolled in U.S.

colleges and universities at both the undergraduate and graduate levels, reflecting a 7% growth from the previous year (IIE 2013a).

According to the U.S. Department of Commerce, international students contribute more than $22.7 billion to the U.S. economy. Enthusiastic supporters tout international education as a vital builder of global business ties, promoter of cross-cultural collaboration, and supporter of knowledge exchange between global communities. Signaling the relatively low participation of American students in international education, policy makers have issued recommendations that Americans make a more concerted effort to avail themselves of opportunities to study abroad (IIE 2013b).

Developing countries like China, India, South Korea, and Saudi Arabia have contributed most to the recent surge in international students (MPI 2012). Asians make up more than 63% of the international student population with China and India alone claiming 40% of the international student body (IIE 2013a). Developed countries send a very small percentage— France 1%, Germany 1.2%, United Kingdom 1.2%—whereas Eastern Europe sends approximately 3% of the total number of international students to the United States (IIE 2013c).

Drawing on Anna's real-life experiences, this chapter highlights the uniquely vulnerable position of international students from developing and underdeveloped countries who come to the United States with no source of financial support besides a research or teaching assistantship. Often recruited as tokens of cultural diversity or talent presumably difficult to find domestically, many of these students embark on legally and financially unsustainable academic trajectories that can become veritable *weak links* in a higher education system increasingly called upon to reconcile internationalization imperatives with dwindling institutional resources.

LEGAL IRON CAGES AND FINANCIAL BOTTLENECKS

To come to the United States as an international student, applicants must secure a letter of acceptance from an American university, which allows them to apply for an F-1 visa at the American consulate in their home country. The applicant must bring evidence that they possess sufficient funds to support themselves in the United States during their studies.

Although some international students are self-payers, approximately 21% obtain the nonimmigrant F-1 visa based exclusively on the assistantship offered from the accepting American university (IIE 2013a). This arrangement is often encountered among graduate students from developing and underdeveloped nations who do not count among the local elites. As their families cannot offer financial support, the risk of insurmountable financial problems during their stay abroad is considerable.

The appeal of studying in the United States or even finding a legal immigration path, however, is often too strong to deter such students from seizing the opportunity. Intentional or not, both individual and institutional underestimations of the real cost, time, and effort required of a foreign student to complete a graduate degree have become increasingly visible and problematic.

A graduate assistantship typically includes tuition exemption and a small stipend paid in exchange for 20 hours of research/teaching activities per week. The student is not legally allowed to work off campus, and the university cannot employ the student for more than the maximum of 20 hours a week. Working anywhere else is illegal and can result in visa annulment and immediate deportation.

Yet most academic departments do not guarantee more than three to four years of funding. This assumes it will be possible for the student to complete the graduate program during this period, despite evidence that the average time to complete a PhD program in the United States is six to ten years (Gravois 2007). Unlike their American counterparts, international students do not qualify for student loans, and credit card limits seldom exceed $500. With much less generous lines of credit than American banks, financial institutions in less developed nations do not typically grant student loans.

Although assistantships include tuition waivers, institutional fees are not subject to exemption. These dues have been escalating at similar rates as tuition; often reaching amounts as high as double the graduate monthly stipend. As resorting to alternative sources of income is legally impossible for such international students, their academic careers are often at risk of turning into financial bottlenecks long before graduation is on the horizon.

HOUSING BLUES AND FRUGALITY OLYMPICS

International students must obtain their visas several months ahead of program start dates, yet they cannot enter the country earlier than 30 days before that date (U.S. Department of State 2014). This forces them to find a roommate on the Internet without meeting them prior. Anna reflected on her experience, saying, "First, you cannot meet the person you will live with. Yet a roommate is an absolute necessity because the graduate stipend does not allow for independent living arrangements. As the university is not involved in these private arrangements, the personal risks associated with setting up something from a distance cannot be underestimated.

"Second, you must pay the deposit and the one-month-rent online. The international transaction adds substantial fees to the original amount. With the Romanian average monthly net income of approximately $400, a deposit of $300, a rent of $800 and bank fees of $150 are virtually impossible to pay in one installment.

"If this little fortune can somehow be produced, the fear that the apartment complex found online may be a scam can easily turn into sheer panic.

"Despite these risks, one must take the leap of faith. You tell yourself the opportunity is for the seizing and is worth taking any risk, after all."

It is difficult to know where to begin, so the first instinct was to look for a co-national in the university area.

Although Anna knew it was high-time to switch to a more self-reliant mindset, she did not have the luxury to take on an individualist's identity just yet. She felt incredibly lucky to find a Romanian graduate student in the Biology Department who turned out to be providentially helpful.

Andreea picked Anna up from the airport, allowed her to stay in her apartment on campus and eventually transferred her apartment lease to Anna's name as she had to move to another city. She even left her bed and a few cooking utensils, which Anna later shared with her Greek roommate.

As the semester unfolded, Anna learned to perfect the art of frugality. As a graduate student she had expected to take a poverty vow. She took pride in the modest meals she prepared with very basic ingredients, her habit of never leaving a light on unless in use and her ability to clean just about anything with vinegar and baking soda. Purchasing a clothing item had to be absolutely necessary and only from Goodwill.

Their room had no furniture besides the bed left from Andreea, but they had heard other international students talking about "dumpster treasures." Anna and her roommate began watching the garbage area in the apartment complex in the hope of finding some unwanted pieces. Soon enough, the patron saint of trickle-down furniture heard them, and they were pleased to bring in a study desk and a table.

But wait, there was more. They soon discovered the patron had also thrown in a bonus. Unable to identify the source of a tormenting itchy rash that had set in all over their bodies, Anna and her roommate ended up at the university's medical office where they were prescribed a topical treatment for scabies. It was a violent hit to their budget, but there was no other way to address the problem. Per practitioner's instructions, they applied the cream all over their bodies and left it on without removing clothes for 48 hours.

Having made the unfortunate mistake of applying the cream before bed, Anna realized she had to walk to school the next day in pajamas. After all, American children had Pajama Days at school sometimes. Why not them? It turned out acculturation came in many different shapes and sizes. As weeks went by without any sign of treatment success, Anna began to investigate the appearance of their blisters on the Internet.

Begging to differ from the diagnostic they had received, Google said "bed bugs." The only way to find out for sure was to catch them in action right before dawn. Armed with an alarm clock and a borrowed flashlight, they woke up at night to find the culprit of their dermal sorrows frolicking in their beds. After a futile battle against the invaders they moved out of the apartment.

BLOATING TERMINAL FEES

Financially limited international students must engage in extreme frugality Olympics to save for the bloating and mandatory institutional fees due at the beginning of each semester. These fees include items such as sports and recreation, athletics, student activities, global learning, wellness center, and excellence fees. Health insurance premiums make up the largest percent of the fee total (approximately 50%), and they are mandatory despite poor coverage.

In the past, the fees represented a small enough percent of the graduate stipend to allow the student to save for them during the previous semester. Currently, these fees have reached amounts that can no longer be controlled with savings, no matter how ruthless. It is not unusual that a graduate student will net a monthly stipend of $1,200, only to be required to pay $2,200 in institutional fees per semester.

Although some universities allow students to pay these fees in monthly installments, others require the full amount upfront. This translates into a situation where the international student without supplemental funds is eventually faced with not being able to eat, pay rent, or pay for transportation for sixty days in a row.

Financial problems further escalate over the summer when fewer employment opportunities are available. With the need for teaching/research assistants declining, many international students are left without the only legal employment they can hold. Although larger universities may have some on-campus job opportunities in their international offices, cafeterias, or janitorial/custodial services, these opportunities have been drastically affected by recent budget cuts, and many universities do not have them at all.

While American students and international students with supplemental financial resources may opt for working off-campus summer jobs, using student loans, relying on parental financial help, or simply going home, assistantship-dependent international students cannot consider trips home, given the onerous price of plane tickets.

When a more seasoned fellow-Romanian student asked Anna how she was going to pay the rent over the summer she replied that she was going to be a teaching/research assistant for the next four years. Anna was not aware that assistantships were not available during the summer. She had to figure out something on her own. Her friend advised her to apply for a custodian position like other internationals she knew. By the time she applied, the positions were filled, and she was left with no income for the summer.

INTERNATIONAL STUDENTS AT THE INTERSECTION OF SOCIAL SUPPORT DISRUPTION AND ACCULTURATIVE STRESS

One of the most significant challenges international students encounter is a severe disruption in social support networks. While regular immigrants may arrive accompanied by family members, international students often experience a complete loss of social support in addition to their financially and legally circumscribed trajectories. Social support has been defined as: important instrumental, informational, and emotional functions performed for the individual by a variety of primary or secondary *others.*

These functions may encompass a wide array of supportive behaviors including material help, informational guidance, companionship and demonstrations of caring, empathy, and opportunity to relate (Cohen and McKay 1984; House et al. 1985). The culturally universal importance of social support has been confirmed by decades of research and has been repeatedly linked to increased quality of life, mental health, and longevity (Helgeson 2003; Uchino 2004; Cohen and Janiki-Deverts 2009; Umberson and Montez 2010; Thoits 2011a).

Recent findings reveal that the impact of social relationships on mortality risk is comparable with that of well-established risk factors such as smoking and alcohol consumption and may even exceed the influence of other factors such as physical inactivity and obesity (Holt-Lunstad, Smith and Layton 2010). Sources of social support can include both *significant others*—family, close relatives, and close friends—as well as secondary groups such as colleagues, mentors, or members of voluntary organizations.

The former are generally deemed to be more emotionally invested in the individual's well-being and more likely to extend assistance; both routinely and in times of need (Messeri, Silverstein, and Litwak 1993). Thoits (2011b) argues, however, that there are situations when the well-meaning contributions of significant others may have limited value due to experiential dissimilarity with the receiving individual's circumstances. Instead, stress-buffering help may be available from *socially similar* others who are often members of secondary groups.

Having been in a similar situation, members of secondary groups may be better equipped to offer informed coping assistance that significant others may be powerless to provide. In fortunate yet rare circumstances, individuals can benefit from the unusually effective help of significant others who are also *socially similar*. In the light of these theoretical considerations, one can argue that international students are faced with a unique deficit of both such sources of social support. Not only do they experience disruptions in primary groups, but they also encounter difficulties in securing support from secondary groups.

The summer was here—Anna's assistantship stipend ended, and she began to think of people she might know in the area. Acquaintances? Maybe a relative who may have immigrated during the communist regime? Any Good Samaritan with whom she could have claimed the weakest association might have been willing to host her for two months, thus saving her from abandoning the program.

After a few days, Anna's mother wrote that she was able to get in touch with Ioana, a distant cousin who was living in a nearby state and who had recently retired. Despite few hopes, Anna contacted her aunt and confessed her situation. Kinship aside, she was a virtual stranger. Yet Ioana turned out to be incredibly kind and hosted her for two months over the summer.

Once again, Anna realized how precarious her situation was. Had it not been for the benevolence of this accidental acquaintance, she would have had to quit her studies, wasting years of effort and resources. Ironically, in the land of self-determination, a Romanian proverb kept ringing in her ears with its relaxed sense of reliance on providential intervention: "God always builds a nest for the one-eyed stork." She was certainly starting to feel like the proverbial one-eyed stork. Yet little did she know the stork was going to become even more disabled soon.

At the end of July Anna returned to the university, where she moved into a new apartment with a co-national student. One day while riding her bicycle to Wal-Mart, she bumped into a sidewalk and fell off the bike. Upon attempting to get up, she realized she could not move her arms. She had broken them both. She was now sitting in the middle of the road waiting for someone to drive by so she could ask them to take the cellphone from her backpack and call an ambulance. Some students stopped soon and called for help immediately.

Anna arrived home around 8 p.m. with her arms bent in casts from the wrists up to the shoulders. She was no longer in pain but it suddenly dawned on her how concomitantly amusing and absurd this situation was. She wondered how many people manage to break both arms at the same time. The stork was now armless, too, and God was going to have to build a very substantial nest for her.

Sipping water from a straw, she did not realize the trip to the bathroom was getting closer with every sip.

Up to that point, her only concern had been how she was going to pull her hair in a ponytail. She had not yet thought of more basal aspects of her human existence: how was she going to eat? dress? wash? visit the bathroom and leave it with dignity?

The next day, it became clear that she was going to need someone at her beck and call until the doctors would decide to remove the casts. Anna didn't know a soul in the world who could possibly perform these types of tasks for her. Her roommate was out most of the day and even if she hadn't been, Anna didn't feel she could have expected this kind of help from her. Neither could she pay for any formal services.

For lack of a viable alternative, Anna called her aunt—again. They had just parted two weeks before, and she was pleased to finally restore her aunt's space and privacy. Embarrassment, frustration, anger, and power-lessness all set in at once. She wanted to throw her hands up, drop it all right then and there, and go home. Yet her hands could do neither throwing, nor dropping, and going home was not an option at that moment.

Due perhaps to a miraculously preserved sense of extended family ties, Ioana turned into a bottomless well of altruism when she drove several hours to help. Anna was at a loss for words when it came to expressing her grati-tude. Here was yet another opportunity to have her faith in humanity but-tressed, yet she felt it was high time for these opportunities to just quit showing up.

Ioana helped her with feeding, dressing, and grooming for a week. Anna's brain, though, was stuck in self-sufficiency mode when it came to handling bathroom-related imperatives, so certain calls of nature were physiologically canceled for eight days.

International students' challenges are not limited to social support defi-cits, however. Albeit less conspicuous, the acculturative stress generated by value clashes related to the individualism-collectivism continuum can have a profound effect on their long-term well-being. Having been described as the most fundamental dimension of cultural differences (Triandis 2001), this continuum sits at the center of the acculturation process. Framed by a rational choice paradigm, the concept of acculturation was originally understood as a linear and relatively uncomplicated process whereby an immigrant adapts to the culture he chose to enter (Sam 2006).

Given prevalent global immigration patterns, the process implied a natu-ral transition from collectivistic to individualistic values, resulting in *assimi-lation*. The success of the acculturative journey was thought to be heavily influenced by language proficiency (Berry 1974).

Over the past several decades more sophisticated theories have evolved to expose the structural constraints, psychological stressors, coping and contest-ing strategies, and identity negotiations inherent in the acculturation experience. The efforts culminated in the bi-dimensional model (Berry 1980), presently the most widely accepted theory of acculturation to date (Rudmin 2003). Depending on the immigrant's orientation toward original and host culture, respectively, four acculturation strategies ensue.

Assimilation results when individuals shed their culture of origin while seeking frequent interactions with the local culture. *Integration* reflects a desire to maintain aspects of original culture and concomitantly adopt various elements from the host culture. When the immigrant values his culture of origin, preferring to avoid other cultural groups, the strategy adopted is *separation*. Often a result of discrimination and exclusion, *marginalization* emerges as the most psychologically vulnerable of the four strategies, with the immigrant separating from both culture of origin and host culture.

Berry (1974) cautioned early on that immigrants do not enjoy absolute freedom in choosing how to engage in intercultural relations because receiving societies may impose political, legislative, or attitudinal constraints. The extent to which a host society may favor a multicultural, *melting pot*, segregationist, or exclusionary approach to immigration impacts the attitudes immigrants develop in the process of acculturation.

Research has confirmed that international students tend to experience more psychological problems than American students, including depression, anxiety, and identity gaps that may lead to feelings of inauthenticity. These can result from the interplay of acculturation-related concerns including language barriers, academic and financial difficulties, interpersonal problems with American and co-national students, racial/ethnic discrimination, loss of social support, alienation, and homesickness (Alvarez and Lindholm 1986; Pedersen 1991; Mallinckrodt and Leong 1992; Sandhu and Asrabadi 1994; Leong and Chou 1996; Mori 2000; Padilla et al. 2007).

International students from collectivistic cultures are more likely than other types of migrants to opt for the *separation* strategy by remaining exclusively within limited groups of co-nationals (Yeh and Inose 2003). Going beyond the presumed sojourner status of international students, which may explain a lack of interest in contact with the local culture, psycho-social factors such as the need for social connectedness, close rapports, or reliable reciprocal arrangements may also come into play.

Social connectedness has been defined as an aspect of the self that manifests the subjective recognition of being in close relationship with the social world (Lee and Robbins 1995, 1998). This trait significantly decreases acculturative stress and plays an important role in the well-being of students from collectivistic backgrounds (Olivas and Li 2006).

As collectivistic students adjust to the strongly individualistic dictates of mainstream American culture, many become confused and eventually discouraged with prescripts favoring independence, assertiveness, and self-reliance in interpersonal relationships. This may cause them to perceive relationships with Americans as superficial and personally unfulfilling and to amplify alienation and perceived loss of social support (Cross 1995).

Not only can this brusque shift accelerate acculturative stress, but also students soon understand individualistic values are all but impossible to maintain without personal financial resources or the structural and legal paths to obtain them on their own.

Anna's progress in the PhD program was steady but slow because of language limitations. She learned there is a significant difference between the English required to score high enough on a TOEFL and GRE test to gain admission into a graduate program and the English necessary for progress in a doctoral social science program at the upbeat pace imposed by funding limitations.

At the pace Anna was progressing, it was becoming evident she could not complete the program during the requisite time frame. Eventually, she had to apply to another program, transfer credits, and move cross-country.

Not without nostalgia for the time spent in the Southwest and the friendships made there, Anna left the city on a rainy day. The weather was clearly not doing much to help her mood, but she had decided to maintain a positive attitude and open herself to the new and exciting academic opportunities in the South. Unfortunately, the weather was beginning to throw a serious tantrum, which culminated in all flights being canceled and passengers being required to leave the airport.

And now what? Anna decided to stay a night in the airport. If it hadn't killed Tom Hanks to live in one for several months, it wasn't going to kill her in one night. But airport authorities ordered everyone off the premise. Completely bewildered, her first instinct—most likely an inopportune cultural legacy—was to reach out to a fellow human as opposed to relying on a bank account or a credit card.

Anna called the only person she knew who was living close enough to the airport, a colleague in a nearby city. Although sympathetic to her conundrum, he was confused about her apparent inability to solve the problem with a taxi call and a quick trip to a nearby hotel. Anna knew immediately she had some more acculturation to do. Unfortunately, between the taxi and the hotel bill for one night, her wallet passed away, and her determination to follow the cultural prescriptive of self-reliance died along with it.

When the flight was postponed again the next day due to stubbornly bad weather—the hotel was no longer an option. As elegant, dignified, and strings-free self-reliance was, it was now back to fellow humans. Strings or no strings. Anna ended up calling another colleague back at the university who gave her the phone number of an acquaintance in the area.

Without the luxury of considering gender-related "stranger danger," she spent the night in the house of a man she didn't know. He turned out to be yet another reminder of the fact that most people, whether men or women, are ultimately decent human beings, and that scary stories are more likely to happen on one's screen than in one's reality. God had built yet another nest for the "one-eyed stork."

OPPORTUNISTIC ASSIMILATION AMONG INTERNATIONAL STUDENTS

Despite its appeal, the strategy of separating from mainstream American culture into the comfort zone of co-national or other culturally similar groups may have limited value for some international students. First, such relationships may be exclusively based on students' membership in *culturally captive* groups and may not necessarily involve personal affinities (Mori 2000). Second, fellow international students' ability to provide support as *socially similar others* is reduced due to their own vulnerable status in the host society.

Finally, the separation strategy can be unrealistic for internationals whose countries send a relatively small number of students to the United States. In the absence of a large enough ethnic community, such students face the risk of adopting the marginalization strategy, which has been associated with negative mental health outcomes (Berry 2002).

When compared to international students from collectivistic backgrounds such as Asia, Central/Latin America, and Africa, European students are fewer in number, they appear to experience less acculturative stress (Yeh and Inose 2003; Olivas and Li 2006), and are more likely to assimilate or integrate. Having being socialized into values closer to the individualist end of the cultural continuum, they experience less contrast in cultural patterns (Carter 1991). Literature suggests that European students also face fewer language barriers and may even benefit from positive ethnic discrimination (King 2000).

Eastern European and Balkan students, however, may constitute an exception. Uniquely positioned at the crossroads of civilizations, these cultures have historically maintained a contradictory amalgamation of traditional Christian-orthodox and Byzantine cultural heritage on the one hand, and aspirational, philo-western attitudes on the other. Thrown in the mix is a unique tendency toward negative national self-stereotyping and a constant need to negotiate the *eastern* identity (Sibii 2011).

Moreover, students from countries such as Romania, Bulgaria, former Yugoslavia, or Ukraine came of age during highly anomic decades marked by tumultuous transitions from socialist to free-market capitalist arrangements. Arriving with conflicting cultural identities and faced with a relatively small number of culturally similar fellow internationals to congregate with,

Eastern European and Balkan students may be most prone to adopting the *marginalization* strategy.

While it is entirely possible for the acculturating journeys of international students from collectivistic backgrounds to result in assimilation or integration outcomes, it is important to acknowledge that the authenticity of such outcomes often involves complex psychological and socio-cultural prerequisites. Clashes between personality and home culture, negative national identities, and cross-cultural perceptions of western superiority are all examples of such factors.

For example, the personality–culture clash hypothesis (Caldwell-Harris and Aycicegi 2006) suggests that individuals from a collectivistic background with an idiocentric personality may find the opportunity to assimilate into western society personally liberating. An idiocentric personality has been associated with inborn traits such as competitiveness, achievement orientation, self-reliance, and emotional distance. By contrast, allocentrics tend to value tradition, social connectedness, and emotional closeness (Tirandis 1995).

Students whose cultural background and personality type are both inconsistent with American society's values may be at risk of identity gaps when opting for an assimilation or integration path. These gaps result from attempts to enact and present a self fundamentally different from one's personal makeup and self-view (Jung and Hecht 2004; Jung, Hecht, and Wadsworth 2007). In such situations, assimilation or integration may amount to little more than a pragmatic, socially desirable yet psychologically inauthentic project, conducive to permanent internal conflicts and ultimately, depression (Spencer-Oatety and Xiong 2006).

The legally, financially, and culturally vulnerable status of many international students may conspire with their relative lack of power in the university structure and a general lack of social support to produce opportunistic assimilators. This acculturative strategy may display or communicate a conspicuously assimilated or integrated self that presents significant discrepancies with one's inner self. Incentives to opt for this strategy abound.

Not only do these students' legal status and livelihood depend exclusively on how competent and culturally adjusted they are perceived to be by faculty, colleagues, and their undergraduate students, but also the prospect of having to return home due to inability to adapt to the American culture may induce shame, embarrassment and a deep sense of failure.

In the Deep South it was summertime and the livin' was indeed easier. Far from being an inherently better place than the Southwest, Anna simply knew more people from her country here, including a close relative whom she could count on during "one-eyed stork" episodes. Many of her co-na-

tionals had formed cozy networks of friends and acquaintances, and it felt natural for Anna to simply join in.

Despite sundry personality types, family backgrounds, and political orientations, shared nationality seemed the main glue of these communities. Some individuals appeared to live in a small American Romania, which allowed them to successfully pursue economic opportunities without intense acculturation efforts in the private sphere. Yet others professed appreciation of the American way of life while limiting personal interactions largely to the Romanian community.

Anna remembered one of the few Romanian international students she had met at her previous university in the Southwest. Stefan was always sure to affirm what he believed to be an American identity. "Are you cooking again?" he would scoff when dropping by for a quick visit. "You know Americans don't waste their time cooking from scratch, right? You need to be more pragmatic."

Despite intense admiration for Americans' goal-oriented lives and enviable efficiency, and despite frequent complaints against antiquated Romanian mentalities, Stefan's frustrations were mounting every day. Seven years after immigrating, doctors advised him to change his diet to bring down high cholesterol levels.

He had no American friends and later confessed it took him eight years to finish his doctoral program. His committee chair was allegedly ignoring him due to who he was, including his political views. Over time Anna learned that international students must tread carefully in any interactions involving power dynamics. After all, a single C grade can cause them to lose the vital assistantship and be sent straight back home.

FINAL THOUGHTS

This chapter comprises a narrative on the backdrop of legal, institutional, and theoretical considerations that are overlooked or played down, whether intentionally or not, by enthusiastic proponents of international education. While each international student's journey is a unique experience marked by a complex interplay of individual, cultural, and socioeconomic factors, a variety of stakeholders can benefit from increased awareness of the obstacles bedeviling the international student prototype highlighted in this chapter.

Not only does the *triple whammy* of legal and financial restrictions, lack of social support, and acculturative stress destabilize the academic path of many international students, but these individual vulnerabilities can also have insidious systemic implications.

First, institutions of higher education will be prone to resource waste and possible failure in their mission to internationalize higher education if they focus exclusively on the front end of this mandate. Recruitment should be accompanied by realistic estimations of the amount of resources and efforts international students need to complete their graduate programs. As many rely exclusively on the funding package provided by the university, it is important that departments ensure assistantships will be available for realistic periods of time as long as the student remains in good academic standing.

Moreover, departments must reevaluate the often unchallenged assumptions that all international students can progress at the same pace as their equally talented American counterparts simply because they passed an English-language proficiency test. In reality, many international students make progress at a significantly slower pace than their American colleagues due to comparatively lower language proficiency and reduced cultural dexterity in securing a valuable mentorship. Financial, legal, and psychological pressures can further slow down their progress.

Assistantship-dependent internationals cannot opt for reduced class loads or breaks in the program to address personal problems, and they are also less likely to contest any perceived misevaluations of their performance. Nor should universities assume that all international students can easily acculturate or that they will all embrace the process without reservations. While formal support for the acculturation process can be helpful, encouraging informal mentor-mentee relationships between international students and interculturally competent faculty and staff might bear more fruit.

Second, American consulates and universities must share more information and better coordinate efforts in the admission and visa-granting process. When evaluating prospective students' financial resources, both academic and diplomatic institutions must remain mindful of the ever-spiraling costs of higher education, budget cuts, and stipend/fees ratios.

If consulates approve student visas based on financially unsustainable paths through the program, retention and graduation rates of international students may suffer, and resources may be wasted, to the political frustration of American constituencies. The trends can fuel anti-immigration and anti-internationalization sentiments and may even result in attempts on the part of desperate international students to resort to illegal immigration paths including fraudulent marriages and illegal employment.

Finally, we advise international students to carefully consider the overall cost of living they will face in the United States and to know exactly where funds will come from every semester, including summers. As difficult as it might be to secure additional financial resources at home before departure, it will likely be even more difficult to secure them in the United States, given legal restrictions of the right to work.

Enlisting a university's help to research supplemental funding opportunities such as grants or fellowships remains a worthwhile endeavor. It is also wise for international students to look for interculturally competent faculty mentors who are both willing and able to take the time to provide substantial feedback on projects and to offer guidance for program navigation and career planning.

Ultimately, we would caution against approaching acculturation as a choice to be made abruptly, that would invariably culminate in a socially desirable outcome. Contrary to popular opinion, acculturation, like happiness, is not a choice people make in a vacuum. It is rather a monumental psychological journey in which personality type, personal convictions, aspirations, and ideologies are delicately woven into cultural and national identities, early childhood socialization, and youth memories.

As America is becoming an increasingly diverse society, opportunities to forge relationships with both American-born individuals and internationals who can accommodate their true self are becoming more plentiful. Rather than enacting rigidly defined patterns of assimilation to fit preconceived notions of *true American-ness*, international students should be open to experience the unparalleled diversity of contemporary America and allow enough time to understand its exceptional cultural dynamics.

REFERENCES

Berry, John, W. 1974. "Acculturative Stress: The Role of Ecology, Culture and Differentiation." *Journal of Cross-Cultural Psychology* 5:382–405.

Berry, John, W. 1980. "Acculturation as Variety of Adaptation." Pp. 9–25 in *Acculturation: Theory, Models and Some New Findings*, edited by A. Padilla. Boulder, CO: Westview.

Berry, John, W. 2002. "Conceptual Approaches to Acculturation." Pp.17–37 in *Acculturation: Advances in Theory, Measurement, and Applied Research*, edited by K. M. Chun, P. B. Organista, and G. Marin. Washington, DC: American Psychological Association.

Caldwell-Harris, Catherine L., and Ayse Aycicegi. 2006. "When Personality and Culture Clash: The Psychological Distress of Allocentrics in an Individualist Culture and Idiocentrics in a Collectivist Culture." *Transcultural Psychiatry* 43(3):331–61.

Carter, Robert, T. 1991. "Cultural Values: A Review of Empirical Research and Implications for Counseling." *Journal of Counseling and Development* 70(1):164–73.

Cohen, Sheldon, and Denise Janicki-Deverts. 2009. "Can We Improve Our Physical Health by Altering Our Social Networks?" *Perspectives on Psychological Science* 4 (Special Issue):375–78.

Cohen, Sheldon, and Garth McKay. 1984. "Social Support, Stress and the Buffering Hypothesis: A Theoretical Analysis." Pp. 253–67 in *Handbook of Psychology and Health*, edited by A. Baum, S. E. Taylor, and J. E. Singer. Hillsdale, NJ: Lawrence Erlbaum.

Cross, Susan E. 1995. "Self-Construals, Coping, and Stress in Cross-Cultural Adaptation." *Journal of Cross-Cultural Psychology* 26(6):673–97.

Gravois, John. 2007. "In Humanities, 10 Years May Not Be Enough to Get a PhD." *The Chronicle of Higher Education* 53(47):A1.

Helgeson, Vicki, S. 2003. "Social Support and Quality of Life." *Quality of Life Research* 12(1):25–31.

Holt-Lunstad, Julianne, Timothy B. Smith, and Bradley J. Layton. 2010. "Social Relationships and Mortality Risk: A Meta-Analytic Review." *PLoS Med* 7(7):e1000316.

House, James S., Robert L. Kahn, Jane D. McLeod, David Williams, and Sheldon Cohen. 1985. "Measures and Concepts of Social Support." Pp. 83–108 *in Social Support and Health*, edited by S. S. Leonard. San Diego, CA: Academic Press.

Institute of International Education (IIE). 2013a. "Open Doors Report on International Educational Exchange." Retrieved April 27, 2014 (http://www.iie.org/Research-and-Publications/Open-Doors/Data/International-Students/Infographic).

Institute of International Education (IIE). 2013b. "Open Doors 2013: International Students in the United States and Study Abroad by American Students Are at All-Time High." Retrieved April 27, 2014 (http://www.iie.org/Who-We-Are/News-and-Events/Press-Center/Press-releases/2013/2013-11-11-Open-Doors-Data).

Institute of International Education (IIE). 2013c. "Open Doors Data. International Students: Leading Places of Origin." Retrieved April 27, 2014 (http://www.iie.org/Research-and-Publications/Open-Doors/Data/International-Students/Leading-Places-of-Origin/2011-13).

Jung, Eura, and Michael L. Hecht. 2004. "Elaborating the Communication Theory of Identity: Identity Gaps and Communication Outcomes." *Communication Quarterly* 52(3):265–83.

Jung Eura, Michael L. Hecht, and Brook C. Wadsworth. 2007. "The Role of Identity in International Students' Psychological Well-Being on the United States: A Model of Depression Level, Identity Gaps Discrimination and Acculturation." *International Journal of Intercultural Relations* 31:605–24.

King, Desmond. 2000. *Making Americans: Immigration, Race, and the Origins of Diverse Democracy*. Cambridge, MA: Harvard University Press.

Lee, Richard, M., and Steven B. Robbins. 1995. "Measuring Belongingness: The Social Connectedness and the Social Assurance Scales." *Journal of Counseling Psychology* 42(2):232–41.

Lee, Richard, M., and Steven B. Robbins. 1998. "The Relationship between Social Connectedness and Anxiety, Self-Esteem, and Social Identity." *Journal of Counseling Psychology* 45(3):338–45.

Leong, Frederick, T. L., and Elayne L. Chou. 1996. "Counseling International Students." Pp. 210–24 in *Counseling Across Cultures*, edited by P. B. Pedersen, J. Draguns, J. W. Lonner, J. E. Trimble. Thousand Oaks, CA: Sage Publications.

Mallinckrodt, Brent, and Frederick T. Leong. 1992. "International Graduate Students, Stress and Social Support." *Journal of College Students Development* 33(1):71–78.

Messeri, Peter, Merril Silverstein, and Eugene Litwak. 1993. "Choosing Optimal Support Groups: A Review and Reformulation." *Journal of Health and Social Behavior* 34:122–37.

Migration Policy Institute (MPI). 2012. "International Student Mobility Rises, and Countries Seek to Capitalize." Retrieved April 27, 2014 (http://www.migrationpolicy.org/article/top-10-2012-issue-9-international-student-mobility-rises-and-countries-seek-capitalize).

Mori, Sakurako, C. 2000. "Addressing the Mental Health Concerns of International Students." *Journal of Counseling and Development* 78:137–44.

Olivas, Monique, and Chi-Sing Li. 2006. "Understanding Stressors of International Students in Higher Education: What College Counselors and Personnel Need to Know." *Journal of Instructional Psychology* 33(3):217–22.

Padilla, Amadon, M., Monica Alvarez, and Kathryn J. Lindholm. 1986. "Generational Status and Personality Factors as Predictors of Stress in Students." *Hispanic Journal of Behavioral Sciences* 8(3):275–88.

Pedersen, Paul, B. 1991. "Counseling International Students." *The Counseling Psychologist* 19(1):10:58.

Rudmin, Floyd, W. 2003. "Critical History of the Acculturation Psychology of Assimilation, Separation, Integration, and Marginalization." *Review of General Psychology* (1):3–37.

Ruiz, Neil, G. 2013. "American's Foreign Students and Immigration Reform." Brookings. Retrieved April 27, 2014 (http://www.brookings.edu/blogs/up-front/posts/2013/04/09-foreign-students-ruiz).

Sam, David, L. 2006. "Acculturation: Conceptual Background and Core Components." Pp. 11–26 in *Acculturation Psychology*, edited by D. L. Sam and J. W. Berry. Cambridge: University Press.

Sandhu, Daya S., and Badioolar R. Asrabadi. 1994. "Development of an Acculturative Stress Scale for International Students: Preliminary Findings." *Psychological Reports* 75(1):435–48.

Sibii, Razvan. 2011. "National Indemnity through Prototypes and Metaphors: The Case of Romanianness." *Journal of Global Initiatives* 6(2):13–30.

Spencer-Oatety, Helen, and Zhaoning Xiong. 2006. "Chinese Student's Psychological and Sociocultural Adjustment to Britain: An Empirical Study." *Language, Culture, and Curriculum* 19(1):37–53.

Thoits, Peggy, A. 2011a. "Perceived Social Support and Voluntary, Mixed, or Pressured Use of Mental Health Services." *Society and Mental Health* 1(1):4–19.

Thoits, Peggy, A. 2011b. "Mechanisms Linking Social Ties and Support to Physical and Mental Health." *Journal of Health and Social Behavior* 52(2):145–61.

Triandis, Harry, C. 1995. *Individualism & Collectivism*. Oxford, Boulder, CO: Westview Press.

Triandis, Harry, C. 2001. "Individualism-Collectivism and Personality." *Journal of Personality* 69(6):907–24.

Uchino, Bert N. 2004. *Social Support and Physical Health: Understanding the Health Consequences of Relationships*. New Haven, CT: Yale University Press.

Umberson, Debra, and Jennifer Karas Montez. 2010. "Social Relationships and Health: A Flashpoint for Health Policy." *Journal of Health and Social Behavior* 51 (Special Issue):S54–66.

U.S. Department of State. Bureau of Consular Affairs. 2014. "Student Visa." Retrieved April 27, 2014 (http://travel.state.gov/content/visas/english/study-exchange/student.html).

Yeh, Christine J., and Mayuko Inose. 2003. "International Students' Reported English Fluency, Social Support Sanctions and Social Connectedness as Predictors of Acculturative Stress." *Counseling Psychology Quarterly* 16(1):15–28.

Chapter Three

Gritty Tales of Tenure-Track Job Seekers in Higher Education

Thomas R. Hochschild Jr.

Ever since Hannah took that Introduction to Sociology course during her freshman year, she was hooked. She was amazed to find that people systematically study society and social groups. She always thought about that stuff anyway, so why not get the degrees necessary to teach it? Little did she realize that the next twelve years of her life would be a blurred haze of Emile Durkheim, Karl Marx, Max Weber, statistics, research methods, countless books, a mountain of articles, comprehensive exams, and a dissertation.

But these are not gritty tales of how one earns a PhD in sociology. Rather, the purpose of this chapter is to provide gritty tales of academic tenure-track job seekers in the current job market. These funny and disheartening stories derive from personal experiences, interviews, and conversations with job seekers from around the United States. Names have been changed to protect the innocent (and guilty).

For tenure-track job seekers these tales can be used as a primer to ready themselves mentally and spiritually for possible tribulations ahead. More importantly, these tales are a call for reflection on the part of university administration and academic search committees.

THE MCDONALDIZATION OF HIGHER EDUCATION

Much has been made about the fact that there are a large number of PhD holders in the job market and a limited number of tenure-track jobs. The displacement of tenure-track by adjunct positions, the large number of baby boomer professors who have not retired, and an increase in online degrees taught by non-PhD faculty have all been cited as reasons for the large number of PhDs without tenure-track jobs (Cross and Goldenberg 2009; Jaschik 2013; McCluskey and Winter 2012; Weinberg and Scott 2013; Wheeler 2013).

As a consequence of the large number of PhD job seekers, colleges have become increasingly selective in whom they hire. Highly qualified candidates who may have had little difficulty securing a tenure-track position 10, 20, or 30 years ago now find themselves bypassed year after year. It is not uncommon for these job seekers to get rejection letters that read, "Thank you for your application. Although we are impressed with your credentials, there were over 300 well-qualified applicants for this position." One of the consequences of the disproportionate PhD-to-job ratio is that the professionalism required to woo a candidate has waned.

As in so many aspects of our society, higher education is increasingly characterized by what sociologists call *McDonaldization*—a social situation characterized by attempts at efficiency, calculability, predictability, depersonalization, and increased control (Hayes and Wynyard 2006; Ritzer 2012). Vast bureaucracies, institutional effectiveness reports, loss of academic autonomy, standardized tests, and quantified course assessments are all geared to impart *value* in the education marketplace. The personalized touch is being replaced with the more cost-effective *one-size-fits-all* approach to higher education.

McDonaldization often seeps down to academic searches. Formally educated and industrious job candidates who may have once been treated with high levels of respect and consideration are often tossed around the job market circuit like Big Macs.

Academic search committees are typically made up of department faculty members charged with advertising job openings, collecting application materials, vetting candidates, creating itineraries, organizing teaching or research demonstrations, and setting up meetings, meals, and sleeping arrangements for candidates. All this while conducting typical teaching, research, advising, and other service activities. It comes as little surprise that overextended faculty are often negligent in giving adequate attention to candidate searches.

To be fair, not all search committees have succumbed to McDonaldization. Some members take the time to learn that a candidate prefers *Bill* rather than *William*. They make flight arrangements for candidates. They provide clean hotel accommodations for candidates. They provide candidates with an itinerary well in advance of their campus visit. They ask if candidates have any dietary restrictions. They allot candidates a little time alone to catch their breath during the daylong interview process.

Other colleges make candidates feel like a burger being passed from one set of hands to another. "Are you taking her?" "Put her in the conference room." "I think Gary's supposed to take her to lunch." "No, I'll take her." Impersonality rules as candidates get shuffled from the department head, to various professors, to the dean, to students, to human resources, to the associate vice president of something or other.

APPLICATION PACKETS

In addition to taking classes, studying for comprehensive exams, and working on a dissertation, PhD graduate students must allot many hours to organizing applications. The word *application* does not really capture all that is required to be considered for a tenure-track position. Outside academia, an *application* typically refers to a piece of paper that allows an applicant to express interest in a job while providing basic personal and professional information.

When applying for a faculty position, however, colleges typically require an application, curriculum vitae, three letters of recommendation, statement of teaching philosophy, research agenda, copies of student evaluation scores, copies of research publications, and any other evidence of the applicant's qualifications, including doctoral grade transcripts.

Additionally, it is always a good idea for a candidate to provide a personalized and signed cover letter with each application. Alluding to family or friends within driving distance of the college can convince search committee members that a candidate is looking to put down roots. At approximately $5 per application packet, the United States Postal Service undoubtedly appreciates the numerous items required by college search committees.

Many colleges have particular specifications about page length, which requires revision on the part of the applicant. Other universities require candidates to answer specific questions in order to be considered for the position. For the applicant, these requirements translate into additional work.

Tenure-track seekers in many disciplines rely on the *job bank* of their flagship organization. However, cash-strapped graduate students may have difficulty coming up with the money for the membership fees required to access these job banks. Although there are free websites with job postings such as *InsideHigherEd.com* and *HigherEdJob.com*, not all universities post openings on these sites. Job seekers should check all of these sites at least once a week because some colleges only post job openings three weeks before the application deadline.

Increasingly, colleges are accepting application materials online, which reduces expenses and footwork for the applicant. However, in order to apply, a candidate must set up an account for each college, which requires a user name, password, and security question(s). The online templates allow colleges to be more specific regarding page and word limits for each document, which occasionally necessitates rewriting.

One hindrance of applying online is that the candidate is often prohibited from sending additional materials regarding professional aptitude. A candidate wanting to include photographs of class activities or media recognition of their work is out of luck. While mail-based applications allow candidates to include these materials, most online application systems do not. Not surprisingly, candidates with these additional supporting materials receive more attention from colleges by using mail-based application systems.

Many search committees require official transcripts from all of the colleges an applicant has attended. With some colleges charging up to $20 per transcript request, applying to more than a handful of positions can be cost prohibitive. For those without the means, fewer applications translate into decreased odds of acquiring a job.

Some seasoned faculty members recommend acquiring a credit card with at least a $5,000 limit. In addition to paying transcript fees, a credit card is useful when universities require candidates to pay for their own flight, hotel, and meals up front, with the promise of reimbursement. When universities do not reimburse candidates in a timely manner, credit card debt can accumulate quickly.

Some PhD candidates are instructed by academic advisors to increase their chances by applying for as many positions as possible. In some academic fields, a job seeker may apply to over 100 positions in an academic year.

One of the more uncomfortable aspects of sending out application materials is asking overworked faculty to write and send out recommendation letters. Technically, letter writing for tenure-track job seekers is a voluntary activity, although the norm in academia is to accept these requests. Many faculty members try to increase a candidate's chances by personalizing these letters for each school.

As others have suggested (e.g., Flaherty 2013), it would be more considerate for search committees to request recommendation letters once a candidate makes it onto a short list. If 150 applicants in the original candidate pool send three letters of recommendation, the search committee collects 450 letters. Unless they are a glutton for punishment, no faculty member is going to thoroughly read 450 letters of recommendation.

ANNUAL MEETING INTERVIEWS

Many disciplinary organizations host job interview sessions at their annual meeting so that departments with tenure-track lines and job seekers can meet in what is the academic version of speed dating. In a handful of minutes, a candidate is expected to make a great impression and answer all of the interviewer's questions pertaining to teaching, research, service, strengths, areas for growth, aspirations, and just about anything else the interviewer can think of. Job interviews are stressful enough, but add face-to-face encounters with your competitors and these interviews rival the intensity of *The Hunger Games*.

In Jennifer's first year on the job market she was granted an interview with a Tennessee college at the American Sociological Association's job interview session. When she walked into the conference room, she saw about 15 small round tables where interviews were taking place. She sat in a chair along the wall with 20 other candidates until it was time for her interview. Here, candidates were forced to watch competitors trying to win over interviewers. Then, through the conference room speakers, a loud trumpet note rang out. Interviewees sat up straighter and, in a panic, tried to inject all of their attributes into the final minute of the interview.

Another anxious candidate sitting along the wall tried to ease the tension: "When I dreamed of becoming a professor, this isn't what I had in mind." Several candidates let out a nervous laugh. Then, three trumpet notes rang out across the room. Those who had just been interviewed relinquished their chairs and were herded toward the door. Simultaneously, candidates along the wall made a beeline toward the appropriate interview table.

Jennifer was in the last interview time slot of the day, as the interviewer's face made very clear. After a handshake and feigned smile, he proceeded with a barrage of rapid-fire questions. He did not make eye contact as Jennifer deftly zigged and zagged through his minefield of questions. He was going through the motions, but she was determined to show him that he saved the best for last. When the final trumpet note sounded, he let out a relieved gasp and Jennifer was pleased with her performance. She left the interview with mixed feelings of relief, hope, confusion, and discomfort.

A few weeks later, Jennifer received a personalized rejection letter. Although she was disappointed that the school did not request a campus-visit interview, she appreciated that the interviewer took the time to thank and encourage her.

It is sadly ironic that organizations such the American Sociological Association and the American Psychological Association, with their vast knowledge of how social structure can harm individuals, create social situations that are so stressful and demeaning.

PHONE INTERVIEWS

Phone interviews are a key hurdle to getting the coveted campus-visit interview request. Many job seekers do not consider phone interviews *real* interviews and therefore do not take them very seriously. Many candidates refrain from any special preparation for them and some even participate in phone interviews while driving their car or shopping. An effective phone interview system can significantly increase a candidate's chances of procuring a campus-visit request.

Gary, a PhD candidate in psychology, developed a phone interview system that centered around eight pages of bullet point reference notes. If a search committee member asked him a question that he was having difficulty with, Gary's trusty notes provided cues for a thorough and thoughtful answer. He even conducted research on each university and its mission statement so that he could tailor responses to each school.

Sitting at his desk at home with eight pages of notes, a hands-free headset, closed curtains, his dog in her crate, and a *do not disturb* sign on his front door helped him control the setting and interview. Partly because of this system, Gary was asked to fly out to seven of the nine colleges that interviewed him by phone.

Some phone interviews are extremely businesslike and tense. No chitchat, no humor, just questions and answers. This interview approach is off-putting because the underlying connotation is that a faculty member does not have to be likable and that the candidate is on trial. Many candidates feel pressure to lighten up a tense interview with chitchat or a joke and feel terrible when the search committee is unresponsive. Many search committees do not realize that a personalized comment about the weather or the candidate's home state can go a long way to reduce awkward tension.

Other phone interviews are too relaxed. In these situations, search committee members talk with candidates as if they are longtime friends, and every response receives glowing affirmation. During one phone interview, almost every one of Michelle's responses garnered an exuberant affirmation: "Interesting!" "Wonderful!" "Your research is very innovative!" "Your students are lucky to have you as their teacher!" With comments like these, it is easy to feel great about the chances for a campus-visit interview. And it makes rejection all the more painful when a candidate does not get such a request.

During one phone interview with a Colorado college, Michelle told the story of two students who met during her Race and Ethnic Relations class, became fast friends, and made a short film about what Jonathan Kozol (1991) calls *savage inequalities* in the education system. These students presented the film to Michelle's Introduction to Sociology students the following semester. Students becoming teachers—a great story. As Michelle delivered this tale, the search committee head interrupted with a cracking voice, "Hold on, I'm getting choked up." Michelle was confident that she would make the short list for a campus-visit interview.

After many days of anticipation, she heard through the grapevine that the search committee had already extended invitations for candidates to visit the campus. Michelle spent a lot of time over the next year trying to figure out why she did not get invited. Several months later, she found out that the winning candidate had had a one-year contract as a full-time lecturer at the university the prior year.

CAMPUS-VISIT INTERVIEWS

The campus-visit interview is the final hurdle to acquiring a job offer. Typically, a school will invite two or three candidates out for one position. Making the cut from the entire candidate pool down to two or three is a great accomplishment and can provide a candidate with some reassurance. At this point, however, the pressure to perform well increases drastically as this may be the candidate's only campus visit for the year.

Added to this pressure are flight arrangements, taking care of academic obligations before departure, packing, handling affairs at home, rehearsing, researching the university, jet lag, taxis or car rentals, strange hotel smells, and an unfamiliar bed. Job seekers with children have even more logistical hurdles to overcome.

It goes without saying that it is extremely important for a candidate to dazzle the search committee during the campus visit. To even be considered for a tenure-track position these days a candidate must be a supercharged, turbo-talking, Bloom's (or Anderson's) Taxonomy–using, service-learning, rubric-creating, student-coddling, pedagogical machine. PowerPoints must entertain like Pixar movies. Prezis should zip students around like Tilt-a-Whirls. The days of chalkboard, chalk, and lecture have gone the way of the leisure suit.

Colton, a PhD candidate in sociology, was excited to get a request for a campus visit to a community college in Michigan. Having attended a community college, he figured it might be a good fit. They asked him to provide a teaching demonstration in front of students about the sociology of the family. Colton spent two weeks meticulously refining and rehearsing a PowerPoint lecture. He even developed an engaging small-group activity about the effects of technology on family bonds and family interaction.

Having made the flight from the Northeast to Michigan, Colton still had to catch a puddle jumper to a small airport near the college. After waiting 45 minutes for the connecting flight to take off, the pilot announced that the airplane was experiencing mechanical problems due to freezing temperatures. Everyone on the plane disembarked and boarded another plane. After another 30 minutes, the pilot made the same announcement. Once again, passengers disembarked and were told that they would receive hotel vouchers.

Colton and his fellow passengers arrived at a nearby hotel at 3:30 in the morning. Because there was no flight to the college the following morning, he reserved a taxi for the two-hour trek. After two hours of sleep, the taxi picked Colton up and transported him into the frozen Michigan tundra.

Several cups of coffee increased his alertness slightly but did not eliminate the bags under his eyes. He was too tired to panic when they told him there was a mix-up and that he would be giving his teaching demonstration to faculty rather than students. As he was being shuffled from interview to interview, he tried to figure out how to alter his presentation in light of the fact that there would be no students.

During the teaching demonstration, Colton jumbled words and repeated himself. He was sure that a giant hook would emerge to pull him off the stage at any moment. Despite Colton's word salad, he received several compliments upon completion.

One committee member was annoyed at one PowerPoint slide that depicted family members each using technology in separate rooms of the house. She felt that the slide was *too stereotypical*. Colton explained that he used the visual depiction because data indicate that family members are indeed spending less time interacting with one another and more time staring at electronic screens. She was not pleased with his response but allowed other faculty members to ask questions. After a few minutes, she blurted out, "I still think that slide is too stereotypical." There was an awkward silence as everyone looked at her and then at Colton. Fortunately, they were out of time.

Not only did Colton not get the job offer, but the search committee did not even contact him to tell him that they hired another candidate. He only discovered this information after calling the secretary two weeks later to inquire about the status of the search. She informed him that the committee made their decision, and the candidate accepted the offer a week after Colton's interview.

She apologized and said that the committee must have forgotten to inform him. Because many search committees do not have the courtesy to let candidates know that a position has been filled, it is a good idea for candidates to ask for the status of the search a few days after a campus visit.

DO NOT OVERANALYZE COMMENTS

Overanalyzing comments from committee members or administrators can cause emotional and cognitive turmoil for job candidates. Reading too much into a casual conversation can give a candidate a false sense of assurance or a lost sense of hope. It is important for candidates to understand that there are no guarantees until a contract is signed or a rejection letter arrives.

Phillip visited a South Carolina college that was hiring a sociologist to teach Race and Ethnic Relations, a course he taught once before. He was pleasantly surprised to be picked up at the airport by a chauffeur in a Cadillac. Dinner with faculty was splendid. "You're vegetarians? So am I!" They exchanged recipes and gritty tales of vegetarianism. The collegiality was overflowing.

The next morning, he enjoyed a tour of the campus. Prestigious buildings with white columns, beautiful landscaping, a modern recreation center that was free for faculty and most importantly—windows in all faculty offices!

Students were highly engaged during his teaching demonstration. A classroom full of White students below the Bible Belt engaged in an intellectual discussion about racism—not an easy task.

As the department head drove Phillip back to the airport, she seemed to give me him subtle cue, "You brought out the best in them." Bingo! A clear signal that he was their candidate. A good teacher is supposed to bring out the best in his students.

Phillip told the head of his dissertation committee about the department head's secret cue and waited confidently for the call. How surprised and honored he would be when they called. He began looking online for vegetarian restaurants around his new campus.

A week later, Phillip received a generic e-mail thanking him for his candidacy but informing him that they had hired someone else. Not getting the job was bad enough, but receiving the same rejection e-mail as all of the other applicants made it much worse. The strong bonds created over tofu spinach dip apparently did not garner a more personalized rejection.

When the department posted the winning candidate's information on their website the following fall, Phillip discovered that the winning candidate graduated from that very college. An article on the college's website read, "Local Student Comes Home to Teach."

ACADEMIC-IMPRESSION MANAGEMENT

Graduate students should understand that academic-impression management begins once graduate school starts. With proper mentoring, graduate students should be making good impressions at conferences, through communication with others in their field and with strong work habits.

Once on the job market, search committees can develop impressions of candidates based on seemingly insignificant things such as font style, signature, letterheads, or even the placement of a staple. Most job candidates realize that professional clothing is important for on-campus visits, but many do not realize that an unkempt background during a Skype interview reflects poorly. With so many candidates to choose from, even minor sloppiness or oversights can get a candidate cut from a short list.

Although it is not supposed to occur, many search committee members independently research candidates online. It is imperative that any unprofessional photographs or comments are removed before the job search begins. Shutting down or restricting access to Facebook profiles decreases the chance of search committee members discovering something discrediting. Some candidates go as far as to use an alias as a primary profile for family and friends.

It is also a good idea for candidates to set up a professional website that highlights skill sets and accomplishments. In this way, the candidate has some control over what committee members find online.

Michelle, who was passed over for the one-year lecturer position at the Colorado college a year earlier, received a request for another phone interview with the same college. This time, she received a campus-visit request. As the department head provided a tour of the campus, he casually justified last year's selection: "We like to hire from the inside." Michelle wondered, did he really say that? Isn't that illegal or something? Doesn't he remember that she was passed over because she was an "outsider"?

Despite having completed her PhD, Michelle was commonly referred to as *Mrs.* rather than *Dr.* by faculty members and administrators throughout her visit. "I know I'm not supposed to ask this, but what does your husband do?" "How will you be able to balance motherhood with academic life?" Fearing reprisal for pointing out these sexist faux pas, many female PhDs tolerate this treatment.

During her interviews with deans, provosts, and the department head, Michelle smiled in all the right places. Her nods were synchronized perfectly to the interviewer's conjectures. Her furrowed brow made it look as though the interviewer was stating something thoughtful and interesting. She peppered interviews with an occasional "Wow!" or "Really!" to convey enthusiasm.

Adept job seekers know that it is important to allow interviewers to talk a lot. Most academic interviewers revel in impressing candidates with their research, thoughts on teaching, knowledge of the university, and day-to-day activities. Active listening is an art form that should not be underestimated.

Candidates cannot rely solely on active listening skills, however. A useful technique is to make safe declarative statements. "I really think it's essential that students apply what they learn in class to the real world." Groundbreaking. "I truly believe that you really don't get the meaningful face-to-face interaction from online universities that you do at a brick-and-mortar college." Duh. Administrators and search committees delight in these types of comments as they feel they share common beliefs and values with the candidate.

After Michelle finished her research presentation, the department head declared to everyone in the room that it was the "the best job presentation I have ever seen." Although Michelle was honored, she was a little uncomfortable knowing that the department head had seen the job presentations of several other faculty members in the room.

Strong impression-management skills are vital but do not guarantee job offers. Despite her strong campus visit, the search committee did not select Michelle. They informed her that they made this decision because, unlike Michelle's, the other candidate's dissertation was complete. Curiously, the search committee knew that Michelle was working on her final chapter when they invited her for the campus visit.

PAY ATTENTION TO DETAIL

With so many obligations and so much pressure, it is easy for job candidates to overlook minor details. Forgetting a third recommendation letter or computer cord for a campus visit can cost a candidate a job. Keeping lists in conspicuous places can help with the particulars. For each college of interest, candidates should maintain a *to-do* list on a dry-erase board, refrigerator sheet, or Excel spreadsheet. It is also a good idea to create a checklist of everything that needs to be packed for a campus visit.

After a successful phone interview with the history department's search committee at a Texas college, the department head gave Brandon six days to book a flight, rent a car, and reserve a hotel room. He jumped at the chance and hurriedly clicked on Expedia.com to make arrangements. In his haste, he failed to realize that Expedia's online default month was March, despite the fact it was the middle of February. The department head asked Brandon to fly out on Tuesday, February 22. Unfortunately, the 22nd of March and the 22nd of February were both Tuesdays.

When Brandon arrived at the airport, the woman at the check-in counter seemed to have a gleam of satisfaction as she informed him that he had booked a flight for March instead of February. When Brandon explained that he had an interview the next day, her smile widened even more, akin to the Grinch plotting to steal Christmas.

Nothing prepares a job candidate for an interview like a $1,164.77 mistake. Rather than focusing on the task at hand, getting a job, Brandon contemplated how much fuss would be made if Expedia's website designer went missing.

Once Brandon arrived at the college, the department head picked him up at the hotel for dinner. As is customary, Brandon expected to meet other faculty members when he arrived at the restaurant. The department head informed him that none of the other faculty members would be attending dinner. No reason was given for their absence. Perhaps it was Shark Week on the Discovery Channel.

Brandon tried to make the best of the situation by winning over the department head with great conversation. The department head was a no-nonsense woman who told Brandon that one of her favorite pastimes was reading demography journals. In their 90-minute conversation, she barely made eye contact, talked little about herself, and avoided talking about the position. Instead, she kept steering their discussion to the delicious food.

The next morning Brandon was scheduled to give a research presentation to faculty. As he prepared, he noticed that the projector made all of his color slides and vibrant photographs appear a blurry shade of gray. After unsuccessfully trying to adjust the projector, he asked the secretary if she could send someone to fix it. Unfortunately, the technology repairman was not on campus that day. Despite the blurry slides, Brandon's presentation was a hit with faculty members.

Brandon had informed the department head of his vegetarianism but got shuffled over to Porky's Restaurant for lunch anyway. Porky's did not have any vegetarian options but improvised and brought him a grilled vegetable sandwich that was apparently sautéed on a grill with pork grease residue. Brandon was too hungry to complain. During his afternoon interviews Brandon's stomach made noises akin to a distressed sea otter.

After Brandon's teaching demonstration, one student implored, "Please, please come teach here" as if it was completely his decision. Despite the lackluster meet-and-greet dinner the night before, the enthusiasm from faculty and students increased Brandon's confidence.

Three days later, Brandon received a generic rejection letter thanking him for applying to the school. When he checked the department's website several months later, he discovered that the winning candidate had had a one-year teaching position at the university the year before. Brandon felt as though he was part of a dog-and-pony show designed to satisfy the job-search requirements of the university.

CRONYISM

Tim was excited to receive a campus-interview request from a sociology search committee in California. The school was far away from his family on the East Coast. However, he was impressed with the campus, faculty, students, and surrounding area. The school is nestled within a landscape of breathtaking mountains. With the ease of flight travel, perhaps this was a place Tim and his wife could put down roots.

While interviewing Tim, an assistant professor confided that she got the job because she had the inside track a year before as a one-year temporary faculty member. She added that once a full-time lecturer proves to be a "good egg," search committees are more likely to write a job description to match the lecturer's strengths the next time a tenure-track position opens up.

Many people think that higher education is a place where cronyism is frowned upon. After all, institutions of higher learning espouse ideals of justice, fair play, and meritocracy. As many faculty members know, however, there is a strong incentive to hire from the inside. Inside hires are known entities that reduce the risk of hiring a *bad egg* who does not get along with others.

The culture of many departments has been ruined by a single faculty member who constantly complains, says and does inappropriate things, or gossips. Even if the inside hire is not as strong a teacher or researcher, many departments prefer the less talented candidate who plays well with others.

If a search committee is intent on hiring someone *from the inside* there is little a candidate can do. However, some candidates will request that they not be invited for a campus interview if one of the other finalists is a current lecturer, adjunct, or graduate of the college. Doing so is bit audacious and risky but can save the candidate time, stress, and money.

After his morning interviews, Tim had lunch with two committee members. One was an activist scholar who maintained that she did her best work outside the walls of academia. The other was an erudite theorist who liked to impress with his knowledge of social history. Instead of poignant questions and conversation with Tim, the two committee members spent the entire lunch complaining about academia and engaging in a "pissing contest" about whether activism or social science is better suited to address the afflictions of society. After watching two scholars trying to impress each other for an hour Tim was ready for his teaching demonstration.

For his demonstration on research methods, Tim used Prezi, which was cutting-edge presentation software at the time. He had spent many hours carefully constructing the presentation so that photos and text swirled around and students could visualize small ideas within a big-picture framework. Tim also created an engaging group activity where students would conduct a rudimentary content analysis of popular magazines.

Tim's itinerary only allowed 15 minutes to prepare for his presentation. While testing out the technology, he noticed that a majority of the photographs and diagrams in his presentation appeared fuzzy and pixilated on the overhead screen. The university's projector was fairly old with a fan that sounded like it was overheating. In a panic, Tim hurriedly reduced the size of the photos and diagrams so that they did not appear quite so pixilated.

Students and faculty were mesmerized by the swirling images. There was also a buzz in the room and laughter when faculty joined in the group activity. Students and faculty clapped and cheered when Tim finished.

The day after he arrived home, Tim received a job offer from California. Although he was excited, he needed to focus on a campus visit to Alabama in two days. With an offer in hand, he felt much more at ease about the upcoming interview.

Tim's research presentation in front of faculty and students in Alabama generated enthusiasm and praise. He even taught a few faculty members how to use Prezi. With only one other candidate in contention, Tim liked his chances.

MYTHOLOGY OF THE ACADEMIC BIDDING WAR

Conventional wisdom suggests that job candidates should try to get universities in a bidding war to drive up the negotiated salary and perks. Such a strategy, along with corresponding folk stories, appeals to the capitalist ethic and can excite candidates looking for the payoff at the end of many years of hard work and sacrifice. While senior faculty may recall a few stories about bidding wars from the old days, these scenarios are rare in modern academia.

The reasons that universities rarely compete for candidates are twofold. First, with a large number of highly qualified PhD holders looking for jobs, schools do not feel much pressure to pander to requests. Requests for a higher salary, moving expenses, course reduction for the first year, computer and other equipment, or office space are often dismissed. Some schools will even withdraw an offer if a candidate attempts to negotiate (Flaherty 2014). Deans, department heads, and search committees are often just as happy with the second or third choice as the first.

The second reason is that when a university makes a decision on whom to hire, the candidate typically gets between 48 hours and two weeks to make a decision. The odds of obtaining another offer within exactly the same period of time are low, especially in a highly competitive job market.

An additional disadvantage for job candidates is that many in higher education consider it unethical to accept an offer from a school with the hope of using the job to negotiate with another school. According to folk tales, the professional stigma associated with such a ploy could have dire consequences. Because of this institutionalized taboo, universities have a significant advantage over candidates when entering negotiations.

With the offer from California in hand and the strong interview in Alabama, however, there was a small possibility that Tim could actually get two universities in a bidding war!

No bidding war occurred. The California college gave Tim three days to make a decision, and the Alabama school would not be interviewing its next candidate for another week. Then it would take Alabama's search committee another two weeks to meet and make their decision. Tim successfully requested more time from California twice but was backed into a corner to make a decision by the department head on his third attempt.

Because Tim was partial to the Alabama college, which was closer to his family, he declined California's offer with the hope of receiving an offer from Alabama. Tim endured a stressful two weeks wondering whether he was foolish for turning down a job offer. Sleepless nights ensued as he wondered whether he would be spending another year trying to piece together a living as a graduate student. Tim eventually received the offer from Alabama. He didn't get an office window but feels fortunate to have survived the enormous amount of work and mistreatment while in the academic job market.

FINAL THOUGHTS

When academic job candidates are not treated with consideration and respect, academia, the status of *professor*, and academic disciplines are devalued. When a lack of professionalism, impersonality, and cronyism reign during academic job searches, the reputation of higher education is tarnished in the eyes of academic job seekers, students, and the general public.

Ironically, institutions that partake in these practices run contrary to the very values they espouse. In academia, students are taught that hard work is the key to success, that they should play by the rules, that they should work for justice, and that they should show respect to others. Unfortunately, these are not the practices of some colleges.

At a time when the knowledge and critical-thinking skills acquired at college are of paramount importance, universities cannot afford to dissuade promising scholars from pursuing careers in higher education. These scholars have already endured the turmoil of graduate school, and many are saddled with significant debt. When also considering lagging faculty salaries, increased class sizes, larger advising loads, more committee work, and greater expectations to publish, universities run the risk of discouraging the best and brightest from leading the next generation.

Faculty members and administrators should reflect on these gritty tales to ensure that up-and-coming scholars do not endure similar indignities. Academic search committees are ideally situated to ensure that professionalism, high ethical standards, and humaneness are incorporated into the search process. Hopefully, as social media and books like the one you are reading bring stories of academic mistreatment to everyone's attention, positive changes will occur in the way academics are treated.

REFERENCES

Cross, John G., and Edie N. Goldenberg. 2009. *Off-Track Profs: Nontenured Teachers in Higher Education.* Cambridge, MA: MIT Press.
Flaherty, Colleen. 2014. "Negotiated out of a Job." *Inside Higher Ed* (March 13).

Flaherty, Colleen. 2013. "Recommendations for Letters." *Inside Higher Ed* (September 4).

Hayes, Dennis, and Robin Wynyard. 2006. *The McDonaldization of Higher Education*. Charlotte, NC: IAP.

Jaschik, Scott. 2013. "They Aren't Retiring." *Inside Higher Ed* (August 2).

Kozol, Jonathan. 1991. *Savage Inequalities: Children in America's Schools*. New York: Broadway Paperbacks.

McClusky, Frank B., and Melanie L. Winter. 2012. *The Idea of the Digital Universe: Ancient Traditions, Disruptive Technologies and the Battle for the Soul of Higher Education*. Policy Studies Organization.

Ritzer, George. 2012. *The McDonaldization of Society*. Thousand Oaks, CA: Sage Publications.

Weinberg, Sharon L., and Marc A. Scott. 2013. "The Impact of Uncapping of Mandatory Retirement on Postsecondary Institutions." *Educational Researcher* 42(6):338–48.

Wheeler, David R. 2013. "Will Online Classes Make Professors Extinct?" CNN (February 3).

II

Now That You Have the Job

Chapter Four

Paperwork, Meetings, and Program Review

The Challenges of University Teaching in the 21st Century

Deborah L. Smith and Brian J. Smith

Tenured professor positions come with a level of security and freedom that rarely accompanies other professions. Professors enjoy the challenges and learning opportunities that are inherent in teaching and research and see the value in serving their university and professional communities. Many cherish the opportunity to work with students, encourage their learning and development, and, ultimately and hopefully, positively impact their lives. Most professors understand the importance of engaging in meaningful service work that contributes to their university and the academic profession.

Child rearing can be made simpler when, thanks to the flexible schedules of the profession, children never spend a day in child care, and time for family can be set aside each summer as well as other time dedicated to not engaging in any of the work associated with being a professor. In many ways, being a professor is an incredible career. The benefits include a comfortable living, flexible schedule, status, and the opportunity to work in a stimulating environment.

This description from *The Princeton Review* (2014) (princetonreview.com/Careers.aspx?cid=127) is not far off the mark:

> College professors organize and conduct the functions of higher education. They engage in a variety of activities, from running laboratory experiments and supervising graduate student research to conducting large undergraduate lectures and writing textbooks.

With the exception of scheduled classes—which can consume as few as three hours a week in graduate universities or up to twelve to sixteen hours per week for undergraduates—a professor's time is largely spent on research, preparing class material, meeting with students or however else she chooses.

The description continues:

This profession is thus best suited for motivated self-starters, and its highest rewards are given to those who can identify and explore original problems in their fields. Tenured professors have relatively high job security and professional freedom. Once tenured, a professor can largely set his own responsibilities and decide to a large extent how to divide his time between teaching, writing, researching and administration.

It is understandable when Kensing (2013) reports that the field's high growth opportunities, low health risks, and substantial pay provide a low-stress environment that is the envy of many career professionals and why CareerCast.com rated *professor* as the least stressful job of 2013. So, one may be hesitant to write this chapter about the challenges one may face in this profession.

While many professors have true horror stories to share, the experiences cited herein are generally positive. However, the horrors presented here detract from the career and from the true value of the professor role. Furthermore, there is reason to be concerned that the profession is in danger of being eroded, given current trends in education. It is for that reason that the horrors of the profession are shared here despite an understanding that a great majority of professors are generally satisfied with their position(s).

What are the negatives for professors who have had a positive experience overall? The paperwork, meetings, and constant program review/assessment are three areas that top the list. If one does not learn to say no quickly in academia, it is possible to get so bogged down in minutia that there is no time left for the more substantive and higher pursuits.

Finding the balance between being a considerate coworker who does their fair share of the tasks involved in keeping the department going and being a *yes-man* or a *yes-woman* who spends so much time in meetings or completing paperwork that there is not time for other pursuits is a constant struggle. If the paperwork, meetings, and program review/assessment were all obviously wasted efforts, then this struggle would not exist. But some of it is valuable and distinguishing between what is worthwhile and what is not complicates the decisions that must be made.

In this chapter, the aim is not just to point out the pitfalls of academia, but to suggest ways to navigate them with finesse. The ability to *separate the chaff from the wheat* is a valuable skill, and nowhere is it more needed than in the role of professor. Professors must be able to determine what is worthwhile, how to approach those tasks, and then have the confidence to say *no* when asked to complete tasks that are not within that realm.

Only by identifying and avoiding the pitfalls can the majority of a professor's time be spent conducting meaningful research, working with students, and engaging in worthwhile service. While the positives of being a professor (both on a professional and personal level) are immense, the pitfalls must be considered so that this role can be preserved. Professors are the true foundation of our higher education system.

PAPERWORK

One of the challenges of being a professor is more mundane than expected. The constant pile of paperwork that must be dealt with is overwhelming and can consume so much time and energy that little else is accomplished. A short list of the paperwork done in just one week includes:

- grading assignments (on paper and online) and recording points;
- reviewing colleagues' personnel files;
- developing meeting agendas;
- writing a draft of a Teaching Table presentation;
- scheduling a visit/timetable for an external reviewer;
- ordering textbooks;
- administrative e-mailing;
- curriculum committee proposals;
- graduate committee proposals;
- nominations for awards;
- academic affairs newsletters;
- processing fieldwork calendars and creating an observation calendar;
- meeting minutes, and so on.

This week is typical, with a mix of paperwork from teaching, research, and service, but with most of it relating to service. Some of these tasks can be completed quickly. For example, writing an agenda for a meeting only takes thirty minutes. One simply looks over the previous agenda and considers what upcoming events/tasks that particular committee needs to complete and writes up a list of action items to discuss or make progress upon at the upcoming meeting.

Some tasks are more laborious. For example, the draft of a Teaching Table presentation can take several hours to complete. Some presentations require multiple revisions. Each revision may be accompanied by an e-mail thanking the committee member for their input and then an e-mail with the revised draft sent back out for further input.

Even the paperwork that is not time-consuming may snowball and impinge greatly on a workday if clear priorities are not set. Professors are expected to produce, read, review, and comment on all this and more in a timely fashion. This, in addition to answering a constant barrage of e-mail, can consume an inordinate amount of time if left unchecked.

Tovani (2004, 118) shares a memo from her mailbox that reads, "If you witnessed the urinating incident last week, please write up a statement." This serves as a reminder of how difficult it can be to sort out what is truly important in teaching from what is pointless busywork. This task is even harder in academia because there often is not a clear boundary between what the role entails and what it does not. Teachers at the K–12 level know that the true focus of their profession needs to be on educating students.

Universities typically divide the professor-role responsibilities into three areas: teaching, research, and service. At most universities, faculty can easily be overloaded with service responsibilities if they don't learn to say no. And in the final analysis, service is simply not weighted very heavily in tenure and promotion decisions at most institutions. At the university level, teaching is part of the mission statement, but at many universities it is not even the primary focus.

While certain numbers must be maintained on student evaluations, the focus for promotion at many universities is clearly on research productivity. This ambiguity makes it difficult to determine how much emphasis to put on the various paperwork components of the position. While providing valuable feedback to students is an important part of the learning process, professors also know that providing individualized feedback on assignments is time-consuming.

If too much time is spent providing feedback and completing other paperwork tasks, there is not enough time in the week to make progress on improving a course by analyzing the assignments or for research interests such as reading the current literature, writing grant proposals, conducting research, or writing up research results. The constant need to balance is clearly evident when it comes to paperwork.

So, how can it be managed? While keeping lists of *items to do* might be useful, it is clearly not enough. Here are practical tips for managing paperwork:

1. If you keep a *to-do list*, think about each item before you add it to the list. Is it worthwhile and/or necessary? Could you do it in less than five minutes? If so and it fulfills the first criterion, just do it. If it is not important, put it in the recycle bin.
2. Prioritize your paperwork based on importance and deadlines. Remember, when determining your prioritization, that feedback to students is most valuable if received promptly (Chickering and Gamson

1987). While this is a valuable step to managing your paperwork, it is also complicated by the fact that this daily busywork can take up far too much time. Grading, prepping, answering e-mail, and completing the materials with upcoming deadlines can be considered much like household chores such as dishes, cooking, and laundry.

3. Set a schedule with specific times allotted for teaching activities, research activities, and service activities. Obviously, a schedule like this needs to be flexible and can change on a weekly basis. For example, the first week of class of each semester may include increased time for faculty-student interactions. Time to get acquainted with students as learners is worth prioritizing and allotting extra time for, despite the schedule adjustments required.

4. Some professors dedicate one (or more) day each week to research pursuits. This weekly commitment can lead to remaining up-to-date on the latest research, conducting research, and writing grants. The dedicated time keeps it prioritized and doesn't allow for other duties to impinge on the research focus. Determining what is worthwhile and dedicating more time to those tasks is part of the process of evaluating your schedule. Each semester, reevaluate the schedule that you set, your dedication to adhering to the schedule, and revise to make the next semester even more productive.

5. This profession is cyclical and, as such, there is a certain amount of repetition that cannot be avoided. As far as paperwork is concerned, streamlining the processes can lead to time saving. In order to do this, keep very organized folders for various tasks and file items so that previous work can be used as a template. This is not an excuse to cut corners—freshness is needed for many tasks.

Knowing when to streamline requires reflection and decision-making skills to determine what was valuable enough to reproduce and what needs revision or, in some cases, a clean start. Having the work from a previous semester available allows for the reflection necessary to decide what improvements need to be made.

Keeping on top of the endless paperwork associated with being a professor is difficult but important. Determining what is truly worthwhile, prioritizing, scheduling time to be sure to include all aspects of the position, and organizing are the keys for keeping paperwork reasonable. While everyone makes mistakes over the years, like sending out an agenda with the wrong date or missing a deadline, these steps can make that a rare occurrence and can allow you to keep the paperwork under control.

Many years ago Northcote Parkinson (1957, 2) stated, "The man whose life is devoted to paperwork has lost the initiative. He is dealing with things that are brought to his notice, having ceased to notice anything for himself."

This quote is still true today and serves as a reminder to limit paperwork and spend time on the larger issues within each discipline. Professors earn doctorates and teach at the university level to impact students' lives and society in general; they strive to be leaders and groundbreakers in their field, and this cannot happen if they spend time bogged down in paperwork.

MEETINGS

Meetings in academia pose an interesting conundrum. One of the reasons professors are expected to attend so many meetings is because their input is sought on a variety of topics and also so that there is transparency in the decision-making process. Universities with strong unions have clear processes in place for tenure and review and have safeguards in place to ensure there is transparency. Transparency and involvement are also expected for curriculum changes, contract ratification, personnel decisions, scheduling, and more.

Not only do professors have access to the guidelines but they are also often involved in the process of developing the guidelines for academic departments and work at institutions where everyone is encouraged to take part in important decisions. The negative aspect of all this is that continuous involvement in the process can be time-consuming and feel pointless when meetings are not run efficiently or seem to have no meaningful purpose.

Many professors could fill page after page with horror stories just based on meeting experiences. Experiences with boredom, frustration, being put on the spot, and feeling restless and overwhelmed are all commonplace. Meetings with no clear purpose, meetings where all of the work accomplished was swept aside because it was not supported by the administration, and meetings that could have easily been accomplished with a memorandum are the norm.

Colleagues who talk rudely and disrespectfully, scream, yell and argue, cry, lecture, and storm out of meetings can lead one to feel like doing the same. Department meetings with the same cast of characters can be predictable. What each participant will say on any given topic and how long the spiel will last is known beforehand. It is hard to not have a knee-jerk negative reaction when someone, once again, requests setting up a meeting.

The skills necessary for running effective and efficient meetings are not taught to professors; instead, leadership skills are learned (or not) by observing when participating. It is evident that meetings should only be held when there is a clear purpose, and that purpose should be presented on the agenda and focused upon throughout the meeting time. A meeting, just like a class session, should be well prepared and organized, and everyone attending should have something that she or he could contribute toward meeting the objectives for the meeting. Even though there is a leader or chairperson for a meeting, the hierarchy is often not evident.

Meetings attended in higher education tend to be run by colleagues, and this makes the task of keeping the meetings focused more of a challenge. A strong meeting leader knows how to keep a meeting flowing and moving through the agenda while balancing the need to value the input from the participants. One way to accomplish this is to stress timeliness during a meeting. Limiting discussions that seem unproductive or off topic can be daunting, but reminding meeting participants of the purpose of the meeting and making it clear that you don't want to waste their valuable time is one way to keep the meeting on track.

If a meeting is well prepared and has an obvious purpose and the participants agree that the purpose is valuable, then that meeting is much more likely to run smoothly. The final component necessary for a successful meeting is follow-up after the meeting. The leader of the meeting must let participants know what course of action was determined and what steps have been taken toward accomplishing the meeting's purpose. So, before you attend a meeting, here are some questions to ask:

Is this meeting valuable/worthwhile/necessary for me?

Just as with paperwork, prioritize and learn to say no to meetings that are not of interest or importance. To do this, you must examine your own interests and your departmental needs like, for example, prioritizing meetings where considerations of personnel decisions are an agenda item. The advantage of attending this type of meeting is that you will possibly serve on search committees and other committees that will make decisions regarding tenure and promotion.

Working with colleagues and administrators who are likable and who do their fair share of work is also important. So participation in meetings where the decisions are made about who is hired and retained within your department, colleges, and at the university level can be valuable service.

Each individual faculty member has varied interests, and there are enough service opportunities available that this component of the position can often correspond with personal interests. Unfortunately, professors must also attend meetings that are not of particular interest but that are important based on department needs. For example, countless meetings on curriculum, syllabi, university-level issues, accreditation procedures, and data collection for program evaluation must be attended. While improving programs is an important departmental function, these meetings are often attended out of duty rather than individual interests.

Is the purpose of the meeting clearly presented?

Even when a proposed meeting is related to professional interests, the meeting is only valuable if it is organized and focused. Choose to not attend meetings based on the agenda items or the lack of an agenda. Most professors have attended meetings that felt like a waste of time because the facilitator was not prepared or did not follow the agenda. A possible example is that of a college-level meeting on improving scores on a statewide test for certification as recounted by Claire.

The meeting included representatives from around the university, whose students would take this test. The initial meeting was productive and began with an analysis of data and compared how students performed in relation to students from other universities in the state. The meeting next included groups brainstorming ideas for raising students' scores. The follow-up was effective—a list of ideas from the first meeting was sent around and the steps being taken toward implementing the ideas were presented.

Unfortunately, the subsequent meeting was not as well organized. New data were presented and analyzed, but the discussion and questions mimicked the first meeting and no new progress was made toward the goal of improving test scores. In order for meetings to be productive, each one needs clear objectives and a focus on meeting those objectives. If this is not evident in the agenda, then asking for clarification can help both you and the facilitator. If a clear purpose is not shared, then declining to attend is one way to protect your time.

Is it clear why you have been asked to attend?

For many committees, the reasons for the invitation are clear. If you teach online, then inclusion in the new university technology committee makes perfect sense. When one is selected *teacher of the year*, inclusion at a college meeting regarding teaching and learning curriculum is a good fit. But when the connection is not evident as to why you were asked to participate, consider carefully before committing.

A committee forming to consider e-portfolios may be valuable and may make decisions on which tool might be selected for students to use across the campus. But unless this is truly going to impact your program or is a topic that you find interesting, there is no need to agree to sit on this committee. If you ask "will this impact me?" and the answer is *yes* then you will need to protect your time. There are too many topics with possible impact for you to sit on all the committees, and if you don't protect your time in academia, then it will quickly fill with meetings about meetings and other nonsense.

Will you be able to make a valuable contribution to this meeting?

This question is another important one to consider. Professors must find meetings that align with their area(s) of expertise and talent(s) so they can make valuable contributions. For example, volunteering regularly to serve as the assessment coordinator for a program. This is not a task of choice, but collecting data and writing reports is a skill set that serves the department. A colleague, who serves as chair, may not be as skilled at writing reports so this division of duties works to the benefit of the department.

Beyond the match with talent, your ability to contribute could be sorely limited if your schedule is too packed to dedicate the time necessary to make a valuable contribution to the goals of the committee. Spreading yourself too thin by attending more meetings than you can contribute to in a valuable way is unproductive.

If you limit your meeting attendance based on asking yourself these questions, then often you will find service work that is fulfilling and constructive. Volunteering to chair a committee is one way to ensure that the work done aligns with your interests, and it has other advantages such as your setting the frequency of meetings and scheduling. Be aware that the extra duties that come with chairing are often time-consuming, and the added responsibilities can be onerous.

It is recommended that you only volunteer to chair if the duties clearly align with your own teaching and research interests. For example, a research interest on metacognition in education might lead you to say yes to chair a committee on how to increase student reflection. Combining research and teaching interests with service work makes for more productive use of time and leads to service work that is of interest and is a worthwhile pursuit.

PROGRAM REVIEW/ASSESSMENT

In some ways, program review could have fit into the earlier discussion of paperwork and meetings. It definitely generates more than its fair share of these, but it is so tedious and time-consuming that it warrants its own section. Additional concerns are raised about program review because it represents a move toward the standardization of education in the United States, which has grown out of the K–12 standardization movement and the culture of accountability that sees assessment as a tool for measuring success. Of course, the only success that is evident from an assessment is the success of scoring well on an assessment.

This drive toward reviewing our programs, whether it be from a national accreditation body or an internal audit of programs, must be handled judiciously. Academic freedom is a tenet of the university system in the United States, and it is threatened by the push toward standardization that often accompanies program review.

For obvious reasons, program review can have a positive impact on the programs offered at many universities. Reviewing programs to ensure that students are learning and that courses are aligned with the overriding concepts in the field can build stronger programs and lead to continuous growth and improvements. Even though the structure involved in program review is often restrictive, there are often ways to make it personal and turn it into a true endeavor for improving curriculum and teaching. This may feel a bit forced, but it is worthwhile since so much time is often dedicated to program review.

The difficult task with program review is determining what is reasonable and right while not just accepting standardization. A program reviewer reported that a university suggested that all faculty teaching a particular course give students the same exam question in order to create better assessment data. Certainly there is nothing wrong with considering such an approach, but it does fly in the face of individualized pedagogy, academic freedom, and creativity.

Faculty are the backbone of the university and will only keep the profession as a place to be creative and innovative if they refuse to *follow along*. Academic departments are often asked to design new programs, but when research-based options are presented, they are deemed not feasible. More often than not, this is because the administration does not want to fund programs that are less profitable, because of the infamous SCH issue (student credit hours—how many are you producing?).

Professors, as content experts, must continue to struggle to provide programs for students that will increase their critical thinking and learning in the discipline. Part of what makes academia great is the focus on academic freedom and individual research agendas. Program review can enhance this, or it can stifle it, and professors must remain vigilant of the potential pitfalls.

FINAL THOUGHTS

Paperwork, meetings, and program review/assessment are all components of the professor role. There is nothing inherently horrifying about any of them. But allowing these pursuits to dull the thirst for knowledge would definitely be a horrible detriment to what is inherently a very important and fulfilling career. Professors, generally, seek to teach well, be productive researchers, and engage in meaningful professional service. If this leads to becoming overwhelmed with paperwork, meetings, and program review activities, then the professor role loses some of its quality and value.

According to Siddique (2011, 187), "If [professors] are free to make their decisions and [are] given autonomy, then they feel more satisfied with their jobs and put more efforts in accomplishing work related goals." If paperwork, meetings, and program review/assessment take up too much time, then professors are less likely to feel autonomous and free to make decisions. Taking charge is the best way to stay focused on what it important and thus spend time engaged in the pursuit of academic interests.

REFERENCES

Chickering, Arthur, and Zelda Gamson. 1987. "Seven Principles of Good Practice in Under-graduate Education." American Association of Higher Education 39:3–7.

Kensing, Kyle. 2013. "The Ten Least Stressful Jobs of 2013." Retrieved February 28, 2014 from: http://www.careercast.com/jobs-rated/10-least-stressful-jobs-2013.

Parkinson, Northcote. 1957. *Parkinson's Law*. Boston: Houghton Mifflin.

Siddique, Anam, Danial Hassan, Mannan Khan, and Urooj Fatima. 2011. "Impact of Academic Leadership on Faculty Motivation and Organizational Effectiveness in Higher Education System." *International Journal of Business and Social Science* 2(8):184–92.

Tovani, Cris. 2004. *Do I Really Have to Teach Reading?: Content Comprehension, Grades 6–12*. New York: Stenhouse.

Chapter Five

Honeymooning Alone

*On the Challenges of Dual-Career Long-Distance
Academic Couples*

Breanne Fahs

Imagine sitting on a beach chair in South Florida on the last day of your honeymoon watching the ocean waves and nibbling on some cheese and crackers that you snagged from the hotel lounge. A hotel staff person, noting the absence of your spouse and remembering your identity as honeymooners, asks about him. Imagine smiling uncomfortably and realizing that for today you would be honeymooning alone. This would be an odd predicament for a newly married woman. How could this arrangement be explained to strangers?

If you were to tell someone that you dropped your husband off early that morning so that he could catch his plane back to teach at a university in the South while you now waited for your late-night flight back to the Southwest, this would sound absurd to the average hotel worker. Imagining having to live away from your partner so that you could continue your academic career in Arizona while he maintained his academic career in the South is something that could make someone cringe when explaining her life to an inquiring employee.

Imagine being newly married and not able to see your husband again for weeks. Imagine having over 80 publications between the two of you and substantial teaching responsibilities, while straddling multiple obligations— to yourselves, to your jobs, and to your gender politics. To ask one spouse to simply give up his or her career to follow the other may not be plausible. Plus, they refused to ask for such a thing. Imagine your response to the inquiring hotel staff person, "I'm honeymooning alone today." This narrative is collected from a respondent who is part of an academic couple engaged in a long-distance relationship, and it forms the core of this chapter.

THE STRUGGLES OF ACADEMIC COUPLES

Having a long-distance marriage whose distance has no expiration date truly exemplifies the epitome of an academic horror story. Those who do are not crippled by unemployment or underemployment, are paid above the exploitative wages and miserly benefits offered to adjuncts and lecturers, and have more vacation time than almost every other occupation. However, they remain trapped by the restrictions of tenure and the politics of academia. In this way, they are not alone (not by a long shot).

A recent study of over 30,000 academic couples working at research institutions across the United States found that 36% of academics were coupled with other academics, with more women than men choosing academic spouses (Girod et al. 2010). A study conducted 13 years earlier found that a full 40% of women academics were married to other academics (Astin and Milem 1997), though those numbers had risen markedly for the 2010 sample (Girod et al. 2010). Ten percent of all faculty members across all disciplines are now *dual hires*, with numbers increasing from 3% in the 1970s to 13% since 2000 (Schiebinger et al. 2008).

Further, academic couples employed as professors had higher odds of applying to other academic positions and engaging in job searches (Girod et al. 2010). This is, in part, because a large proportion of these couples live geographically separated from their spouses.

Accounting for non-married partners and same-sex couples whose data are often invisible in these assessments, those numbers increase exponentially. Among scientists, one study found that a whopping 70% had chosen another scientist as a partner (Goodman 2005). This fact raises questions about how faculty and universities will manage the ever-increasing needs of faculty to balance family and job responsibilities for dual-career academic couples.

Shockingly little scholarship has examined the phenomenon of academic couples living apart. One notable study of married couples from the general population found that, while both long-distance and geographically close relationships both had high satisfaction, couples in long-distance relationships had high relationship investments in comparison to geographically close relationships (Pistole, Roberts, and Mosko 2010). This suggests that distance relationships need strong commitments to survive and can foster serious investment and commitment in partners and also that they will likely continue to seek jobs in geographically closer locations until they succeed in doing so.

Consequently, recognition from universities at the administrative level that this quest is real, painful, and ongoing would in all likelihood lead to more faculty staying in their jobs, fewer resources devoted unnecessarily to job candidates who primarily want geographical proximity to their partners and fewer costs to the university. That is, of course, if universities care about issues such as faculty morale and faculty retention.

In studies of academic couples, nearly all have focused on academics working at the same university (Sweet and Moen 2004; Girod et al. 2010; Schiebinger et al. 2008). This creates a notable gap in the literature concerning those who endure long-distance marriages or partnerships, even though a few studies have documented that this is quite a common arrangement for university faculty (Wolf-Wendell, Twombly, and Rice 2000; Pistole et al. 2010).

This blind spot in understanding these relationship stressors, particularly because academic jobs are given to one person and the assumption is that all family members will follow, seems all the more bizarre given how many academics, especially women, find themselves living apart from their partner. Perhaps academics are too upset or afraid to even study the social problems of their own profession, despite the overwhelming frequency of distance relationships.

Academics all over the country are plagued with such arrangements and are expected, much like military wives and husbands, to live happily and productively away from their partners in order to maintain their academic jobs. These expectations, when coupled with the demanding expectations of university life—publishing, committee work, excellence in pedagogy, student mentoring, and intensifying demands to attend conferences and make a nationally recognized presence for oneself—can become overwhelming.

THE HIDDEN CHALLENGES OF DUAL LIVES

Long-distance couples face a plethora of challenges that are often invisible to those who have never grappled with this oddity. Contemporary university practices routinely over-rely upon contingent and non-tenure-track faculty and often have over 100 applicants per tenure-track opening. This sets up terrible odds for academic couples attempting to secure two tenured positions.

In terms of the sorts of challenges academic couples face, each member of the couple must find a job (itself a huge obstacle in today's economy), work toward tenure, ensure constant research productivity and teaching success, provide mentoring to students at their university, maintain communication with their partner (e.g., phone, texting, Skype) that often takes place across different time zones, and establish community in the place where they live as well as the community where their partner lives (Stuck and Ware 2005).

Essentially, these couples must lead two separate but integrated lives with two sets of friends, different contexts and social lives, and different university expectations and procedures. This is accomplished often with wildly different support networks, break schedules, and official arrangements with university administrators.

The financial costs also present a staggering challenge as couples must operate two full-time households, often with two mortgages, two cable payments, two electric bills, two medical insurance premiums, two car payments, two sets of home repairs (and so on), and the massive costs of travel and plane tickets. If the couples need to see each other urgently (e.g., death in the family or medical emergency) these financial and emotional costs rise even more.

For gay and lesbian couples, struggles with coming out (often twice), finding a gay and lesbian community and combatting heterosexist hiring practices often compound the existing difficulties of long-distance relationships within academia (Stuck and Ware 2005). Additionally, lesbian and gay couples often cannot invoke the sorts of privileges that heterosexual married couples have, including the ability to utilize the Family Medical Leave Act or each other's health insurance while living in long-distance partnerships.

Often couples have the tasks of weighing priorities, balancing work and life, and ensuring commitment to the university and their partner. For example, picture an academic couple that is trying to plan their wedding. In so doing, they have to choose an appropriate time to get married in Phoenix, Arizona. This means that a summer wedding would be far too hot for their guests and yet a fall and spring wedding would be impossible, given the distance between the two and their inability to see each other for longer than a weekend. They are left with Christmas break as their only viable option and are married immediately after finals ended.

For one spouse, this arrangement means having to juggle grading final exams, familial logistics, wedding preparations, and student needs simultaneously. Specifically, the spouse wrote several student letters of recommendations the morning of the rehearsal dinner and received phone calls the morning of the wedding day asking them to complete an urgent Skype interview for a potential job; they declined the interview.

They ultimately ended up interviewing via Skype for a job at a Big Ten university during the first day of the honeymoon (a job they ultimately did not get, in part, because, as the chair later informed, the candidate was *underprepared* during the interview to answer site-specific questions about their research centers). These challenges, far from insignificant, signify the imbalances, intrusions, and impossible choices that dual-career couples often experience.

INVESTING IN DUAL-CAREER HIRES

The invisibility of these challenges can often lead to blind spots and inconsistencies with regard to who offers institutional support for hiring both partners as an academic couple. Although most universities will proclaim that they value academic-couple hires, only 24% reported having a policy-level infrastructure to support these types of hires (Schiebinger et al. 2008).

Most universities also show no flexibility about scheduling or other aspects that would help long-distance couples negotiate their travel and commuting needs. And yet, such refusal to formally support academic couples goes against the interests of the university as dual-career academic hires bring many benefits to the university.

One recent study indicates that academic couples were far more productive than married non-academic couples (Girod et al. 2010). This implies that universities that care about improving productivity should see academic couples as worthy of investment. Notably, new assistant professors hired under a spousal hire policy were 30% more likely than their peers to earn tenure (Woolstenhulme et al. 2011).

Another study of academic couples found that they formed highly productive collaborative partnerships based on egalitarian values, complementary and overlapping collegial networks, and similar training and interests and that they were highly supportive of each other (and their colleagues) both on and off the job when at the same university (Creamer et al. 2001).

While some problems have been noted for heterosexual academic couples—particularly related to husbands advancing more quickly than wives or women being accused of over-relying on their husbands' academic contributions (Bird and Bird 1987; Smart and Smart 1990; Horning 1997)—most people's experiences remained quite positive.

Reactions by chairs, directors, and deans have ranged from wholly empathic and sympathetic to callously indifferent and apathetic. Those university administrators who have struggled with an academic long-distance relationship of their own have often shown far more support, empathy, and care for these difficult arrangements than those who have not. Understanding the emotional, financial, time, and personal costs of a long-distance marriage seems to require personal experience with its unique horrors.

A university dean aptly described a long-distance academic relationship as similar to delivering a baby and being in a labor that you're not sure will ever end and also to running a grueling marathon without a finish line in sight. A colleague described her long-distance marriage as cruel and unusual punishment and cited the fact that such assaults to family life would never be tolerated in most other professions. Still another female colleague told me that she put off having children for a long time because of a long-distance academic relationship and that she is now too old to begin the process (something she regrets deeply).

Understanding the ultimate costs to faculty members who have to commute, not to mention bottom-line costs to the university in terms of competition for time and resources, should inspire university administrators to take these challenges seriously. Often, and unfortunately, however, they routinely do not. Many universities have no policies in place to support dual-career academic couples. As a result, spousal hiring is only sometimes available as a means to recruit potential job candidates and *not* as a means to retain outstanding existing faculty.

THE COSTS OF DISTANCE

Research suggests that living apart like this hurts job satisfaction, lowers investment in the workplace, and makes people less likely to stay put and more prone to leave their jobs (Canary and Dainton 2002). This sometimes occurs at considerable cost to both members of the couple as people sacrifice their own careers at the expense of their partners' or take jobs they do not necessarily desire in order to live closer to their partner.

Depressingly, having a PhD was sometimes even a deterrent to finding good jobs closer together. A study of economists found that married couples who both had a PhD had a harder time securing their preferred job than married economists who both had MA or BA degrees (Helppie and Murray-Close 2010). Gender biases centered on who has the power to negotiate a partner hire is also a significant factor as men more often negotiate partner hires for their female partners than the opposite.

Consequently, women unable to secure jobs for both spouses, particularly at the senior level, reported considerable bitterness and frustration with the university, while those who did secure dual-career employment at the same university reported positive experiences overall (McNeil and Sher 1999). One study found that, when comparing couples who both worked for a single university (one in seven of their sample) and couples where only one partner worked for the university, coworking couples showed more work commitment and family success (especially for husbands), more family and marital satisfaction (especially for wives), and overall benefits to institutions (Sweet and Moen 2004).

Institutions that support dual-career hiring, often by having dual-career programs in place to help with targeted hires, end up with greater investment in the university by their faculty (Sweet and Moen 2004). While some administrators have rightly noted that policy-level changes are difficult and often do not account for the unique circumstances of individual faculty members (Hornig 1997), other universities have celebrated success with such blanket policies. For example, the University of Nebraska at Kearney has an 85% rate of placing the academic spouse in a desirable job in their field within eight weeks; something that has helped them attract top faculty and keep them loyal (Goodman 2005). Explicit policies for spousal and partner hires could also entice talented faculty. One recent study found that 72% of academics had an employed partner whose career needed to be taken into account when either of them applied for a job (Schiebinger et al. 2008).

Further, universities that supported partner hires for both heterosexual and same-sex couples—something that occurs seldom within academia, particularly at the policy level—may end up securing more *buy-in* from the broader faculty, who may see such measures as an indicator of positive climate.

One study found that the heterosexist premises of spousal hiring that only helped heterosexual married couples often stood in direct contrast to a university's supposed commitment to diversity, equality, and anti-homophobic practices. As a result, Chantal Nadeau (2005) argued that queer faculty should *not* support spousal hiring policies until universities fully account for the needs of all committed couples regardless of gender.

GENDER POLITICS AND THE *PROGRESSIVE* UNIVERSITY

The complications of academic couple life can also place more strain on women faculty than men as academic couples also face sexism when seeking dual hires at the same university. First, highly educated women, especially heterosexual women, often have a harder time finding suitable partners, often because men prefer partners who have less education than themselves (Regan et al. 2000; Greitemeyer 2007). Women have also typically been socialized to value their male partners' careers over their own, thus setting lower career aspirations or taking worse jobs than men typically do.

When women do partner with other academics, this can be perilous in terms of finding dual-employment opportunities at the same university. A study of women physicists found that while 68% of these women married other scientists, their and their spouses' needs for dual appointments were rarely supported (McNeil and Sher 1999). Among physicists, one study found that 6% of married male physicists married another physicist while a full 43% of female physicists married another physicist (Ouellette 2007). This signals, again, why dual-career hiring is an issue that disproportionately affects women faculty.

Similarly, in a recent study of medical school faculty, women were far more likely than men to be employed at their current institution as part of a dual hire, especially at senior levels (13.6% of women versus 6.3% of men at the full professor level) (Girod et al. 2010). Women academics also reported that they turned down jobs because their male spouse was not offered *satis-factory employment* far more often than did male academics.

This implies that women either settled for less appealing spousal-hire jobs more than men did or that men could more successfully negotiate for their female partners than women negotiating for their male partners.

Either way, this does not bode well for senior-level academic women. As Girod et al. (2010, 317) wrote, "Fewer women enter a dual hire as the first hire in a couple, despite being more likely to have an academic partner. Why this is is so unclear—it is possible that dynamics within couples and traditional recruitment processes are simultaneously at work."

Notably, academic couples also tended to differ from couples with only one academic in important ways, primarily around equality and gender politics. While faculty in general experienced work and family strain, sometimes along gender lines where women felt more family strain and men felt more work strain, academic couples faced both at the same time (Elliott 2008). Compared to couples with only one academic partner, dual-career academic couples had more education overall, and they reported less likelihood to prioritize one spouse's career over that of the other (Sweet and Moen 2004).

Academic married couples working at the same university also prized more egalitarian parenting relationships than other dual-career couples as their schedules and career aspirations formed a *give-and-take* relationship that valued both men's and women's roles (Sweet and Moen 2004). This suggests that these couples can help support the progressive politics of the university on both a personal and professional level.

Still, universities will have to make accommodations in order to retain academic couples on their faculty. Two studies found that academic couples were far more likely to resign from a current job, or to take a new job, based on their partner's employment opportunities. Several studies found that one in five resignations and hires has of primary importance the partner's dual hire (Wilson 1996; Ferber and Loeb 1997).

SYMBOLIC AND EMOTIONAL STRAIN

These macro-level analyses of the stressors of long-distance academic couples do not fully account for the difficulties present in actually managing a long-distance academic lifestyle. Stuck and Ware (2005) pointed out that distance can create strain on the quality of life for academic couples as distance exacerbates the difficulties of day-to-day hassles (e.g., maintaining two homes and not having a partner's help when doing house or car repairs). Couples often struggle with split loyalties and cannot find a single *home*. This can present important symbolic challenges to one feeling comfortable, secure, and relaxed.

As Stuck and Ware (2005, 46) wrote, "If one values eating meals together, enjoying a fireplace, talking over the day's events, and falling to sleep together, even perhaps sharing the joy of having a family pet, the biggest cost in a distance relationship is exactly that—not sharing the same physical *home* during the week."

One couple reported on their struggle with not sleeping beside each other, not being able to enjoy their pet together, not preparing meals together, not deconstructing the day's events together, not being able to visit friends and attend social events as a couple, feeling less joy at simple entertainment options like watching movies or enjoying a sports game, and ongoing feelings of missing each other. The *two-body problem* becomes challenging in ways that geographically close married or partnered couples rarely even think about.

This couple also reported that while seeking jobs at each other's universities, they faced barriers because they are *both* senior-level hires. Typically, spousal hires have a clearly demarcated senior-level and junior-level person, or one partner may be more accomplished or famous than the other. This couple truly embodied a partnership based on equality, including their rank, salary, and accomplishments.

Neither of them wants to leave academia or to ask the other partner to do so. Further, they have each met with the force of institutional barriers to helping them find adequate solutions to their family/work needs. Each struggles with cycles of feeling powerless and hopeless, followed by feelings of renewed optimism and resilience. Ultimately, this challenge has required them to demonstrate courage and perseverance while not crumbling under the weight of their two-body problem.

PROPOSALS FOR CHANGE

In order to lessen the stress on academic couples, break this silence, and work toward rectifying the fundamentally important inequities present in the current system of dual-career academic hiring, the following solutions are proposed:

1. Universities should establish and adequately fund policies that make partner hires easier and more routine in university employment practices. For all the reasons outlined in this chapter, universities need to offer solutions that do not require couples to live apart for years on end, as this is an inhumane and inadequate way of addressing faculty needs.
2. Job candidates should be advised, from graduate school and beyond, to never take a job without negotiating a partner hire up front. Most

jobs will never offer a partner hire after you have already taken a position.

3. University hiring committees should state in their job advertisements whether they have a dual-career hiring program in place and whether they support partner hires. Search-committee chairs should also make clear (without prompting or questions from job candidates) that they support these policies and would be willing to negotiate and discuss a partner hire if the candidate needed one.

4. For people who become partnered after taking a tenure-track or tenured position, universities should put policies in place about the procedure for *then* securing a partner/spousal hire so that the needs of these faculty can be recognized. Universities should not imply (or require) that faculty should seek academic jobs elsewhere as a means of securing leverage for spousal hires, as this is both unethical and destructive to the limited resources of other universities and to the faculty members themselves.

5. Partner/spousal hiring policies should be absolutely clear about their politics and should clearly and plainly support same-sex committed couples, non-married committed opposite-sex couples, and married opposite-sex couples equally. Special provisions should *not* be given to married heterosexual couples above other kinds of couples, and marital status should not matter in these regards at the policy level.

6. University administrators should pay special attention to equity and fairness in gender, race, and sexuality with regard to partner hiring. Women faculty, compared to men faculty, are often disadvantaged in their ability to successfully lobby for partner hires. This fact should be documented and rectified by the university. Similarly, universities should carefully attend to whom they consider *attractive* faculty to retain, especially along gender and race lines, so that women and people of color are not disadvantaged.

7. For couples who have not yet secured a partner hire or dual careers at the same university, policies should be put into place that allow for these couples to receive special accommodations from the university in the form of temporary pay increases to help offset commuting and dual-household costs until the partner hire can be implemented; extra periods of research leave relative to other faculty or allowances for non-residential status while teaching online courses; unpaid leaves when requested by faculty; and allowances for more telecommuting.

Ultimately, like many other challenges in academia, the problems dual-career academic couples face are not simply inevitable or without solution. Faculty must break the silences so often enforced around poor quality of life within academia rather than enduring them in silence or with resignation (Gill 2009).

Instead, universities have an obligation to recognize the unique burdens placed upon faculty in today's job market as many (or most) academic couples have to negotiate living apart for sustained periods of time. Policy-level implementation of measures to support dual-career academic couples will help to partly alleviate the burdens that faculty members, as individuals, too often negotiate alone and without institutional support.

Further, given that the literature suggests that these problems disproportionately affect women faculty and that the humanities and social sciences lag behind the *hard* sciences and medical schools in advocating for spousal hiring (Schiebinger et al. 2008), universities must recognize dual-career policies as an indicator of positive climate and progressive politics.

Not only will faculty benefit from having better work/life balance and by being able to live in one household with their partner, but universities, too, will benefit through increased productivity (academic couples already are more productive than their peers, and living without extra strain increases this even further); more solid commitment to the university; and, ultimately, a chance to demonstrate progressive gender, race, and sexual orientation politics at the policy level. With an increasingly vicious job market displacing more academic couples to separate states and separate households, the need for these policies has become ever more urgent.

REFERENCES

Astin, Helen S., and Jeffrey F. Milem. 1997. "The Status of Academic Couples in U.S. Institutions." Pp. 128–55 in *Academic Couples: Problems and Promises*, edited by Marianne A. Ferber and Jane W. Loeb. Chicago: University of Illinois.

Bird, Gloria W., and Gerald A. Bird. 1987. "In Pursuit of Academic Careers: Observations and Reflections of a Dual-Career Couple." *Family Relations* 36(1):97–101.

Canary, Daniel J., and Marianne Dainton. 2002. *Maintaining Relationships through Communication: Relational, Contextual, and Cultural Variations*. New York: Routledge.

Creamer, Elizabeth G. 2001. *Working Equal: Academic Couples as Collaborators*. Florence, KY: Psychology Press.

Elliott, Marta. 2008. "Gender Differences in the Causes of Work and Family Strain among Academic Faculty." *Journal of Human Behavior in the Social Environment* 17(1–2):157–173.

Ferber, Marianne, and Jane W. Loeb. 1997. *Academic Couples: Problems and Promises*. Chicago: University of Illinois Press.

Gill, Rosalind. 2009. "Breaking the Silence: The Hidden Injuries of Neo-Liberal Academia." Pp. 228–44 in *Secrecy and Silence in the Research Process: Feminist Reflections*, edited by Róisín Ryan-Flood and Rosalind Gill. London: Routledge.

Girod, Sabine, Shannon K. Gilmartin, Hannah Valantine, and Londa Schiebinger. 2010. "Academic Couples: Implications for Medical School Faculty Recruitment and Retention." *Journal of the American College of Surgeons* 212(3):310–19.

Goodman, Sally. 2005. "The Family Balancing Act." *Nature* 433:552–53.

Greitemeyer, Tobias. 2007. "What Do Men and Women Want in a Partner? Are Educated Partners Always More Desirable?" *Journal of Experimental Social Psychology* 43(2):180–94.

Helppie, Brooke, and Marta Murray-Close. 2010. "Moving Out or Moving Up? New Economists Sacrifice Job Opportunities for the Proximity to Significant Others and Vice Versa: A Working Paper." University of Michigan, Department of Economics.

Hornig, Lilli S. 1997. "Academic Couples: The View from the Administration." Pp. 248–69 in *Academic Couples: Problems and Promises*, edited by Marianne A. Ferber and Jane W. Loeb. Chicago: University of Illinois Press.

McNeil, Laurie, and Marc Sher. 1999. "Dual Science Career Couples." Accessed November 26, 2015. http://www.physics.wm.edu/dualcareer.html.

Nadeau, Chantal. 2005. "Unruly Democracy and the Privileges of Public Intimacy: (Same) Sex Spousal Hiring in Academia." *Journal of Lesbian Studies* 9(4):89–105.

Ouellette, Jennifer. 2007. "Scientists in Love: When Two Worlds Collide." *Nature* 445:700–702.

Pistole, M. Carole, Amber Roberts, and Jonathan E. Mosko. 2010. "Commitment Predictors: Long-Distance Versus Geographically Close Relationships." *Journal of Counseling & Development* 88(2):146–53.

Regan, Pamela C., Lauren Levin, Susan Sprecher, F. Scott Christopher, and Rodney Cate. 2000. "Partner Preferences: What Characteristics Do Men and Women Desire in Their Short-Term Sexual and Long-Term Romantic Partners?" *Journal of Psychology & Human Sexuality* 12(3):1–21.

Schiebinger, Londa, Andrea Davies Henderson, and Shannon K. Gilmartin. 2008. *Dual-Career Academic Couples: What Universities Need to Know*. Palo Alto, CA: Stanford University Press.

Smart, Mollie S., and Russell C. Smart. 1990. "Paired Prospects: Dual Career Couples on Campus." *Academe* 76:23–27.

Stuck, Mary Frances, and Mary Ware. 2005. "We're Both Tenured Professors . . . but Where Is Home?" *Journal of Lesbian Studies* 9(4):41–56.

Sweet, Stephen, and Phyllis Moen. 2004. "Coworking as a Career Strategy: Implications for the Work and Family Lives of University Employees. *Innovative Higher Education* 28(4):255–72.

Wilson, Robin. 1996. "Weary of Commuter Marriages, More Couples in Academe Make Career Sacrifices to Be Together." *Chronicle of Higher Education* 43:A10–A13.

Wolf-Wendel, Lisa, Susan Twombly, and Suzanne Rice. 2000. "Dual Career Couples: Keeping Them Together." *Journal of Higher Education* 71(3):239–321.

Woolstenhulme, Jared L., Benjamin W. Cowan, Jill J. McCluskey, and Tori C. Byington. 2011. "Solving the Two-Body Problem: An Evaluation of University Partner Accommodation Policies." Accessed October 26, 2015. http://dualhire.org/s/Solving-the-Two-Body-Problem-AFW.pdf.

Chapter Six

Who Publishes in Leading Sociology Journals (1965–2010)?

Robert Perrucci, Mangala Subramaniam, and Carolyn C. Perrucci

Although not a central topic in the current sociological literature, the sociology of sociology has long been concerned with the stratified nature of universities and academic departments. Interest in the prestige ranking of universities and academic departments has produced a number of national ranking schemes that serve as proxy measures for the quality of academic programs and critical reaction to such rankings (Carter 1966; Knudsen and Vaughn 1969; National Research Council 1995; Burris 2004).

The existence of national rankings has also generated scholarly research devoted to examining the possible basis for a stratified system of higher education, examining the role of research funding and faculty research productivity in shaping the prestige hierarchy in academe (Crane 1965; Gross 1970; Hagstrom 1971; Pfeffer, Leong, and Strehl 1976; Long 1978; Keith and Babchuck 1998).

The question of why universities and academic departments across disciplines have taken a stratified form has received less attention. One of the early efforts in this regard is the 1963 publication of *Little Science, Big Science* by Derek J. de Solla Price, a Yale historian of science. Price was concerned with the long-term shift from solo-scientist, small-lab research to collaborative teams with extensive corporate-government funding. Price's primary attention was devoted to the growth of publications, scientific journals, increased specialization, the search for new ways for scientists to communicate, and increased competition among scientists.

As almost an aside, Price noted the appearance of what he called *invisible colleges*, or informal networks of elite scientists and their followers with common interests that would facilitate the sharing of information much faster than what was provided by scientific journals. Price's observations about the *hard* sciences soon spread to the social sciences.

Competition for funds and for professional recognition among individual scholars was soon supported by their universities and academic departments, leading to institutional forms of competition with emphasis on external funding for research, citation counts for publications, impact scores of journals, and prestige rankings of universities and academic departments. Recognition of the growing competition among scholars and departments was related to research on the stratification system in sociology and how it has affected the production and placement of new PhDs (Baldi 1994) and the increased pressure for productivity and promotion (Perrucci, O'Flaherty, and Marshall 1983).

The expanding body of empirical research on the link between scholarly productivity and competition among universities and academic departments has led to the recognition of the importance of the idea of *social closure*, first introduced by Max Weber and discussed most fully by Frank Parkin (1979, 44), and is defined as "the process by which social collectivities seek to maximize rewards by restricting access to resources and opportunities to a limited number of eligibles." Some analysts have proposed using a social-closure perspective to understand a wide array of practices in the profession of sociology associated with the increasing competition among scholars (Murphy 1983).

This chapter is drawn from a larger project examining the publication practices in four leading sociology journals from 1960 to 2010 (Perrucci, Subramaniam, and Perrucci 2013). This project examines the publication practices of faculty from elite departments (top 20) and those from non-elite departments (about 200 departments) in order to uncover the existence of a pattern of social closure reflected in the domination by elite faculty of the publication outlets in four leading journals.

The theoretical framework distinguishes between several forms of social closure, including *demographic social closure*, which reflects the numerical composition of faculty and graduate students across several hundred graduate departments of sociology; *competitive social closure*, which reflects a shifting advantage between elite and non-elite departments that is revealed in the number of faculty and graduate students in all graduate departments of sociology; and *knowledge social closure*, which reflects the differential use of theoretical and methodological paradigms across departments of sociology.

Thus, examinations of the question of competition in the discipline of sociology are continued by examining the publication practices of faculty from elite and non-elite academic departments. Specifically, data are provided from four leading sociology journals over a 50-year period that identify the authors of published articles who are on the faculty of elite departments of sociology and those on the faculty of non-elite departments.

Beyond the affiliations of elite authors, authors are identified who are on the faculty of non-elite departments but who received their PhDs from elite departments and may therefore be considered to be *hidden elites*. The combination of authors from elite departments and authors from non-elite departments who received their PhDs from elite departments will provide a better measure of the extent of social closure that may exist in leading sociology journals.

GETTING PUBLISHED: THE PEER-REVIEW PROCESS

Scholarly journals have as their stated goal to identify and publish the highest quality papers they receive. Usually they receive several hundred papers a year. A small percentage of these papers are deflected or not sent out for review by the editor because the paper is believed to be well outside the guidelines for the journal. Most papers received by the journal are sent out by the editors in what is called a "double-blind review process" (i.e., the reviewers do not know the identity of the author, and the author does not know the identity of reviewers).

The review process is a self-regulating system that protects the autonomy of the journal and emphasizes the values of objectivity and fairness in the review process (Chubin and Hackett 1990). This process is important to scholars in the discipline because publications in peer-reviewed journals are linked to a wide array of rewards including promotion and tenure, merit raises, and professional reputation (Clemens, Powell, McIlwaine, and Okamoto 1995).

Despite these universalistic and meritocratic goals, the journal review process has been subjected to research and commentary that has examined possible sources of bias and particularism in the process of selecting manuscripts for publication (Bakanic, McPhail, and Simon 1987; Miller and Perrucci 2001)

Since the focus here is on papers that have already been published in leading journals, many of the issues raised in the literature about biases in the review process may not apply. Yet there may still be some basis for the exercise of particularism in the range of actions available to journal editors and perhaps even to external reviewers. So the question of interest for this chapter is, "In what ways may an editor, or advisory editors, privilege authors from elite departments, or authors who have received their PhD's from an elite department?" Consider the following possible answers.

1. Since the editor alone knows the identity of the author, an editor's academic ties to an elite department may influence decisions made about external reviewers and the decision made to accept, reject, or call for the author to revise and resubmit the manuscript in light of the comments and criticisms of external reviewers. There is some research indicating the existence of editor-author institutional network ties that may influence the publication process (Willis and McNamee 1990).

2. The advisory editors and external reviewers are in the double-blind mode, so they do not know the author of the manuscript they are being asked to review. However, as most scholars who have reviewed papers know, almost all papers have an early footnote thanking colleagues for their various forms of support regarding the current paper. Such information provides indications of the author's network of colleagues and perhaps provides clues to the academic department of the author.

   The double-blind condition may also be vulnerable to reviewer knowledge of who among their colleagues publishes in distinctive areas, data sources, or methodologies. Thus, it is often possible to link certain areas of research or research methodologies to specific persons or groups of persons known to have publications with a distinct focus.

3. When there are split decisions by external reviewers (one says accept, one says reject, and one says revise and resubmit), the editor has the discretion in making a final decision based on the quality of the positive or negative reviews, or in seeking additional reviews. Editors may seek additional reviews for papers they believe have merit or for any other reason that may reflect particularism.

   Editors may have greater influence over the final decision in cases of split decisions by external reviewers. Since split decisions are often the case for most manuscripts (Miller and Perrucci 2001), the influence of the editor is increased.

DATA AND METHODS

Three data sets were created and used, in part, for this chapter. The first data set is based on a sequential sample of issues from the *American Sociological Review (ASR), American Journal of Sociology (AJS), Social Forces (SF),* and *Social Problems (SP)*. The journals were ordered by decade between 1960 and 2010, and a sample was drawn from each by, for example, the first decade (1960), the fifth year of the decade (1965), and the last year of the decade (1969).

For each year selected, all issues of the journal were selected for coding (six issues each of *ASR* and *AJS* and four issues each of *SF* and *SP*). The final sample consisted of 20 issues of the four journals per sampled year for a total of 300 issues. The total number of issues published by the four journals from 1960 to 2010 is 20 issues per year, for a total of 1,000 issues. The sample of 300 issues constitutes a 30% sample.

Every article in each sampled issue was subjected to coding operations, excluding presidential addresses and research notes. The coding most relevant to this paper was the academic affiliations of the journal editor, associate editors, and authors. Department affiliation of editors and authors was coded as elite or non-elite based on the Carter (1966) ranking of the top 20 sociology departments and the National Research Council (1995) ranking of the top 23 departments for 2005 and 2010. For purposes of this chapter, this data set was used to identify authors with faculty appointments in elite and non-elite departments of sociology.

The second data set was based on information extracted from ASA Guides to Graduate Departments from 1965, 1975, 1985, 1995, 2005, 2010. We summarized the demographic composition of faculty at over 200 sociology departments, including total number of faculty, number of female faculty, number of graduate students and number of PhDs produced. These data are useful indicators of the extent of demographic social closure (i.e., whether the representation of elite authors in the four journals was a numerical expression of their representation in the total number of academic departments).

A third data set was created to identify the extent of *hidden elite* authors in the four journals, that is, those authors who were currently employed in non-elite departments but who had obtained their PhDs from elite departments. This measure was obtained from a separate sample of all articles published in the four journals for the years 1965, 1975, 1985, 1995, 2005. Authors with a current non-elite department affiliation were examined to see if their PhDs were earned at an elite department, thus being identified as hidden elites.

ELITE AND HIDDEN ELITE AUTHORS

The data analysis will proceed by examining all of the authors who have published articles in each of the four sociology journals under consideration for the mid-decade points in the years 1965 through 2005. The current academic department affiliation of each author is classified as elite (a top-20 department) or non-elite (all other departments), and they will be referred to in the analysis as *elite authors* and *non-elite authors*.

In addition, all non-elite authors will be examined for the departments from which they obtained their PhD. Those authors currently employed in

non-elite departments but who have received the PhD from an elite department will be classified as *hidden elites*.

The following analyses include a summary of the authors of articles in the
four journals for the six mid-decade years that were sampled. It is important
to consider some of the similarities and differences among the four journals.
All four journals are considered to be general journals, meaning that they
consider manuscripts for publication from a broad array of sociological topics, although *SP* may be less general than the others as its manuscripts are
expected to deal with some form of social problem.

The *ASR* and *AJS* are generally viewed as the top two journals in the
discipline, based on a variety of citation scores (Jacobs 2011). *SF* and *SP* are
ranked lower than *ASR* and *AJS*, but they are among the highly ranked
general journals. A point of difference among the four journals that may be
important is that the *ASR* and *SP* are official journals of professional associations, the American Sociological Association with about 14,000 members
and the Society for the Study of Social Problems with about 3,000 members,
while *AJS* and *SF* are independent journals.[1]

Simon (1994) has suggested that journals affiliated with professional associations may place greater constraints on the freedom of editors because of
the need for the journal to be responsive to, or representative of, the broad
interests of the association membership. The implicit hypothesis in Simon's
discussion is that professional association journals should be more universalistic in their selection of editors, authors, and topics for publication.

Data garnered for this study clearly indicate that about 50% of all authors
of articles published in *ASR* and *AJS* hold academic positions in an elite
department of sociology. While the percent of elite authors varies from a low
of 33% (*AJS*-2005) to a high of 64% (*ASR*-2010), the modal pattern is about
50%. The percent of elite authors in the *ASR* and *AJS* far exceeds their
proportion among all faculty in about 200 graduate departments of sociology.
For example, the highest proportion of elite faculty to all faculty is at a high
of 27% in 1965. For all remaining decades, the percentage of elite faculty
hovers around 15%.

Another relevant demographic statistic is the percent of PhDs in sociology awarded by elite departments versus all departments. This is important
since it is argued here that it is the new PhD who may be more likely to
submit articles based on dissertation research to either the *ASR* or *AJS*. In
1965, elite departments awarded a high of 58% of all PhDs and declined to
about 30% for all remaining decades. This percentage comes closer to the
percent of elite authors who publish in *ASR* and *AJS* but it does not quite
represent a case of demographic social closure.

The percent of elite authors in *SF* and *SP* is somewhat lower, with modal
patterns closer to about 30% of all authors coming from elite departments. *SF*
has a high percent of elite authors in 2005 (35.3%) and a low of 26.2% in

1985. *SP* has a high of elite authors in 1965 (57.1%) and a low in 1985 of 17.8%. The 1965 elite author percent for *SP* seems to be an outlier as most of the years reveal about mid-20% of elite authors in this journal. The general pattern across the four journals is that there is a much higher percent of elite authors in the two top-ranked journals, *ASR* and *AJS*, and somewhat lower percentages of elite authors in *SF* and *SP*.

However, in all cases, the percent of elite authors in the four journals far exceeds the demographic representation of faculty and graduate students in top-20 elite departments compared to all faculty and graduate students in about 200 departments of sociology. As noted above, in 1965, the percent of elite faculty to total faculty in all graduate departments of sociology was at a high of 27.2%, and this percentage declines to 14.6% in 1975 and remains at about the 15% level until 2010. Thus, the demographic composition of elite faculty, relative to total faculty, could not account for their high level of authorship in the four leading journals.

When considering PhD production in elite departments compared to PhD production in all graduate departments of sociology, the data tend in the direction of a demographic explanation for the high rate of elite authors, but not entirely. Data garnered for this study indicate the production of PhDs from elite departments is about 30% of all PhDs produced in each decade from 1975 to 2010.

Assuming that most PhDs may potentially be involved in publication efforts, the comparatively high level of PhD production by the top 20 departments increases the chances that those graduates would become faculty in elite departments and become authors of articles in the leading journals. Evidence from other research (Perrucci 1974; Burris 2004; Subramaniam, Perrucci, and Whitlock 2014) indicates that about eight in ten faculty in the top 20 elite departments obtained their PhDs from that same set of departments.

Also gleamed from the data is the percent of authors who received PhDs from elite departments but are now on the faculty in non-elite departments, or hidden elites. Among *ASR* authors, the percentage of hidden elites typically matches or exceeds the percentage of elite authors. In the case of *AJS* authors, the percent of hidden elite authors always exceeds the percent of elite authors with the low percent being 60% and the high of 88%.

In *SF* and *SP* the percent of hidden elite authors exceeds the percent of elite authors in all but one year (1965 for *SP*). The percent of hidden elite authors is about 50% across the six decades and, although the percent is somewhat lower than for *ASR* and *AJS*, the differences are not large.

When the percent of all authors in the four journals who are elites or hidden elites is combined for the *ASR* and *AJS* across all decades from 1965 to 2010, about eight out of ten authors are either on the faculty of an elite department or have obtained their PhD from an elite department. There is a low percent of 73.4 (*AJS* in 2005) and a high of 94.6% (*AJS* in 1985). For *SF* and *SP*, the combined percent of elite and hidden elite authors is lower than for *ASR* and *AJS*, 67% and 59.9%, respectively. However, these figures on the percent of authors with elite department ties in all four journals far and away exceed the proportion of all faculty at elite departments and PhD recipients from elite departments.

FINAL THOUGHTS

This chapter began with the stated goal of examining the extent of *social closure* in the discipline of sociology and undertook this task by asking, "Who publishes in leading sociology journals?" The answer is quite clear. But what is not known for sure is *why* faculty at elite departments and graduates of elite departments dominate the publication venues of the four journals.

The possibility of *demographic social closure* is not supported by the aggregate data on all graduate departments of sociology. The percent of authors in both leading journals with elite ties far exceeds their proportions in the population of all graduate departments. This leaves *competitive social closure* and *knowledge social closure* to account for the patterns in our data here. A case may be made for increased competition among departments that accompanies the expansion of departments, faculty, and graduate students.

This expansion must lead to greater competition for critical resources like research funds, top graduate students, and publication venues. And it must certainly be part of the reason for the concern over prestige rankings and metrics for performance by departments and faculty. Less well understood may be the operation of *knowledge social closure*, and this requires an examination of the relationship between gatekeepers and authors. But that is the subject for another paper.

NOTE

1. There is some ambiguity about the status of *Social Forces* as an independent journal or a publication of the Southern Sociological Association. Issues of the journal in the 1960s and 1970s make no mention of SSA. Then in 1990, the cover for *SF* states: "Associated with the Southern Sociological Society." The current official website for the journal makes no mention of SSA, but lists the connection with the University of North Carolina at Chapel Hill.

REFERENCES

American Sociological Association. *Guides to Graduate Department,* 1965–2005. Washington, DC: American Sociological Association.
Bakanic, Von, Clark McPhail, and Rita J. Simon, 1987. "The Manuscript Review and Decision-Making Process." *American Sociological Review* 52:631–42.

Baldi, Stephane. 1994. "Changes in Stratification Structure of Sociology, 1964–1992." *The American Sociologist* 25:28–43.

Beyer, Janet. 1978. "Editorial Policies and Practices among Leading Journals in Four Scientific Fields." *Sociological Quarterly* 19:68–78.

Burris, Val. 2004. "The Academic Caste System: PhD Prestige Hierarchies." *American Sociological Review* 69(2):239–64.

Carter, Alan Murray. 1966. *An Assessment of Quality in Graduate Education.* Washington, DC: American Council on Education.

Chubin, Daryl F., and Edward J. Hackett. 1990. *Peerless Science: Peer Review and U.S. Science Policy.* Albany: State University of New York Press.

Clemens, Elizabeth S., Walter W. Powell, Kris McIlwaine, and Dina Okamoto. 1995. "Careers in Print: Books, Journals, and Scholarly Reputation." *American Journal of Sociology* 101 (September):433–94.

Crane, Diane. 1965. "Scientists at Major and Minor Universities: A Study of Productivity and Recognition." *American Sociological Review* 30:699–713.

de Solla Price, D. J. 1963. *Little Science, Big Science.* New York: Columbia University Press.

Fyfe, James J., and Rita J. Simon (eds.). 1994. *Editors as Gatekeepers: Getting Published in the Social Sciences.* New York: Rowman & Littlefield.

Gross, George R. 1970. "The Organization Set: A Study of Sociology Departments." *The American Sociologist* 5:25–29.

Hagstrom, Warren O. 1971. "Inputs, Outputs, and the Prestige of University Science Departments." *Sociology of Education* 44:375–97.

Hargens, Lowell L. 1988. "Scholarly Consensus and Journal Rejection Rates." *American Sociological Review* 53:139–51.

Keith, B., and Nick Babchuck. 1998. "The Quest for Institutional Recognition: A Longitudinal Analysis of Scholarly Productivity and Academic Prestige among Sociology Departments." *Social Forces* 76:1495–533.

Knudsen, Dean D., and Ted R. Vaughn. 1969. "Quality in Graduate Education: A Re-Evaluation of the Rankings of Sociology Department in the Carter Report." *The American Sociologist* 4:12–19.

Long, J. Scott. 1978. "Productivity and Academic Position in the Scientific Career." *American Sociological Review* 43:889–908.

Miller, Joann, and Robert Perrucci. 2001. "Back Stage at *Social Problems:* An Analysis of the Editorial Decision Process, 1993–1996. *Social Problems* 48:93–110.

Murphy, Raymond. 1983. "The Struggle for Scholarly Recognition: The Development of the Closure Problematic in Sociology." *Theory and Society* 25:28–43.

Parkin, Frank. 1971. *Class Inequality and Political Order.* New York: Praeger.

Parkin, Frank. 1979. *Marxism and Class Theory: A Bourgeois Critique.* New York: Columbia University Press.

Perrucci, Robert. 1974. "On the Liberation of a Liberating Discipline. *Sociological Focus* 7: 1–12.

Perrucci, Robert, K. O'Flaherty, and H. Marshall. 1983. "Market Conditions, Productivity and Promotion among University Faculty." *Research in Higher Education* 19:230–44.

Perrucci, Robert, Mangala Subramaniam, and Carolyn C. Perrucci. 2013. "Big Science and Social Closure: Publication Patterns in a Sociology Flagship Journal, 1960–2010." Presented at the annual meeting of the American Sociological Association, New York.

Pfeffer, J., A. Leong, and K. Strehl. 1976. "Publication and Prestige Mobility of University Departments in Three Scientific Disciplines." *Sociology of Education* 49:212–18.

Simon, Rita J. 1994. "An Effective Journal Editor: Insights Gained from Editing the *ASR.*" In *Editors as Gatekeepers,* edited by Rita Simon and James Fyfe, 33–44. Lanham, MD.: Rowman and Littlefield.

Subramaniam, Mangala, Robert Perrucci, and David Whitlock. 2014. "Intellectual Closure: A Theoretical Framework Linking Knowledge, Power, and the Corporate University." *Critical Sociology* 40(3): 411–30.

Willis, Cecil L., and Stephen J. McNamee. 1990. "Social Networks of Science and Patterns of
    Publication in Leading Sociology Journals, 1960 to 1985." *Science Communication* 11:
    363–81.

III

Challenges in Academia

Chapter Seven

The Tyranny of the Majority

A Case Study of Intellectual Exclusion in Sociology

Joseph Michalski

Alexis de Tocqueville ([1835] 1994) did not invent the phrase the *tyranny of the majority*, but his commentary on the often-corrupting influence of majority rule offers a prescient reminder that those of minority status typically lack the resources to challenge the moral authority of the claims, rights, and privileges exercised by those in power. Those who dissent may plead their cases in democratic systems, but the majority's decisions can render those voices rather inconsequential.

The same principle applies in academia despite the supposedly more enlightened nature of the professoriate, the recognition of historic inequities, and active attempts to be more inclusive and build more diverse departments. The key issue, though, pertains to the potential for hegemonic control of intellectual production. In a multiple-paradigm discipline such as sociology, which perspective occupies a privileged place within the academy? Furthermore, how are institutional hiring practices affected?

The central thesis here suggests that academic departments often exercise intellectual control through a dominant culture that perpetuates certain paradigms to the detriment and possible exclusion of other perspectives. Departmental hiring practices thus largely reflect and reinforce specific forms of intellectual hegemony.

Historically, hiring exclusions tended to be linked to status advantages in the forms of social class, gender, race/ethnicity, and age, as well as other personal distinctions and structural constraints. While such minority statuses continue to disadvantage some segments of the population in the labor markets, these are somewhat less relevant today in academia as compared with other hiring arenas.

Instead, the more salient problem relates to intellectual hegemony, whereby the dominant discourses within departments and among those in power help frame the hiring agenda to precipitate new forms of exclusion. Left unchecked, one could anticipate that an entire department might be subjected to the *tyranny of the majority*; eliminating anyone who does not provide the proper intellectual fit, regardless of the individual's knowledge or other markers of academic excellence. The evaluation of this thesis stems mainly from a case study examination of the exclusionary practices of one Canadian university's Department of Sociology.

LITERATURE REVIEW

Previous research has highlighted that the main sources of discrimination in university hiring practices are against those occupying a range of minority statuses (Kennelly, Misra, and Karides 1999). Much of the initial work focused more on salary discrepancies linked, for example, to gender discrimination (Brewton and Freiberg 1995). Even in recent years the problem of gender discrimination has persisted with women severely underrepresented among hires in the University of California system following the passage of Proposition 209 in 1996 (which essentially abolished affirmative action).

Coinciding with a series of hearings, the proportion of females hired started to rise again, up to about 40% by the mid-2000s—a figure still far below the relative proportion of women earning PhDs in the 1990s (West 2007). American Sociological Association (2014) data reveal that women earned more than 60% of all PhDs awarded in sociology in 2011 while the wage gap has nearly disappeared, and women are moving to the forefront in terms of recent hires. Many departments, and the discipline as a whole, appear to continue apace with an inexorable shift toward gender equity.

On the other hand, Takara (2007) has argued that structural and institutional roadblocks have ensured that African Americans have not earned proportionately their share of advanced degrees. Moreover, a persistent tokenism and a relative lack of supportive networks have meant that Black females continue to be severely underrepresented among tenured faculty. Burns (2009) further confirmed that the relative proportion of African Americans at southern community colleges has remained low despite the proportionate increases among African American students attending such colleges.

At the same time, even the *experiences* of African American women gainfully employed in academia can be problematic, with identities and cultural locations often at odds with the traditional administrative, pedagogical, and interactive frameworks already established in White-dominant institutions (Beoku-Betts and Njambi 2005). Some research reveals that classroom environments can prove rather chilly for minority instructors, and women of color in particular, as White students may offer resistance to the teaching styles, perceived differences, and specific course content (Grahame 2004).

Doorewaard (2008) has explained that the challenges women of minority status face reflect the hegemonic power structures that preceded their hires coinciding with and exacerbated by the intersectionality of multiple forms of status inequalities.

The one issue that does *not* receive as much discussion as personal status characteristics or human rights concerns the right to one's intellectual orientation, which tends to be subsumed under the rubric of the debates about *academic freedom*. The discipline of sociology, for example, has been characterized as a multiple-paradigm science that embraces a range of intellectual traditions (Ritzer 1975), but that has not always been entirely true. Early American sociology boasted an unequivocal positivist orientation and the dominance of structural-functionalism, which meant that various perspectives within the academy remained on the margins for decades (Cortese 1995).

The preponderance of White males populating the academy in the first half of the twentieth century did not provide a fertile context for promoting the diversity or the genuine emergence of the multiple-paradigm discipline that one observes these days. Lamont (2000) argues that among the elite institutions, American positivism, empiricism, and pragmatism continue to predominate, especially in the form of quantitative hegemony, at least in contrast to French intellectuals' preoccupation with metatheoretical issues.

The case of Canada straddles both of these positions in part because of an influx of American sociologists in the postwar era *and* a continental bias that reflects English and Francophone influences on the academy north of the 49th parallel. Could there be new bases for intellectual hegemony in the 21st century, especially in view of the diverse range of contemporary influences on intellectual production? In Canada there have been some rather compelling departmental struggles, but the likelihood that one dominant approach would characterize all of Canadian sociology appears unlikely (Davies 2009).

Michalski's (2005) study of a random sample of Canadian sociologists, however, determined that two-thirds of respondents identified first and foremost with various types of critical and/or feminist paradigms. Nearly one in three claimed an allegiance to some form of interpretive or hermeneutic approach (often combined with a *critical* approach) while only about one in five identified primarily with positivism or scientific sociology.

Nearly 10% of respondents acknowledged a post-modernist or post-structuralist approach, but usually with a critical orientation embedded in their descriptions of sociology's mission: "To produce research and teaching which will increase critical understanding of sociocultural reality and relations of power and how our subjectivities are constituted" (Michalski 2005, 3).

The differences have generated real hostilities between members of different camps, commencing with the radical critiques of the 1960s and 1970s. The battles sometimes led to departmental divisions that have resonated across the social sciences down through the present era (Davies 2009; Gordon 2013; Wadsworth 2005).[1] To assess who, if anyone, *won* the war would be difficult and too far removed from the current analytic focus. Rather, the important *sociological* issue involves the underlying theoretical and epistemological diversity within the field or the degree to which competing groups establish any type of intellectual hegemony.[2]

More immediately, where does one's intellectual orientation rank among the factors to be considered in hiring advertisements and the actual interview process? The content of job advertisements naturally delimits the range of potential applicants, especially in terms of substantive expertise. Many individuals must decide *a priori* if their work can be framed in a manner reasonably consistent with the areas advertised. Yet departments can choose not only to define the specific subject matter but may even narrow the search further in terms of epistemological frameworks.

For example, Davies (2009) discovered that nearly 30% of Canadian sociology advertisements that appeared in *The CAUT Bulletin* from May 2005 to January 2008 contained *critical* categories that include terms such as *critical, social justice, equity studies*, and *racialization* (among others). Davies (2009, 632) argues that as conventional job classifications recede, Canadian sociology job advertisements increasingly use "an explicit language that requires candidates to adopt a critical approach."

Similarly, the mainstream approaches to job advertisements arguably privilege dominant theoretical and methodological frameworks by *not* stating these criteria explicitly—and the same argument applies, therefore, to the intellectual reproduction that occurs elsewhere (see Johnston 1998).

Do departments these days ever tilt *entirely* in one particular direction, à la the Chicago school, or are there corrective measures or homeostatic processes that kick in to help rebalance academic units? The most dramatic skews occur, one might hypothesize, under conditions of elite control of intellectual agendas within specific departments and their impact on hiring processes that unfold over time. The next section explores these issues.

UNIVERSITY HIRING CRITERIA

The key mechanism to ensure that the majority rules in hiring—and that minority opinions lose out on a regular basis—involves promoting the *individual choice* model that eschews any *objective* criteria for hiring, at least beyond the substantive expertise identified in the job advertisement. The standard requirements for most job searches usually include:

1. a cover letter outlining the candidate's strengths and rationale for why she or he would be a good *fit* for the advertised position;
2. the candidate's *curriculum vitae*;
3. three or more letters of reference from respected colleagues or mentors in the field;
4. evidence of teaching excellence;
5. a writing sample.

Presumably candidates are evaluated and potentially short-listed on the basis of some relative weighting and combination of the above items. Regardless of the formalities involved, nearly everyone agrees that these are among the key factors to consider. Beyond anecdotal information, some research confirms that potential employers rank candidates' prior research and teaching experience as the two most important factors to be evaluated, followed by letters of recommendation and publications (Burns and Kinkade 2008). The candidates' demographic profile ranked lowest among factors to be considered.

Enlightened professionals everywhere generally agree that status distinctions relating to race, class, gender, sexual orientation, and physical abilities are irrelevant to the quality or professional competence of candidates.[3] That does not mean, of course, that there has not been considerable status discrimination in the past or that all such practices have been stamped out in the present era. The evidence contradicts such claims as already discussed.[4] The one caveat, though, relates to the extent that university departments might value increased diversity and a pluralism of voices that may not have been represented in historical context (see Gordon 2013).

The conventional wisdom suggests that, all else equal, one should hire the candidate who most enhances departmental diversity. Yet therein lies the ultimate sociological challenge that further helps explain why human rights codes and strict anti-discriminatory legislation are in place; the tendency to select (or to *like*) those more like ourselves. That logic extends even more powerfully to the issue of intellectual orientations. To use an analogy, everyone has musical tastes and preferences, but how does one determine which type of music should be preferred over any other? There are no purely *objective* markers, ultimately, that can be used.

The specific procedures vary across departments, such as whether an entire department participates or strikes a hiring committee to review the applications. But what criteria do individuals actually use to winnow down their short lists from among dozens of qualified applicants? Many times, candidates have several publications, strong letters of reference, an excellent curriculum vitae, and even strong teaching evaluations—but fail to get short-listed. Why might that be?

The typical hiring procedure, for example, does not include formally ranking each individual in terms of criteria such as the number of refereed journal articles candidates have produced. Even the relative weight of the different factors does not usually have any explicit definition. Instead, the members involved argue for why or why not they *like* a particular candidate by selectively identifying evidence from the application package that buttresses their support for specific individuals. Reasonable colleagues can and often do disagree as to the relative merits regarding what each candidate has to offer.

The departmental or committee members vote and, based upon the total votes or some weighting procedure, a short list will be established for potential interviews. Everyone's vote typically counts the same and, with secret ballots, no real public accountability exists beyond that of personal preference or conscience. At the end of the discussion process, each member can choose whomever he or she likes. The criteria arguably do not *really* matter, at least not in terms of *compelling* people to support candidates whom they do not like.

For instance, to support candidate *A* purely on the basis of having *three* publications as compared with candidate *B*'s *two* publications will not likely convince anyone that candidate *A* should, therefore, be hired. The more important factor arguably relates to the orientations and preferences of more senior faculty. These faculty members have more experience and usually more power relative to their junior colleagues.

Another group dynamic operates here, well-known to anyone who has ever worked in a university or almost any larger organization, is the degree to which subgroups or alliances are formed *within* departments to ensure that certain agendas may be realized. Just as some members simply do not like certain candidates for any number of reasons, there are often colleagues within departments who genuinely do not like each other for personal, political, or professional reasons.

Hence the opposition to certain candidates may stem from the particular alliances that have been forged, or whatever orientations had taken root over time. Consider the following example of a scholar well positioned to be hired in the Department of Sociology in southern Ontario.

CASE STUDY: THE UNIVERSITY OF CANADA

In the case of the University of Canada, their Department of Sociology advertised to hire an assistant professor with teaching and research interests in the subfield of criminology. In applying for the position, an academician with ten years of teaching experience felt confident about being short-listed as a result of the five criteria identified previously.

At the very least, the Applicant's[5] teaching and publication record were directly relevant to the position advertised. With more citations in Sociological Abstracts than the other members of the department that year, as well as a forthcoming publication in a respected feminist journal, there could be no question in regard to his scholarly competence.

Moreover, the Applicant had been nominated for three consecutive "Excellence in Teaching Awards" at the university where he had worked immediately prior to the University of Canada in a series of one-year contracts. To help further strengthen his case, the Applicant possessed a stellar record of grant funding over the decade prior to re-entering academia.[6] In short, he put together a compelling application package to secure a tenure-track position. Yet there were some potential obstacles with which many women in particular might identify.

Perhaps most important, the prospective candidate had been a stay-at-home father in the years immediately after receiving his doctorate. That decision resulted in his lagging behind his peers in terms of an academic career path. Hence, the Applicant had worked feverishly in the late 1990s to build a credible teaching and research dossier to be more competitive in a tight academic market. The Applicant certainly empathized with the many women who had interrupted their professional careers to bear and raise young children—and the relative disadvantages that they encountered upon re-entering the labor market.

Having just turned 40, the Applicant felt, too, that his *professional clock* was ticking and that the window of opportunity to secure a permanent, full-time academic position might close before long. He thus did everything possible on the professional front to ensure that he might receive notification of having been short-listed for the coveted position, years after most of the members of his cohort had already achieved tenure. Much to his chagrin, though, the department failed to short-list the Applicant for the position at the University of Canada. Why not? No one ever offered a satisfactory explanation.

First, the chair never explained why the seemingly ideal candidate had not been short-listed despite the evidence outlined in the cover letter, the burgeoning publication record, and his outstanding teaching evaluations in the substantive areas where they planned to hire. After two rather frustrating meetings, the Applicant next requested a joint meeting with the chair and the then academic dean of social sciences to discuss the reasons for having been overlooked.

While they acknowledged the Applicant's excellent publication record, teaching abilities, and obvious qualifications, both offered essentially the same explanation—each member of the department could freely choose to short-list whatever candidates she or he deemed most suitable.

In a nutshell, departmental members used their judgment and whatever standards they preferred to determine the suitability of potential candidates. Certainly, no *objective* criteria forced the issue, such as the number of publications, teaching awards, or funded research projects. In comparing his record on all of these measures with each individual who had been short-listed, the Applicant arguably had the strongest overall record as well as stellar letters of recommendation.

What, then, happened in the hiring committee meetings? Only those who participated more than a decade ago could possibly remember at this juncture. The one fact the chair shared, however, was that *no one* in the department supported the Applicant (i.e., voted to short-list him for the position advertised). Hence, only circumstantial and indirect evidence can be gathered to help recreate a plausible interpretation of what happened.

A DIFFERENT TYPE OF MINORITY EXCLUSION

Prior to his failed attempt to be short-listed, the shunned Applicant had been hired as an assistant professor on a one-year contract at the University of Canada *without* an in-person interview. Over the telephone, the chair expressed genuine enthusiasm, stating that the Applicant had been recommended without reservation by his previous chair.

Based on such an "impressive curriculum vitae," the chair explained that there really were no compelling reasons to do a formal job talk and departmental interview. The Applicant sensed he might indeed be a welcome addition to the department and may have found his professional home at long last. That proved, however, to be a woefully naïve assessment.

The Applicant had not met any of the faculty members prior to his arrival and, with just a couple of exceptions, was not overly familiar with most of their work. Being a commuter faculty member, he did not get to know his colleagues well that year either. Sociologically speaking, the proper strategy would have been to build relationships with departmental members to enhance his chances of being hired permanently. Instead, the faculty members, who were pleasant enough and certainly civil in face-to-face interactions, nevertheless maintained their distance. The reasons only came to light inadvertently through the experience of another part-time colleague.

The colleague in question had lunch with three other departmental members in the fall of 2002. The discussion eventually gravitated to her politics, as she conveyed the conversation, which generated some discomfort for her. Her lunch colleagues could not understand why she was not an avowed *critical-race-feminist*, especially as a woman of color. She reported that she felt as though she had just been interrogated, essentially "failing the political and intellectual litmus test" that she had been given. She ended up being the Applicant's one confidante for that increasingly lonely year as they often shared a coffee together or office time conversing.

As a White male who befriended a female colleague of color with no overtly political agenda framing her scholarship, no one approached the Applicant about his politics or intellectual orientation. The *evidence* was already apparent. One could examine his course syllabi, readings, and publications to confirm the presence of *an American Positivist in Canada.*[7] Thus, none of the full-time faculty invited the Applicant for coffee or lunch that year or expressed any interest in his work. Still, the Applicant continued to be collegial in all settings, though, often speaking up in departmental meetings with humor and constructive comments.

Throughout the one-year appointment, the Applicant maintained a certain optimism regarding his employment prospects. He steadfastly believed that professional competence would be more important than personal issues or even his status as a permanent resident in Canada hailing from the United States. The one factor he had *not* considered, however, related to his particular academic orientation. While there were a great many supporters of a critical perspective in the department, the Applicant reasoned (incorrectly) that they needed sociologists with other orientations to help round out their program.

The evidence revealed that during the 2002–2003 academic year, the active full-time members of the department operated mainly from within one or another critical social science perspective. An analysis of their self-identified interests confirmed that 11 worked almost entirely within a critical framework, while two others operated both from critical and interpretive frames of reference. Only the Applicant and one other active faculty member shared a more scientific orientation toward the discipline.

Three other faculty members were on leave that year, including two senior members nearing the ends of their respective academic careers. These faculty members each shared a somewhat more positivist orientation in terms of their published academic work. Yet these colleagues were not present at any meetings throughout the year. The one other *positivist* had been working mainly with a different department that year and ended up transferring to another university altogether a few years later.

A more in-depth analysis revealed that the faculty members most often endorsed some form of radical feminist or socialist feminist orientation while two members might best have been characterized as Marxist-Socialists. Two faculty members worked from within a critical race and social justice framework while a third faculty member supported critical animal studies. One interpretive theorist staunchly advocated feminism as well. The evidence, therefore, confirmed that the department already had an entrenched majority operating from within a critical paradigm at that time.

Despite the overwhelmingly positive response from students, the reality was that such evaluations held little importance in terms of what might interest the department for their next hire.[8] Who, then, *should* apply to such a department? The answer can be found in the hiring evidence in the dozen years that witnessed the fundamental transformation of the department that occurred from 2001–2012.

In 2001–2002, the department had an equal divide between members practicing mainly with the *positivist* and *critical* paradigms, although three of the five positivists were on leave for various reasons. On the surface, the department appeared reasonably balanced. With a growing interest in building their criminology program, the Applicant was encouraged to apply for the one-year position in anticipation of the future tenure-stream position.

The die had been cast, though, as the main *positivist* exited for a more prestigious appointment the year prior to the Applicant's arrival, while any other colleagues who might be sympathetic to scientific sociology were no longer actively engaged. The net result was that the department hired four more full-time members with *critical* orientations along with one who operated more from within a critical-interpretive framework. In view of the fact that three of the other five positivists remained on leave, the department had a distinctively critical flavor in terms of course content and instruction as well as in the departmental meetings.

In the end, the three presumed positivists who had been on leave retired or had left by 2003–2004. The department had committed fully and firmly to the critical paradigm with 11 of 15 members either tenured or en route to tenure. Two full-timers were critical-interpretive academicians, while only two others aligned with positivism (both had left by 2006).

Perhaps most important, all six senior full professors endorsed a critical approach of some kind or another and provided leadership necessary to ensure the final denouement of the drama that unfolded over the years. For example, the 2002–2003 University of Canada undergraduate calendar under *General Information* opened with the following statement:

> The various disciplines of the [d]epartment . . . are concerned broadly with processes, structure and behaviour conditioned by participation in social groups. The department at (Canada) University is committed to a conception of the social sciences as scientific disciplines and to the belief that sound social action projects should be based on rigorous scientific effort. The department is also committed to the view that social analysis is a complex process and that no one discipline can provide a complete perspective.

The above statement reflected the broader mission that departments often have endorsed to some degree or another, including the commitment to science, an appreciation of the complexity of social processes, interdisciplinary approaches, and, for that matter, a modest commitment to social action based on rigorous research. Contrast that view with the revised statement that first appeared in the same section of the 2008–2009 undergraduate calendar:

> The [d]epartment . . . offers students a unique opportunity to cultivate their intellectual curiosity and social awareness, and to develop their capacity to engage in a critical, informed and self-reflective way with the key social institutions, relationships and processes shaping the world in which they live. Sociology . . . allows students to delve into a rich variety of fascinating topics of the greatest historical and contemporary relevance: animal studies; gender; sexism; family life; sexuality; race and racism; cultural identity; globalization; imperialism and colonialism; immigration; poverty and class inequality; work and the economy; education; religion; the environment; crime, prisons and social repression and social movements.
>
> Underlying the wide range of issues taken up in the department's teaching and research activities is a shared commitment to analyzing inequality, oppression, exploitation in all of their varied manifestations, and exploring the forms of resistance and struggle to which they give rise.

The members changed the narrative to reflect their own intellectual preferences. One might commend the department for the shift toward truth in advertising. Indeed, the "Message from the Chair" posted on the departmental web page displays an even more transparent focus, starting thusly: "The [d]epartment . . . at [the] University [of Canada] is committed to a critical, social justice approach." The entire thrust of the chair's message stresses the exclusive focus on the critique of extant social arrangements and scholarship aimed at creating social change.

The rhetoric and reality of the program, however, contradict in one sense the notion that the department has a "vibrant and diverse faculty (of) twenty-two engaged and diverse faculty members with a wide range of interests." The alleged *diversity* hardly reflects that of sociology as an academic discipline; essentially ignoring altogether the scientific and the interpretive paradigms that form the other main legs upon which the discipline stands. Their diversity reflects perversely only the hegemonic lens through which the entire department frames their intellectual mission; critical social thought. No one else need apply for a position.

With an almost exclusive contingent of critical paradigm supporters, the department hired four new like-minded academicians as junior faculty in 2006–2007. The department boasted, then, a total of 16 members with critical-school perspectives as well as two members with critical-interpretive perspectives. No positivists or purely interpretive thinkers remained. The department had been transformed unabashedly into the "Department of Critical Sociology."

The assistant professors from 2006 had been promoted to associate professors by 2011–2012, yielding a complement of 20 critical academics in total. Perhaps most revealing, the department hired exactly two more junior faculty members in 2010–2011 into tenure-track appointments: the partner of one full-time member (who would receive tenure the following year) and the daughter of one of the six full professors in the department. The added layer of nepotism on top of the exclusivity of those with critical perspectives meant that no one else indeed should have bothered to apply.

One might suggest, though, that the faculty members may have broader intellectual foci or that the interpretation of their publications could be contested if one were to examine the nature of that work by different criteria. That may be the case, though the available publications almost always resonate with the critical perspective. The best and simplest evidence available actually derives directly from their self-descriptions of their academic research and orientations published on the departmental website.

In 2012–2013, the department listed 23 individuals as full-time members, although two were nominal members in that they represented external recruits, serving as the dean of the faculty of social sciences and the university provost, respectively. What language did faculty members use to describe themselves, their research agendas, and orientations? A content analysis helps provide a rather compelling answer.

The faculty members used one or more of the following terms more than 70 times in their web bios: critical, feminist or feminism, gender, race, racism, or racialization. In addition, some form of the term *colonialism* (especially anti-colonialism) arose eight times, as did the term *social justice*. Inequality, oppression, liberation, and rights rounded out the critical orientation of virtually everyone in the department. Only two members used the term *construction* or *interpretive* in their descriptions, while one faculty member utilized the term *symbol* or *meaning* five times. No one mentioned *science*, *social science*, or *scientist* or self-identified as a *sociologist*.

The members no longer feigned support for the scientific mission or, to any significant degree, the interpretive dimensions of sociology as a discipline. The department instead announced their commitment to one paradigm, including their status as the "first university in Canada to offer a concentration in the field of Critical Animal Studies."

The faculty developed too an MA in critical sociology as a natural extension of their intellectual focus: "The emphasis in courses and faculty-supervised graduate research will be on theory, methods and empirical research that prioritize challenges to oppression, disenfranchisement and social inequalities in social arrangements."

Their website continued by stating that the department "encompasses a variety of critical sociological frameworks including, for example, feminist trajectories in sociological thought, Marxist political economy, political ecology, critical race theory, post-colonial theory, post-structuralist and queer paradigms, critical criminology, animal rights work, environmentalism and critiques of and alternatives to current economic arrangements." Most members identified that they participated as well in the interdisciplinary MA in social justice and equity studies.

While these academicians viewed their departmental developments as *progressive*, one might argue that the department actually *regressed* by abandoning any pretensions of being inclusive or representative of the broader discipline. Is such intellectual hegemony inevitable across departments, or are there alternatives? What might a more inclusive and intellectually diverse department look like in sociology?

INCLUSIVE ALTERNATIVES: STRUCTURAL AND CULTURAL APPROACHES

A Structural Alternative

In the late 1980s, the Applicant secured his first full-time teaching position at a university on the American East Coast. The department had been experiencing some tension surrounding core requirements, which included standard courses at that time in statistics and research methods. The positivistic orientation embedded in those courses did not sit well with some of the faculty, who formed a subcommittee to discuss what might be done.

As a result of their collaborative efforts, the members of that department redesigned the program to have a broader, more inclusive focus. For the next two decades, the program required courses that included combination theory-method courses in critical analysis, interpretive analysis, and naturalistic (positivistic) analysis.

The program recently introduced one integrated seminar titled Sociological Inquiry with the following description: "A systematic introduction to various modes of sociological investigation, including positivism, interpretivism and critical analysis. Students learn to evaluate, critique and design original sociological inquiries with special attention to how sociological inquiry is guided by different philosophical and theoretical commitments."

The structural changes ensured that students would be educated in the main traditions that underlie sociology as a multiple-paradigm social science. Furthermore, no *one* perspective trumped the others in terms of relevance or importance despite the fact that the department contained advocates and practitioners working within each of the various traditions.

Consistent with their more pluralistic orientation, the department's website states: "The mission of the sociology program is to develop students' ability to analyze the social world by using diverse sociological theories and research methods that stress the importance of social, cultural and historical contexts for understanding the relationships between social actors and structures." In order to maintain such pluralism and to ensure the proper staffing of their courses, the department has to consider the intellectual orientations of those whom they may be inclined to hire. That has been a key factor in the hiring criteria of this particular university.

A Cultural Alternative

The restructuring of the program at another Canadian institution involved more modest changes that included core requirements of basic and advanced statistics (for honors students), courses in qualitative *and* quantitative research methods, and both classical and contemporary theory courses where professors incorporate a diverse range of theoretical perspectives. Rather than dictate that particular schools of thought or approaches *must* be included, each faculty member defines his or her pedagogical agendas to suit their own expertise and preferences.

Since full-time faculty members predominantly operate within critical, feminist, cultural studies and post-modernist frameworks (8 of 11 members), theory courses tend to be slanted more in those particular directions. One member combines both positivistic and interpretive frames of reference, while the other two members operate within the positivist paradigm. The natural inclination would be to continue to hire future colleagues who share the majority's perspective(s). What would prevent the department from devolving into the similarly narrow-minded critical orientation that characterizes the University of Canada's department?

Perhaps most important, the *culture* of the department allows for a greater appreciation of diverse approaches. The faculty members who work within the various critical, cultural studies and post-modernist frameworks share a more open-minded perspective and have an appreciation for the inherent diversity and pluralism within sociology. That means that in departmental and hiring committee meetings, the faculty members display a somewhat more flexible and, to a certain extent, pragmatic approach.

The focus shifts to the nature of program needs, especially in regard to the courses offered and the type of sociologist who would best serve those needs. As the largest program at the university, their department offers degrees in both sociology *and* criminology. With a staff of scarcely a dozen members (and nearly 30 part-time teachers), the program offers an impressively diverse array of mandatory and elective courses. Faculty members recognize that the success has been built precisely on the diversity of their faculty, and, indeed, the complementary nature of various approaches to sociology and in the courses offered.

The chair attempted to lead by example by stressing complementarity, sharing with his colleagues on more than one occasion the view of sociology as analogous to music, wherein there are many different genres reflecting the variegated tastes of those involved in the endeavor. While the chair practiced and created within one particular *style* of sociological music, he nevertheless listened to and appreciated the many different forms that exist.

Rather than denigrate colleagues or criticize their musical tastes, the chair lauded the diversity and shared with his students the idea that each perspective possessed different nuances and interesting questions that could best be addressed using various styles of scholarship. In contrast to the University of Canada, this particular sociology department has nurtured a safe environment where departmental members and students alike can express themselves within whatever sociological traditions that they prefer. That type of supportive culture clearly requires the conscious effort and commitment of everyone involved.

For example, the chair organized a departmental retreat with a facilitator that allowed everyone to engage in discussions and program-planning meetings in a more informal, collegial setting. The faculty members had the chance to get to know one another, to work collaboratively on various tasks and exercises, and to appreciate the diverse strengths and abilities each member offered. The departmental colleagues effectively built bridges, if not always close friendships, that would allow the faculty to work together in more collegial ways moving forward.

In thinking about hiring decisions, each member still has her or his own preferences, but the chair would attempt to prod the group to think a bit more *outside of the box* by stating categorically something along the following lines: "Well, we already have *me* in our department, so we definitely do not need another *clone* to replicate what I'm doing. Instead, what are the intellectual gaps in our program?" The department has developed, for the most part, a *live and live approach*. Each member pursues their own intellectual agenda without any pressure to conform to any particular intellectual tradition.

FINAL THOUGHTS

Departmental hiring decisions are enormously important investments in terms of the financial, social, *and* intellectual capital involved. The potential *tyranny of the majority* in academic departments has existed for far longer than the current chapter can convey. That said, the above case study at the University of Canada represents the exception rather than the rule. That department offers a cautionary tale, however, that those in positions of leadership may work to establish a culture of exclusivity to help ensure that one specific intellectual orientation prevails.

Without any external oversight or corrective mechanisms in place, the department effectively stamped out any significant intellectual diversity by solely hiring candidates who endorsed the status quo. Perhaps not surprisingly, their program, with twice as many full-time faculty members, has perhaps half as many students majoring in the discipline, compared to the department at the University of Canada.

Having taught at the University of Canada for one year and met many of the students, the subject of this chapter believes there can be no question that the narrow focus on a purely critical orientation has stripped away choice, diversity, and a sense of feeling welcome by anyone who does not subscribe to the tyranny of the majority perspective.

NOTES

1. For example, the University of Alberta's Department of Sociology experienced a massive paradigm shift in the 1990s from a more quantitative department to one with a much more explicit focus on "cultural studies."

2. While some endorse the multiple-paradigm position as a source of strength and diversity, a great many critical theorists argue that the key to advancing sociology as a discipline lies in subverting traditional intellectual power structures to embrace new paradigms focusing on empowerment, resistance, and/or a public sociology that transcends the limited "pure science" approach (Boden and Epstein 2011; Burawoy 2005; Lorber 2006). In the extreme, critical theorists object to conventional scientific approaches to the study of society as inherently conservative, barren, irrelevant, or even immoral (Acker 2005; Beck 2005; see Davies 2009). York and Clark (2006) offer a rare exception, juxtaposing Marxism and positivism to suggest possible ways that these often antagonistic paradigms might be reconciled to the benefit of both.

3. The standard tenure-track advertisement in Canada contains something similar to the following: "In accordance with Canadian immigration requirements, this advertisement is directed in the first instance to Canadian citizens and permanent residents. STM is committed to diversity within its faculty. Women, Aboriginal people, people with disabilities, visible minorities and members of other designated groups are encouraged to self-identify on their application."

4. For example, the Ontario Human Rights Commission determined in 2000 that a junior physics professor had been repeatedly passed over for tenure largely on the basis of "his race, colour, ancestry, place of origin and ethnic origin."

5. The term "Applicant" hereafter refers to the specific individual, the current author, who experienced everything that happened in the remainder of the chapter.

6. The Applicant had been the principal investigator or co-investigator on more than three dozen applied research projects dealing with a range of criminological and legal issues (mainly relating to various forms of family violence) including family conflict, poverty-related issues, and immigrant research totaling more than $1 million in funding.

7. In hindsight, there were some rather obvious alarm bells, such as the one faculty member who stridently posted anti-American "hate literature" on his door, which hardly provided a welcoming environment for a transplanted American positivist. That particular individual quite literally *never* spoke directly to the Applicant the entire year.

8. The students often spoke of how much they appreciated his teaching and balanced perspective, using terms such as "breath of fresh air" and "open-minded" in their year-end evaluations. Their narratives started to make a great deal more sense when the Applicant realized that many of them had been forced to endure all manner of public or intellectual humiliations from *certain* members of the department for having the "wrong perspective." The students, in effect, were responding to a different voice from the one they were hearing in most of their other sociology courses, as well as the sense of openness to exploring diverse evidence and perspectives.

REFERENCES

Acker, Joan. 2005. "Comments on Burawoy on Public Sociology." *Critical Sociology* 31:327–32.

American Sociological Association. 2014. "Changes in Gender Characteristics of the Sociology Discipline and Profession." Accessed April 15, 2014. http://asanet.org/research/stats/gender. cfm.

Beck, Ulrich. 2005. "How Not to Become a Museum Piece." *British Journal of Sociology* 56:335–43.

Beoku-Betts, Josephine, and Wairimu Ngaruiya Njambi. 2005. "African Feminist Scholars in Women's Studies: Negotiating Spaces of Dislocation and Transformation in the Study of Women." *Meridians: Feminism, Race, Transnationalism* 6:113–32.

Boden, Rebecca, and Debbie Epstein. 2011. "A Flat Earth Society? Imagining Academic Freedom." *The Sociological Review* 59:476–95.

Brewton, Audi, and Lewis Freiberg. 1995. "Gender Discrimination and University Faculty Salaries from 1984–1992." *Journal of Economics* 21:65–76.

Burawoy, Michael. 2005. "2004 Presidential Address: For Public Sociology." *American Sociological Review* 70:4–28.

Burns, Annie Lou Brown. 2009. *The Low Percentage of African American Faculty in a Southern Community College: A Critical Perspective*. Published PhD dissertation submitted to Mississippi State University, Mississippi. Ann Arbor, Michigan: UMI Microform.

Burns, Robert G., and Patrick Kincade. 2008. "Finding Fit: The Nature of a Successful Faculty Employment Search in Criminal Justice." *Journal of Criminal Justice* 36:372–78.

Cortese, Anthony J. 1995. "The Rise, Hegemony, and Decline of the Chicago School of Sociology, 1892–1945." *The Social Science Journal* 32:235–54.

Davies, Scott. 2009. "Drifting Apart? The Institutional Dynamics Awaiting Public Sociology in Canada." *Canadian Journal of Sociology* 34:623–54.

Doorewaard, Hans. 2008. "Hegemonic Power and Locality." Paper presented at the 4th Organization, Identity and Locality Symposium in Aotearoa, New Zealand, February 14–15.

Gordon, David. 2013. "The Joys and Sorrows of Diversity: Changes in the Historical Profession in the Last Half Century." *Society* 50:140–51.

Grahame, Kamini Maraje. 2004. "Contesting Diversity in the Academy: Resistance to Women of Color Teaching Race, Class, and Gender." *Race, Gender and Class* 11:54–73.

Johnston, Barry V. 1998. "The Contemporary Crisis and the Social Relations Department at Harvard: A Case Study in Hegemony and Disintegration." *The American Sociologist* 29:26–42.

Kennelly, Ivy, Joya Misra, and Marina Karides. 1999. "The Historical Context of Gender, Race, and Class in the Academic Labor Market." *Race, Gender & Class* 6:125–55.

Lamont, Michele. 2000. "Comparing French and American Sociology." *La Revue Tocqueville* 21:109–22.

Lorber, Judith. 2006. "Shifting Paradigms and Challenging Categories." *Social Problems* 53:448–53.

Michalski, Joseph H. 2005. "La Diversité épistémologique de la Sociologie Canadienne: Quelques éléments de Comparaison entre Professeurs Francophones et Professeurs Anglophones. *Le Cahier de l'ACSALF* 2:2–3.

Ritzer, George. 1975. *Sociology: A Multiple-Paradigm Science*. Boston: Allyn and Bacon.

Takara, Kathryn. 2007. "A View from the Academic Edge: One Black Woman Who Is Dancing as Fast as She Can." *Du Bois Review: Social Science Research on Race* 3:463–70.

Tocqueville, Alexis de. [1835]1994. *Democracy in America*. New York: Alfred A. Knopf.

Wadsworth, Yoland. 2005. "'Gouldner's Child': Some Reflections on Sociology and Participatory Action Research." *Journal of Sociology* 41:267–84.

West, Martha S. 2007. "Unprecedented Urgency: Gender Discrimination in Faculty Hiring at the University of California." *NWSA Journal* 19:199–211.

York, Richard, and Brett Clark. 2006. "Marxism, Positivism, and Scientific Sociology: Social Gravity and Historicity." *The Sociological Quarterly* 47:425–50.

Chapter Eight

Two Professors and Their Stories from a Tiny College

Hamon Ha-am and Malintzin

A case study of faculty struggles against the racial and ethnic dynamics of a predominantly White, small liberal arts college is presented in this chapter. It purposefully oscillates between the separate and collective voices of the subjects interviewed. At the subjects' tiny college, their voices tend to be silenced in various ways. Their hope is that by sharing their story, they will be heard by other colleagues.

The subjects in this chapter seek to not only offer a picture of their experiences but also share the ways they have managed to struggle, in the hope that their story will help others move forward. They joined their small college in the southeastern United States in the late 1990s, convinced they could make the institution better.

The small faculty, staff, and student body of the institution made their presence notable and noticed. They realized they were a small step in diversifying the White college and, as such, agreed to serve on multiple committees and task forces, supported generations of students who saw the potential for positive social change on campus, and authentically believed they could make a difference.

The subjects in this case study offer a sense of their personal experiences, their vision of what a diverse workplace would/should be like, the challenges they face, and their strategies and approaches to confronting these challenges.

MARGINALLY DIFFERENT IN A WHITE INSTITUTION

The First Voice

Diversity in the United States is a debated and contested concept. Developed to explain the goals of going beyond the separations that are the legacies of segregation, diversity illuminates a community that celebrates differences and that recognizes difference as a positive attribute and mystifies the legacies of race.

In the United States, until the civil rights movement, the classification of people into races facilitated exclusion of some from institutions, opportunities, peace of mind, and even drinking fountains. The removal of laws creating separations did not remove the worldview of the individuals actively practicing separation or passively seeking to maintain their privileges.

After the 1960s, organizations were forced, encouraged, or wanted to increase the presence of visible minorities, especially, and arguably, the group most oppressed during segregation—African Americans. Some of the most important organizations for these demographic changes were colleges and universities as they were vehicles for economic and social mobility in post–World War II America. Given the changing demographics, institutions of higher education became sites of struggle over diversity and equality.

For several years, the president of the college investigated and made it clear that he was committed to diversity, and this was a welcomed change for the campus. But the formulation was troubling. He looked around the room at the faculty meeting and said that he wanted to see different color faces. Subject One reported that he had the privilege of intellectualizing and socially contextualizing the dilemmas of difference at his tiny college. He can step away from debates over diversity because he can walk down the halls and pathways of the institution without drawing attention to himself.

Subject One somewhat looks like he fits in. But that does not erase his inherited differences, nor does it take away the pain of knowing what others face, colleagues or students, when they walk down the same halls and pathways, even the same classrooms. So he speaks out through his research, teaching, and by building community-based programs. In the process, he becomes visible, but it is a choice.

Subject One's difference from the campus majority is a strange one, or one might think, for the 21st-century United States—being Jewish. Having completed undergraduate and graduate programs in the United States, it was a shock to find that after accepting a tenure-track position at a small liberal arts college in the late 1990s, diversity was still contested. Even more surprising was the reaction by the majority to the presence of the very few who are different. While two others on the faculty had Jewish ancestry, they put up Christmas trees and did not engage in any Jewish communal activities or life cycle events—Subject One was different.

Being Jewish, Subject One is not a member of a visible minority; it is his name that exposes his ethnic background and membership in an integrated minority group in the United States. Yet early in his first year as a tenure-track professor, he was called a Jewish ethnic slur right outside of his office by a senior member of the faculty. It seemed the gauntlet was thrown down.

Subject One knew his options. He could negate his heritage and be accepted by the majority. Instead, he decided to continue honoring Jewish religious holidays, which were commonly recognized when he was an undergraduate and graduate student in the northeast, and to be an ally to other minorities on campus. Although not a member of a visible minority, students of color and faculty of color welcomed his presence at meetings to strategize on change for the campus. And at every such gathering he made the point of acknowledging the welcome.

But the choice had perils. When Subject One cancels class for his religious observances, even though the meeting is replaced, per college regulations, he is met with a curt, "Don't you want the students to learn?" by faculty members who take it upon themselves to comment on his scheduling. And several times, students have e-mailed him asking for an appointment on Rosh HaShanah or Passover; when he asked one the reason for the specific day, he was told that a faculty member recommended the meeting for that particular date.

Faculty members regularly organized important meetings on Jewish high holidays with the excuse that calendars did not list them. Subject One could laugh off those comments and policing behaviors because he knows the law, as well as common decency, is on his side. The line famously repeated by Martin Luther King Jr., "The arc of the moral universe is long, but it bends towards justice" is a sustaining thought.

But such behaviors are part of a larger project, as became clear over the years. And it was the comments about others, the presumed incompetence of an African American professor, the language skills of a Hispanic faculty member, and a quip about Asian names being too difficult to pronounce, that were the hardest challenges for Subject One. Did he need to educate his senior colleagues on basic polite and collegial behavior? Were they joking or testing him? These experiences make the label *a White institution* very clear as practice. And the challenges increase as Subject One's decisions continue to be on the right side of history.

A White institution describes a place that privileges whiteness. Whiteness, at this institution, is a hegemonic worldview that overtakes common sense and allows unprofessional comments against those outside of Whiteness; the look and behaviors of the majority. Different expectations and reactions, more than exclusion, mark the Whiteness of the college.

Even when he is not the target of the racism, the presumption of incompetence and the meanness to others hurts him as if those proclamations were actually directed at him, which in some ways they were. It hurts him because he has a commitment to social justice that is evident in his academic research, his classroom and experiential learning projects and in his activities in his social and neighborhood communities. Tenured and with academic achievements, Subject One wrestles with his lack of success at the college; all of which was exhausting and so very necessary.

A Second Voice

In the United States, Subject Two has been a Latina in predominantly White institutions throughout her academic career. Arriving at another predominately White space, she believed, should not be much of a change in experience. However, experiencing the Deep South was new. Her White colleagues noted that their workplace felt like a plantation—a place where faculty were the White masters and the predominantly Black grounds keepers and Southeast Asian janitorial workers were the servants.

She was uncertain what her experience would be as the only faculty of color at the institution. Subject Two had not even thought about that when she accepted the job. She had considered a variety of other issues (e.g., possibility for job growth, institutional support, job opportunities in the city for her spouse, etc.), but it seemed that being the only person of color at the institution would be something she should be able to handle.

Although it was somewhat lonely, she did find support in various ways. Her supervisor was careful to not ask that she serve on more committees than her colleagues. Her colleagues were warm and welcoming people with whom she could have warm discussions, even when in disagreement. The people that were most welcoming were the oldest of them; perhaps the least threatened by disagreement. As this generation of scholars retired, the civility and warmth began to fade while acrimony and the search for favoritism increased.

It is difficult to pinpoint the reason for these shifts. Subject Two contributed to the difficulty because once she earned tenure, she was no longer the well-behaved and acquiescent minority. She spoke up, many times and sometimes strongly, in disagreement with what colleagues took for granted. When one is no longer in one's place, understandably, people will feel angered and will respond in kind. Yet she could no longer remain quiet when she could observe privilege at play and how colorblind racism was playing out.

Subject Two still recognized her own privilege and became sharply aware of it when Black faculty members were hired. She had not faced the racist reactions of students and faculty that these colleagues had.

For example, she remembers a time when she was at a public event speaking with a Black colleague when a White colleague approached. The White colleague spoke to Subject Two and immediately left, ignoring the Black faculty member. There was no acknowledgment that a conversation had been cut short on their initiation, no acknowledgment of the existence of this other person, and clearly no acknowledgment that such behavior is not conducive to a welcoming environment.

Soon after, that assistant professor and another Black colleague resigned from the college. Senior faculty members tried hard to blame them for their negative experiences or simply dismissed the racial tensions by claiming they were difficult people to relate with or that they left for personal motivations that had nothing to do with race. As they talked about the situation, some colleagues claimed to not understand why their Black colleagues were so upset. The explanations went on for years, according to Subject Two, and are occasionally raised to show that the blame goes to the victims. After all, why would anyone want to leave such a pleasant place?

Subject Two tried, after lengthy one-on-one conversations, to explain the lived experience of those who left. But most faculty members could not understand or, rather, would not accept their role in pushing these assistant professors out. They see themselves, in principle and with righteous indignation, as tolerant and good people. Niceness comes up a lot, and other White faculty members agree to produce the ruling assumptions.

The characterization by both subjects is, therefore, interpreted as unfair and a misrepresentation of the situation. Clearly, there is no recognition that they believe they have the authority to determine when the interpretation of the world offered by a person of color is legitimate or it is not. They do not recognize the assumption that their Whiteness (or age or gender) should give them the authority to determine whether a person of color is right or wrong.

These experiences have led Subject Two to realize that her voice is not truly heard. The silencing is a sign of disrespect. She is told by some colleagues and administrators that they respect her very much and want to hear what she has to say. So she shares her views. Yet with time, she comes to realize that the behavior is guided more by the worldview of her White male colleagues. Of course, she does not anticipate every aspect of her worldview to predominate in a supposedly democratic environment, yet she did not expect that none of her views would lead to practical implementation.

Both subjects and other minority faculty and staff have consistently argued for the need for a professionally trained expert to lead the college in its goal to diversify the campus. One attempt lasted only two years. The disintegration of this opportunity demonstrated the administration had other institutional interests. With funds tight, as with many colleges in the aftermath of the Great Recession, the hiring line went from a diversity officer to an academic support officer; where the diversity officer was a Black woman, the new position was filled with a young White male.

Diversity is a priority when there is money left over for it—a reflection of the way diversity is performed tongue-in-check. Another example is the discussion that was had when Subject Two's school attempted to hire a scholar with a specialty in race and ethnicity. The applicant pool was the most diverse this institution ever had. Through much push and pull, the search committee's top candidates were all minorities. Yet the top two candidates turned them down and the third was not acceptable to many.

In a meeting with administrators, Subject One was told that perhaps they just simply need to hire a White person if there are not enough minority candidates! They had many equally qualified minority candidates in the pool, so it was clear some members of the administration were ready to give up the effort to increase diversity, even with this unique opportunity of a large body of minority applicants. Eventually top administrators approved the recommendation to bring additional minority candidates to campus. In the end, the position was offered to a well-liked candidate.

A similar example is when a colleague of both subjects expressed disapproval of the use of limited resources for diversity initiatives when the budget was being cut in other ways. To the school's administration, there were more important issues in times of financial crisis than the diversification of the campus, and campus climate did not deserve such attention. This body represented an influential but small group of faculty.

Many of Subject Two's White colleagues have been tremendously supportive and understanding, and it was helpful to her to have them remind her that she is not misunderstanding these *racial* situations. As additional minority faculty members were hired, she soon had others with whom to share her experiences and frustrations and from whom to gain hope. Hence, what Subject Two has learned is the importance of recognizing these individuals in her life and the importance of cultivating those positive relationships.

Two Voices

The dynamics of hurt but possibilities for change kept both subjects optimistic through nearly twenty years. And their analysis followed, although never explicitly, the insight of a Jewish refugee from mid-20th-century Europe; Albert Einstein in 1946 spoke at Lincoln University in Pennsylvania, a historically black college, saying, "The separation of the races (segregation) is not a disease of colored people, but a disease of white people. I do not intend to be quiet about it" (see Jerome and Taylor 2005).

It seemed every new diversity initiative would bring fresh ideas and faculty of color to campus and that the campus climate would become more positive and time would seem to be on the side with new faculty replacing retiring professors. But the changing demographics of the student body and slow changes to the make-up of the faculty led to more micro-aggressions and concerns.

The subjects now share the lessons learned over their years at a liberal arts college. The results have, not surprisingly, been uneven and sometimes bring them to tears. But they remain at the institution and collaborate on some projects, nearly always serving on diversity committees and believing that a diverse college will be a better college and a better place for the undergraduates.

IDEALS, DIVERSE CAMPUS COMMUNITY

One cannot clearly know what a college's work environment is like before having spent one or two years in it. The hope is that one's colleagues will be not only respectful but also welcoming and supportive. Their pathways are meant to illuminate the successes and continuing challenges.

Both subjects seek a community where faculty recognize each other's achievements, help each other grow into better teachers and scholars, and are cognizant and respectful of their strengths and weaknesses. Moreover, they seek a place where they can be seen as whole people with their own kinship networks and beliefs. But most importantly, they seek a place where they do not have to remind White colleagues that they are only *passing* as White and that their commitments to diversity mean that they are allies *of* minority faculty as well as *being* minority faculty.

To lighten the tone of this case study of challenges, there is a scene in the children's movie *Reef II* where the main character, Pi, is organizing all the members of the community in defense of the evil shark. Pi's problem is that he wants to make soldiers of all and have all be able to do the same thing. Eventually, he comes to realize that he is more effective if he uses the different qualities each individual has and directs them to the tasks where they can be most efficient. This allows everyone to be proud of their accomplishments and contributions to the community.

It is a lesson that involves the recognition that everyone has various passions, strengths, and weaknesses. Rather than expect all to do perfectly well in all areas, the leader uses each person's strengths in the areas where they would be most effective in pursuing the institution's goals. This, of course, implies a willingness of all participants to know one another as well as themselves, to value each other's strengths and know how best each participant is contributing to the larger effort.

Contributing to a larger effort is part of being in a community. Most, if not all, colleges consider themselves to be communities. The smallest of such

communities might call themselves a family. The family metaphor illuminates a crucial aspect for the challenges of change.

Bringing someone to the college family implies a distinction between
family and visitor. The visitor respects the family's choice in the organization of the household. The family member has a say and can comfortably
propose changes in that organization. This implies being open to accommodating the needs of the additional members as well as being flexible in being
accommodating to those who are already there. The subjects share the belief
that no member of the family should have special privileges and that all
members have equal access to opportunities offered by the institution.

Family organizations and dynamics, however, are not universal. The
White institution is a White family, despite the fact that most families in
today's United States have members who are minorities; whether as in-laws,
nephews, nieces, or grandchildren. Yet how the dominant group responds to
the new family member(s) varies widely.

Both subjects are reminded of George H. W. Bush in 1988 referring to his
grandchildren, from Jeb Bush's marriage to Columba, who was born in Mex-
ico, as the "little brown ones." He was speaking out of pride for his Mexican-
American grandchildren, but he was also tacitly acknowledging that they
were different from his other grandchildren who were never marked as his
"little White ones." That dynamic from the last century seems ongoing at the
tiny college.

Continuing with the family metaphor, the college has its living room.
Adding new furniture is a change, but living rooms have finite space, and
sometimes new furniture means the entire room needs to be rearranged. This
can sometimes cause tension within the house. The new member needs to
understand the motivation leading to the current arrangement, and the old
members need to understand the needs of the new member. Together, the
group can rearrange the furniture to satisfy most people's needs. Of course,
this implies the openness to have one's routines disturbed to make space for
change.

In authoritarian workplaces, the assumption is that the new adapt to the
old and work around the existing furniture placement in order to achieve
what they seek. In a small liberal arts college, this attitude can be demoraliz-
ing for young faculty and perhaps even impossible for faculty of diverse
backgrounds. When the faculty, however, work from the assumption that
accommodation involves more than goodwill, but willingness to change
some aspects of one's routines, the environment can become more welcoming.

BEING A PROBLEM

W. E. B. Du Bois famously asked, in the 1903 *Souls of Black Folks,* "How does it feel to be a problem?" But when are the general problems of a college also the problems of minority faculty? Lack of communication, (relatively) low salaries, uneven workload, (under)recognition of achievements, and administrative demands exist all across campus.

However, for minority faculty, their exclusion from hegemonic whiteness is an extra burden. That includes places where one can feel at ease versus needing to *perform* a specific identity. It is hard to capture the feelings of being *outside the norm* in White-dominated spaces. But these examples, where they return to separate voices, might illuminate the dynamics for a campus presentation.

Some programs at the college insist that faculty conduct a research presentation before their tenure vote. Many on campus disagree with this approach, especially since research expectations across the teaching-intensive college are great. No one on the faculty produces scholarship on the level of a Research 1 institution; it is not even close. And with tenure and promotion votes being decided by groupings rather than a specific discipline, assessment seems, and has a track record of being, more personal than professional. Yet even with the administration and the faculty union opposed to the practice of having a tenure candidate give a presentation on their research, junior faculty feel they must present.

Within this uncomfortable test, in 2013, the chair of one program announced the schedule for pre-tenure-vote research presentations. As with many announcements, the chair sent out an e-mail inviting all faculty members to attend the presentation. When Subject One responded to the e-mail indicating that the date reserved was Yom Kippur and that the invitation was not inclusive of all faculty, another e-mail was sent to the faculty acknowledging that the presentation was on Yom Kippur, that the event would take place as scheduled, and that everyone else (i.e., those not recognizing Yom Kippur) was invited to hear the presentation.

From the office of the provost . . . silence. A commitment to hegemony overtook support for principles and equal rights. The walls that mark the divides in the campus community are very high walls. Even though Subject One's e-mail was to the chair and not to the e-mail list, the result was predictable. He was told, in passing, that he was overstepping his place on campus. He was, again, told this in passing more than once so that there would be no record, no acknowledgment that the policing even occurred.

Protection for some on campus creates citadels—to protect some and keep out others. There are many more examples Subject One offered, but they cannot be included in this space regarding decision making, timing for events, and basic politeness, but the listing will not contribute anything to the point. While Subject Two contributes to state and federally generated check-lists for diversity, as well as being in the religious tradition of the majority of the faculty, Subject One does not on either count.

In the reorganizing of a space in the college as a family, some differences are too much for the majority. While Subject Two feels unheard but gets supportive statements, the other is excluded to the point that he is not considered a faculty member. The exclusion comes from choices, unlike for visible minorities, but is important to include in consideration of the challenges for diversity.

As bell hooks (2013, 159) recently explained, "Turning our collective gaze away from old assumptions about race and racism, refusing to see the problem as solely about direct discrimination or overt harmful acts, opens the space where white supremacy as it is expressed in everyday racism can be called out, critically examined, and eliminated."

The challenges the subjects face are not only related to their personal experiences and those of faculty. Their minority students also face these challenges, and the subjects find themselves needing to use their privilege as faculty to offer the necessary support to these students. For instance, a minority student explained to Subject Two that in her science textbook some of the examples and images used to illustrate particular ideas were sexist.

Subject Two was surprised to see the use of 1950s gendered images without critical analysis. She encouraged the student to speak with her female professor and, fortunately, the professor did respond positively. Yet it is not clear to Subject Two that a different textbook would be used in the future or that the issue would be a teaching moment beyond the one encounter with concern.

Another student was very concerned with the representation of Latino gay men in one of her social sciences courses. She was upset and felt uncomfortable challenging the interpretations presented in the article. Simply having someone with whom to speak who understood why she was uncomfortable was helpful to her.

A third example is a minority student who told a faculty member of color that she was disturbed by the way she had been treated by a White professor during class—a class where they were discussing issues of discrimination. Although the White faculty member had expertise on the topic, the student felt her emotions and views were dismissed. Speaking with the professor of color helped the student feel supported and validated.

Through these experiences both subjects came to realize that they face more emotional distress than other faculty when students share their experiences with discrimination, racism, sexism, or religious intolerance. When a senior faculty member called to ask Subject One if a student's request to go home for Passover was legitimate, it was interpreted as a test over what was more important, a holiday or a class session—with the simple and honest answer (yes, Passover is an important annual family gathering event) placing the student at risk.

Yet an honest discussion on topics such as this is nearly impossible because so many students also face emotional distress that some of their colleagues believe is exaggerated because they are minority students. Hence, the subjects came to the conclusion that their experiences were not different from many of their students of color and that the demands of the students and themselves were not exaggerations.

As with the example of silencing regarding policy invoked earlier, a significant challenge they face is their colleague's lack of respect for their interpretation of social reality, which results in the denial of the legitimacy of their experiences. These experiences illustrate that Whiteness is not a function of skin color, but of power.

In a small college, some choose to focus on sustaining their social status by excluding the different, even when the differences are modest. With a liberal arts education supposedly being about being able to confront social challenges, how does one's role fit in a White institution? How does one live with the emotional toll of shortcomings, insults, and disrespect? How does one handle the pain from seeing exclusion prevail? Those are their concerns for creating social change, to increase possibilities for differences at the college and beyond.

STRATEGIES

How to confront these challenges varies given their personalities and world outlooks. Both subjects recognize that there is a particular context to the issues at their college that might not resonate for others. And their success in gaining tenure separates them from colleagues who left before reaching that goal; in several ways, this is a plea to sustain the effort for those struggling at their campuses.

For those who are hopeful in trying situations, the suggestions below might be helpful. The subjects seek to contribute to structural change through the committee service that opens doors for diversity and change. Both subjects contribute to change through voicing their opinion to administrators, offering mutual support to each other and to fellow faculty and by supporting their students. It is at times frustrating, at times depressing, but the challenges are reproduced across many institutions.

As a junior member of the faculty, Subject Two seeks to remain focused on her teaching, research, and service and somewhat away from the internal and external politics. She has been very cognizant of the fact that academics are no different from the larger population. While they claim professionalism in their decision making, they allow their emotions to influence their decisions to a much greater extent than they like to admit. Hence, being well liked becomes very important for the tenure process. A well-liked person is less likely to face a focus on weaknesses and more likely to see praise in strengths. It is harder to deny tenure to someone you like than someone you dislike.

Her youth, and perhaps gender and personality, helped in this process because Subject Two was uncertain as to whether her interpretations were accurate—she was still learning. Subject Two, therefore, could more easily remain quiet and avoid too much controversy. Eventually, once she gained tenure and through years of lived experience, she became more outspoken and more comfortable being so.

Yet even then, one must *choose one's battles*. The battles can be very draining to one's spirit. Hence, choosing them is important. Subject Two dismissed the sly comments, the everyday expressions that clearly reflect an individual's bias. These help her to know who her colleagues *really are* without needing to confront them. She does, however, engage in the institutional mechanisms available to fight the injustices she sees around her. For instance, she serves on the college's diversity and multiculturalism committee. Also, she signs up for committees that she knows are addressing issues that she cares about.

While she is not always successful in pushing forward the solutions to the issues identified in this chapter, she is able to influence, to some extent, the way the house is organized. She has come to realize that she is not alone in the need to rearrange the furniture or the understanding that the furniture needs to be rearranged. So, her actions also allow others to gain the strength to speak up in support of these changes.

At a more interpersonal level, Subject Two does not allow academic life to be the whole of her life. She is fortunate to have a family. So she must be home for dinner and spend quality time with her children and spouse. This part of her life, which is contested by some at the college who privilege the institution over family life, forces her to take a break from the all-encompassing work that academe involves.

Subject One diverts from this trajectory because being a man offers privileges but also requires explanations (he has always prioritized family life, even when colleagues assumed his wife would take care of the children, and it especially was challenging when she was willing to take a larger role as he refused to allow gender inequalities in the marriage). He also faced the religious differences, with the Jewish calendar and life cycle events—for a role model for students from multiple religious backgrounds (not just the Jewish students) and being able to play the role of a professor, even when senior faculty members dismissed his accomplishments and skills, seemed important in the long run, for the goal of social justice.

What sustains that goal? Both participate in the activities of their religious community and are partially engaged with some activist networks. Both of them not only offer new friendship networks and support systems, but they also serve as a reminder of the larger picture that in their humane existence there are more important things (e.g., hunger and homelessness in the city or the loss of life due to war in their home countries) than the emotionally wrenching issues at her institution. This distance allows recognition that the small issues of academe are only a small part of a larger picture. From such a perspective, the institutional problems become smaller and hence less emotionally draining.

Management of emotions is a much more difficult task. Subject Two cannot really prevent the anger, disappointment, sadness, or exhilaration surrounding the various social interactions that encompass her. All she can do is try to prevent them from overtaking her behavior. Subject One faces different emotional states but shares those goals. The first thing that each does is become self-analytical to understand what is at the root of the emotions.

Once the root cause is understood, one can better think strategically about how to resolve the situation. At times, the issue is policy; other times it is practice. Some solutions are reached through the administration, others by talking to individual faculty members. Occasionally, both have stood up boldly for diversity at public meetings; other times, symbols on office walls make the point for those who visit during office hours.

If a member of the faculty is making racist, racially or ethnically insensitive comments, most commonly through colorblind racism, they are deeply hurt. And that needs to be acknowledged. When the opportunity lends itself, Subject Two will address the matter in as polite a way as she can, as when a colleague noted that it did not make much sense to put too much energy into attracting students from the local, predominantly Black neighborhood as most of these kids are not the quality of student they seek. She did plainly voice that she found such commentary very troubling.

Subject One is more likely to seek allies to contest such points of view, enlisting administrators, staff, or other faculty members so that the issue is contained and addressed. He recognizes that at times he can use his White privilege to confront racism, but other dynamics require a team effort to reduce the harm to the person's sense of self or to overturn the negative racist dynamics.

There are times, however, when both have lost their patience and offered very direct responses to similarly insensitive comments. Both have noticed that when academics present interpretations of social reality of class, race, and gender privileges that colleagues, and even well-intentioned and progressive academics, benefit from, they become irate. Clearly many academics have difficulty coming to terms with the fact they are living with privilege and managing their sense of guilt that they are, but possibly should not be, benefiting from such privilege.

At each moment in their experience at the college when a diversity hire was promising, White faculty members would turn to Subject One with queries over whether they would be employed if such dynamics had been present when their tenure-track lines were advertised. The implication that they may still benefit as members of the majority is interpreted as an insult. Race, particularly White supremacy and privilege, continue to be an intellectual minefield.

This, however, is not only a challenge with one's White colleagues. Colleagues of color are not uniform in their worldview, nor do they approach each problem with a similar set of solutions. There is disagreement, for example, over terminology.

Should it be *people of color* or should it be *minorities*? Should minorities accept that they will have to work twice as hard as Whites to prove themselves and stop being complainers, or should minorities push with critical analysis against the systems of oppression and, hence, complain about the injustices so these become undone?

Not everyone wanted an ally, which was a challenge for Subject One. And when Subject Two raised awareness of the structural problems, was she interpreted by colleagues as a *cry baby* and embraced by them based on her White colleagues' colorblindness? When their minority colleagues take positions that support the worldview of their more conservative White colleagues, the battle is longer and more difficult.

While Subject Two has not yet found a satisfactory solution to this challenge, she has found that further interpersonal conversations and the sharing of a meal and a conversation helps break down some of the tensions. When the institution does not offer a space nor nurture a culture of communication and colleagueship that encourages colleagues to get to know one another better, it is difficult to move beyond these tensions and obstacles to a more welcoming environment.

Subject One, on the other hand, focuses on supporting student programs, both social clubs and community service learning programs, hoping those structural changes to campus life can be the change that makes the college more welcoming.

The personal matters greatly in creating and sustaining a community, but the challenges and the emotional toll are the reasons for laying out these examples and thoughts from a small college. From their experiences, they have come to value the mixing of different approaches. This chapter concludes with the combining of a Palestinian term and a saying from the Jewish tradition.

Both subjects have learned the need to be steadfast. Arabic has a word for being steadfast—*sumud*. And it is a useful concept. If the goal is to change the institution, to ensure that the ideals for diversity are respected and sustained, one key is to persevere. Being one of the first minority faculty members on campus was challenging for Subject One. Seeing so few visible minorities on the faculty was also a challenge, but it was a start.

After nearly twenty years of perseverance, the results are minor for the subjects, but others are building on the positive dynamics they helped to create. One has to be hopeful, also, as noted in *Pirkei Avot*, of the Talmud's *Chapters of Fundamental Principles*, whose intention is more beautiful than the translated words: "It is not incumbent upon you to complete the work, but neither are you at liberty to desist from it."

REFERENCES

Du Bois, W. E. B. 1903. *The Souls of Black Folk: Essays and Sketches*. Chicago: A. C. McClurg & Company.
hooks, bell. 2013. *Writing beyond Race: Living Theory and Practice*. New York: Routledge.
Jerome, Fred, and Rodger Taylor. 2005. *Einstein on Race and Racism*. New Brunswick, NJ: Rutgers University Press.

Chapter Nine

Down the Rabbit Hole

Racism and Microaggressions at a Public New England University

Shanette M. Harris and Donald Cunnigen

> "When I use a word," Humpty Dumpty said in rather a scornful tone, "it means just what I choose it to mean—neither more nor less."
> "The question is," said Alice, "whether you can make words mean so many different things."
> "The question is," said Humpty Dumpty, "which is to be master—that's all."—*Alice's Adventures in Wonderland*

During Alice's unexpected and confusing interaction with Humpty Dumpty, an underlying truth related to power, authority, and control is revealed that also influences the career success and personal experiences of faculty of color (FOC) who commit to work at predominantly white institutions. The majority of FOC who make this decision will eventually come face to face with their powerlessness in an environment in which their realities are seldom confirmed and often challenged by those who hold power and privilege much like Humpty Dumpty.

This sense of negotiating one's *twoness*, or existence in two worlds, and having to confront an ever shifting set of norms and standards eventually renders many faculty of color traumatized and alienated as they attempt to persist in an unending and complex maze of hostility and bias. Consequently, there is growing interest in research that focuses on the adjustment and experiences of minority faculty on predominantly White American college campuses.

However, experiences of minority faculty do not occur within a vacuum but emerge from interactions between characteristics of university environments and personal and background qualities of individual professors. The identification of institutional qualities that interfere with goal attainment of minority academicians, induce university dissatisfaction, and encourage faculty withdrawal is necessary to develop strategies that may improve higher education for minority graduate students who aspire to the professorate.

The norms, philosophies, and ideologies of educational institutions constitute the culture or climate, which is reciprocally influenced by qualities of the city/town, county, state, and geographical region in which the university is embedded (Rose 1966). Precollege experiences and characteristics of faculty members (e.g., salary, marital status, and academic rank) (Jayakumar, Howard, Allen and Han 2009) interact with college institutional climate and culture that govern faculty behavioral responses and reactions to influence perceptions and affect faculty (Harris and Nettles 1996).

In this chapter, empirical research related to university experiences of African American faculty and microaggressions is reviewed. A discussion of the tenets of the Critical Race Theory (CRT) theoretical framework and the methodology that guides this study is then presented. Next, two case studies for Dr. Humphreys and Dr. Jones (both pseudonyms) are described with empirical research that applies to their experiences. Finally, suggestions are offered for graduate students who seek to work as academicians on similar college campuses.

AFRICAN AMERICAN FACULTY ON PREDOMINANTLY WHITE COLLEGE CAMPUSES

Research suggests that the presence of diverse faculty benefits colleges in several ways, and administrators are quick to articulate a commitment to recruit and retain minority faculty in institutions of higher learning (e.g., Astin et al. 1997; NCES 2008; Ryu 2008). However, findings of quantitative and qualitative studies show that minority college faculty members experience a university environment that is distinctly different from that of their White colleagues.

Stanley (2006) reviewed literature related to faculty of color on predominantly White campuses and noted that certain descriptions surfaced repeatedly (i.e., marginality, alienation, isolation, and invisibility). Based on qualitative data and several different dimensions (e.g., comfort with the culture, habits, decisions, practices, and policies of the academic environment), six themes were identified related to faculty of color experiences: 1) teaching, 2) mentoring, 3) collegiality, 4) identity, 5) service, and 6) racism.

However, the socio-cultural dynamics of racism is the overarching issue that shapes the encounters of faculty of color. Minority professors face discriminatory and stereotypical behavior in most realms of White academia.

Studies report concerns related to racism and marginalization that shape experiences with colleagues (e.g., Johnsrud and DesJarlais 1994; McKay 1997), classroom management (e.g., Hendrix 1998; Harlow 2003; Pittman 2010; Sue et al. 2011), and student evaluations (e.g., Hendrix, 1998; Fries and McNinch 2003; Hammermesh and Parker 2005; Pittman 2010).

Similar experiences influence teaching and service (e.g., Hendrix 1998; Leik and Goulding 2000); research and publishing (e.g., Menges and Exum 1983; Johnsrud and Sadao 1998; Leik and Goulding 2000; Turner and Meyers 2000; Stanley 2006; Turner, Gonzalez, and Wood 2008; Jayakumar, Howard, Allen, and Han 2009); and promotion and tenure (e.g., Leik and Goulding 2000; Fenelon 2003; Jayakumar et al. 2009) decisions and outcomes for professors of minority status.

The negativity of a racial college climate is more exaggerated for Latina/o and African American faculty than Asian faculty, but is positively related to the retention of White faculty (Jayakumar et al. 2009). Harlow (2003) found that African American professors reported disrespectful or inappropriate challenges to their intellectual authority. Other researchers also support African American faculty issues with credibility, particularly, in the classroom. For example, Hendrix (1998) found that White and African American students used more rigorous criteria to assess the credibility of African American professors.

Bavishi, Hebl, and Madera (2010) also found that students evaluated Black professors as less competent and legitimate than White or Asian faculty and saw Black and Asian professors as having less interpersonal skill than White professors. Sue et al. (2011) investigated how minority faculty encouraged and facilitated difficult race-related conversations in the classroom and reported that students direct microaggressions toward them more than other faculty. Racial stereotypes of African Americans held by students and faculty contribute to their difficulties. The low number of African Americans on these campuses makes it difficult to dispel stereotypical beliefs.

The penalty that women of color must pay as objects of both racism and sexism (i.e., gendered racism) can exacerbate the impact and breadth of these concerns. African-heritage women are viewed as *outsiders within* on the White college campus, and their contributions and expertise are undervalued more than those of other faculty, despite the importance of the standpoint and inclusive approach they bring to higher education (Henderson, Hunter, and Hildreth 2010). The intersectionality of race and gender are apparent in the experiences of African American female professors on White campuses.

On the one hand, they are treated as if invisible and relegated to the periphery of academia but, simultaneously, are constantly critiqued and monitored for physical presentation (e.g., clothing, hairstyles, and mood), remarks, language or speech, tone, and even frequency of interactions with specific campus employees and students (e.g., race of students, department of faculty, and race/ethnicity of faculty) (Wright Meyers 2002). Bavishi, Hebl, and Madera (2010) found that female African American professors were rated last in competency, legitimacy, and interpersonal skill compared to males of the same race and those of Asian and White heritage.

Students' prejudicial and racist beliefs contribute to negative impressions of African American women prior to meeting them as a course professor. Colleagues and students often perceive African-heritage women as angry when they present as serious or professional and refuse to behave in a stereotypical *motherly* way (Harlow 2003). These findings are consistent with the modern *mammy* image of Black professional women, which holds that they are easily exploited, expected to place White academia and students above their life and are accepting of abuse, mistreatment, and inappropriate demands but willing to remain silent (Wingfield 2007).

African-heritage female faculty receive more student evaluations that describe them as mean, cold, or intimidating and are the object of more physical or verbal threats by students (Harlow 2003). Student complaints levied against African American female faculty are frequently taken seriously and empowered by White faculty and administrators, which undermines their authority and bestows greater credibility on those who complain (Harlow 2003). Consequently, the White privilege that defends White faculty also protects students in conflict with African American female faculty (Henderson, Hunter, and Hildreth 2010).

Racial Microaggressions

Chester Pierce (1970, 66) coined the term *racial microaggression*, which refers to "subtle, stunning, often automatic, and non-verbal exchanges which are 'put downs.'" More recently, psychologists have defined racial microaggressions as brief and commonplace daily verbal, behavioral, or environmental indignities, whether intentional or unintentional, that communicate hostile, derogatory, or negative racial slights and insults toward people of color (Davis 1989; Sue, Bucerri, Lin, Nadal, and Torina 2007).

Sue et al. (2007) identify three types of microaggression messages: (1) microassaults (explicit displays of racial harm much like *old-fashioned racism*), (2) microinsults (insensitive or rude verbal or nonverbal behaviors that put down a target's heritage or identity and typically occur outside of the perpetuator's awareness), and (3) microinvalidation (actions that nullify, exclude, or dismiss the experiences of a race/ethnic target). According to these theorists, microinvalidations are the most egregious of the three types of microaggressions because they deny, ignore, or exclude the reality of the target.

Consequently, microinsults and microinvalidations are more difficult to identify than microassaults (Sue and Constantine 2007). Given that cross-racial interactions are associated with racist stereotypes and attitudes, it is important to determine if exposure to microaggressions is one potential pathway through which racism impacts the well-being of African American faculty and the *types* of microaggressions most often identified in relation to race and gender in academia.

THEORETICAL FRAMEWORK AND METHOD

Critical Race Theory (CRT) is an invaluable framework that provides meaning to the race and racial power systemic to larger social structures that influence the dynamics of predominantly White American institutions of higher education and dominate the experiences of faculty in the academy. To guide the conceptualization and orientation of this study, we use the tenets of CRT, which originated within legal studies (e.g., Bell 1992; Ladson-Billings and Tate 1995; Tate 1997; Ladson-Billings 1998; Delgado and Stefancic 2001).

CRT has been used in education since the mid-1990s to examine educational disparities and inequities between people of color (POC) and White Americans (e.g., Ladson-Billings and Tate 1995; Ladson-Billings 1998) and provides an orientation that supports examinations of the relationship between racism and institutions of higher education. This theory proposes that racism is not normal, but aberrant, and only appears normal because of historical norms and standards.

A second tenet is that Whites have been and remain the primary beneficiaries of a biased and racist system and will not likely agree to change this system unless it also rewards them. Consistent with these tenets, CRT holds that liberty and equality are not fully understood by the White American majority because of institutional and structural racism that blinds them to seeing inequities. Finally, CRT encourages the voice of those most impacted by the negativity of racism to be heard and utilizes methods that allow personal experiences to be presented with the expectations of eradicating walls of racism. A case study approach is well suited for this theory. In this chapter, a case study perspective is applied to understand African American faculty perceptions of microaggressions. Yin (1994) refers to this type of case study as *exploratory*, which seeks to develop theory. We are interested in African American faculty's "conclusions arrived at through personal engagement in life's affairs" (Stake 1995, 86) in order to gain insight into the experiences of a male and female professor on a New England campus rather than to generalize this information to all minority faculty (Yin 1994). The primary objective is to provide a "study of the particularity and complexity of a single case" (Stake 1995, xi).

CASE STUDY RESULTS AND DISCUSSION

Case Study A (Dr. Aziz Jones)

Aziz Jones is a full professor at a small public New England University and a native of a Deep South state. He received his undergraduate education at a historically Black liberal arts college in the South and graduate degrees from a state and an Ivy League university in New England, respectively. Dr. Jones held two previous faculty assignments at the assistant level, and his current academic appointment is his third position, during which he was elevated to associate professor and most recently to full professor. He is the first African-heritage individual to hold a tenure-track appointment in his department and consequently to serve as full professor.

Soon after accepting his current position Dr. Jones and his wife were invited to dinner by a White male colleague who told a story about threatening the owner of a Black-owned establishment in the presence of Black patrons during a visit through the South as a consultant to an enrichment program at Black colleges. This information was perplexing and particularly upsetting to the Joneses, who had witnessed and were victims of White terrorism in their home state. Another White male colleague highlighted his ancestry in a prominent southern confederate family during a conversation.

At another point, when Aziz inquired of this same colleague about housing during the planning process for a research trip, he was told that this was an unlikely option because his brother did not care for Black people. Similar experiences occurred that related specifically to the work environment. The department held an election for a new chairperson. Because the departmental factions were so obvious and visible, he opted to abstain from voting. Later that day, from his open office door, Dr. Jones overheard three White male colleagues discussing the election outcome in the hallway.

One White colleague voiced loudly and clearly that Dr. Jones could have voted because "no one will do anything to him because he is a *f---ing* minority." However, this group of faculty immediately dispersed when he walked past them in the hallway. Another White male professor assigned as Dr. Jones's mentor, with an office next door, did not speak to him for three years. As a newly minted associate professor, Dr. Jones also discovered that a colleague was teaching sections of the courses that he was hired to teach (courses rarely taught because of lack of interest) and arranged a meeting with the chairperson to inquire about the course overlap.

This meeting resulted in conflict. First, he was informed that professors did not have a *claim* on courses in the department. The chair also reversed a decision from earlier semesters during which he had made an implicit *ultimatum* that one had to offer writing-intensive courses if they wanted to maintain small class sizes. The chair then eliminated the two writing-intensive courses that he had recently insisted that Dr. Jones design. After Dr. Jones presented his perspective on both matters, the chairperson crossed his arms over his chest and whirled around in his chair with his back to him to stare out a large picture window.

Dr. Jones did not speak at this point, although the chairperson asked him to continue with his discussion. During the week, the chairperson attempted via telephone to arrange a luncheon date to continue to discuss these issues. However, Aziz did not return his calls because he was told in the messages *where* he should meet, *what* he could discuss, and *what* he could not discuss during the lunch meeting.

Prior to the submission of the promotion portfolio for full professor, Dr. Jones placed the required materials in five envelopes for the chairperson to mail at a future date to external reviewers. To make certain that the envelopes were not stained or smudged (as noticed in previous cases) and kept in a secure and clean space, Dr Jones requested that the secretary place the envelopes in the office of the departmental chairperson. However, upon seeing the review packets on her desk, this new chairperson accosted him in the hallway and yelled loudly that he had "violated her personal space" by placing the promotion materials in her office.

Dr. Jones felt vulnerable at this point because the AAUP (American Association of University Professors) and university promotion guidelines specified that the departmental chairperson held a major role in the review and promotion of faculty and he did not know, based on her actions, if she would support him. Dr. Jones made an appointment to discuss this interaction with the dean of the college but did not receive supportive information or proactive steps that could be taken to address the situation. The dean concluded their discussion with the question, "What do you want me to do?" Clearly, neither his colleagues nor the chair appreciated the depth or impact of this outburst on him.

Dr. Jones was not satisfied with this meeting and learned that the chairperson and dean were close acquaintances or friends. After several sleepless nights and days without an appetite, he called the president's office, who took action only after he also contacted friends in a professional organization who wrote the president. Dr. Jones received a *cover your A** letter* and the chairperson subsequently resigned. He had requested her resignation and a public verbal apology but never received such an apology. Interestingly, the chairperson accused him of bullying, despite the fact that she initiated the altercation.

Dr. Jones encountered repeated efforts by White colleagues in the department and administration to undermine his authority in the classroom, including illegally changing recorded grades, instructing students not to attend classes, encouraging students not to submit required course work, instructing students not to take examinations, constructing dummy substitute courses for required courses taught by him, and pretending to mediate faculty/student disputes but never consulting with him face-to-face. An internal departmental *kangaroo investigation* was also initiated for a student who acknowledged failure to submit work at the designated time.

University pass/fail policies were violated and Dr. Jones's teaching practices discussed with students. In one situation, the provost changed a student's course grades without informing him and then refused to allow him to read the complaint letter that contained blatant lies until a decision was rendered. This student challenged his authority on a daily basis. She would repeatedly disrupt class by slamming a notebook on the desk, speak in a disrespectful manner, study for other courses during class time, look out the window while filing her fingernails and refuse to cooperate in class discussions.

The repeated offenses by the university's administration and departmental personnel resulted in Dr. Jones filing a human rights complaint for a hostile work environment and racial harassment. He also filed a grievance via the faculty union regarding violation of his academic freedom. The grievance outcome resulted in modifications to the university handbook that Dr. Jones, university faculty, and university administrators found acceptable in relation to policy. Dr. Jones became seriously ill shortly after these experiences and is currently in recovery.

Case Study B (Dr. Sharon Humphreys)

Dr. Sharon Humphreys is an African American, southern born and educated female who received a doctorate in clinical psychology at 28 years old. Upon graduation, she held her first appointment at a major southern flagship institution in the southeast and enjoyed her work and the environment. During these five years, she was nominated by her department as faculty member of the year, received university research and travel support, and obtained a postdoctoral fellowship from the Ford Foundation. She was vice president and president of the Black Faculty Staff Association and served on the University Commission for Blacks.

Sharon joined a midsize, New England state university after being pursued for three years (one contact call per year) and only accepted the offer after the president arranged for a tenure-track line in the department, since the initial offer was based on a soft money contract. Upon arrival in the rural town, there was no one to show her how to acquire a university ID card, parking tag, and other requirements. Surprised, she learned the current department chair was not the same person who assisted with her contract.

Her office was also dirty and dusty, and the agreed-upon computer from months earlier had not arrived. Three days before the start of classes, and still without the agreed-upon computer, Dr. Humphreys felt compelled to personally purchase a computer in order to have syllabi prepared for classes on the first day (the chair implied that *some* faculty held an initial class without a course syllabus). Since Dr. Humphreys and only one other faculty member (White male, tenured at an Ivy League in-state university) were new to the institution, the annual orientation was not held and was replaced with a luncheon.

Information related to institutional rules, regulations, and policies were not discussed during the luncheon nor were related materials provided. At that time, there was only one university manual in print, and that copy belonged to the associate dean, who made it clear that she needed to keep her copy. During this first semester, Dr. Humphreys spent an inordinate amount of time with graduate students of color who were having problems because of racism, studying for state licensure as a psychologist, teaching courses, sitting on various committees, and trying to continue her research productivity despite an absence of support and resources.

The first year in the department, and the first semester in particular, set the tone for future years. Graduate students of color brought her their feelings of frustration and confusion about their perceptions of racism and perceived mistreatment due to their racial/ethnic heritage, but they tended to want to work primarily with White faculty members. This was the first class admitted into the department with a large number of graduate students of color and Dr. Humphreys as the first professor of color. Unbeknownst to the students or professor, an accrediting board had pressured the program area to increase program diversity in accordance with ethical guidelines.

Rivalry among various program areas within the department led to problems for students and Dr. Humphreys. Students were steered away from her, especially those of European heritage. In one case, she worked with a White male on a research topic and was to submit a joint paper for presentation, but he took their work to a female faculty member (White) in another program area. He wrote Dr. Humphreys a letter apologizing for his *mistake*, attributing his actions to being under stress. During a class, one student overtly refused to complete an assignment.

When Dr. Humphreys sought guidance from the program area coordinator, she was told "students usually get A's in the class." Her immediate and direct response to the question was, "Are you suggesting that I give the student an A even though she refuses to do the assignment?" "I'm not saying that," was the chair's response. At the start of the semester in January, the same chairperson had signed a letter of complaint by this particular student as if the professor had not informed her of the matter in advance. At this point, it was becoming more apparent that *something* was not quite right.

Students also complained to the dean of the College of Education, where Dr. Humphreys taught a class for additional compensation, that she did not give them a 15-minute break during class. However, she had no knowledge of such a norm because of the absence of an orientation session and a lack of familiarity with norms of the university culture. Any mistake that could have been attributed to adjustment to a novel work environment was approached by administrators as deserving significant attention.

In one instance a European American male student wrote Dr. Humphreys a note on an exam that commented on her appearance, and he asked for a date. Because she had never encountered this type behavior from a student, she did not know what to do. Given other interactions with administrators about student behaviors, she felt helpless. She remained anxious during the class, would not walk to this student's side of the classroom (i.e., front row to the right), and never reported his behavior out of fear that her report would be considered less valid than the student's.

On numerous occasions, her grading and teaching expectations and standards were challenged, even when opportunities were provided for extra credit and class grades were significantly inflated. Dr. Humphreys eventually became aware that the norms in the department (if not on the campus) included students arriving to class late, failing to submit work on time, directly confronting her during class, and feeling comfortable going to the chair or dean when their demands or expectations for higher grades were not met.

When students were granted a grade of incomplete because they did not finish all of the required course work, she was unaware that the student could graduate without ever having to actually fulfill course requirements. She learned this when she contacted a student to arrange a date for the student to take a missed exam and to submit the required research paper. The student explained that she had already graduated and thanked her for the call. Faculty meetings were just as confusing and hurtful. Remarks made by Dr. Humphreys were basically ignored.

Sometimes supportive faculty would restate her comments, such as, "I think Dr. Humphreys' idea about ... deserves some discussion" in order to call attention to her ignored remarks. In one instance a male faculty member acted in a loud, shouting and finger-pointing manner when Dr. Humphreys disagreed with his comments. However, none of the faculty came to her defense during or after his tirade despite the obvious inappropriateness of his reaction.

Prior to tenure and promotion, the chairperson decided to ask undergraduates to vote or comment on Dr. Humphrey's teaching, which was in violation of the university tenure and promotion guidelines and AAUP policy.

Even after the AAUP director informed this chairperson that such behavior was inappropriate and unacceptable, he still requested a departmental vote to allow undergraduates to vote on her portfolio. When she excitedly told this same chair that she had been asked to serve as an interviewee on a major television news show he replied, "It won't get you tenure."

She learned that an associate dean of the College of Arts and Sciences had two-years-retroactively changed a student's grade of D in her class to a grade of B. The head of the university union stepped in to grieve this situation because Dr. Humphreys was able to produce work submitted by the student, and the grade was eventually changed to the original. She was even accused by one chairperson of interacting with minority students more than White students because she walked with a student to class each day, but the student was actually an Italian female.

During one summer, almost three years after her arrival on the campus, Dr. Humphreys experienced symptoms of dizziness and double vision while driving in another state, while collecting data for a study. She was rushed to the emergency room of a nearby hospital where she was admitted with insulin levels above 700 and, subsequently, diagnosed with diabetes mellitus type 2. Dr. Humphreys was promoted to associate professor with tenure later in the summer after significant stress and hostility from daily battle.

Some of the students that Dr. Humphreys assisted transferred to other institutions, and two graduated from the university—she has not heard from any of them since. The few faculty members who wanted to diversify the department and had offered support retired, and one passed away; new faculty simply represent clones of the existing members. Three faculty of color entered, stayed for a brief time and eventually left for universities in other states. However, this first year continued to repeat itself. For example, students are encouraged not to enroll in her classes and to write negative comments on the website Rate My Professor when dissatisfied or disgruntled.

The current chair continues to drop students from Sharon's courses as late as the final week of class in the semester without sufficient justification or willingness to have them accept a grade of incomplete. Several students are frequently offered the opportunity to write a 10-page paper by the chair in place of the course taught by Dr. Humphreys and with similar course credit despite university policies and norms that do not allow such actions. In addition, the dean has even asked her to modify course requirements, and some students have been allowed to miss classes without necessary documentation.

Dr. Humphreys was diagnosed with diabetes one year before promotion to associate professor. She was diagnosed with hypertension two years after promotion and tenure and hospitalized. More recently, she has been diagnosed with congestive heart failure. When others comment, "but you're so young," she nods and wonders, "but what *if* she is putting her portfolio forward for evaluation and review for full professor this year."

CASE STUDY DISCUSSION

Dr. Humphreys and Dr. Jones stopped attending departmental faculty meetings to avoid feelings of invisibility and to avoid receiving differential treatment when they offered comments. They also slowly dissociated themselves altogether, or as much as professionally possible, from their departments. They reduced their number of office hours and visited the campus only when necessary. Dr. Humphreys has found a *home place* for relaxation and support within her campus research laboratory. In this space, she has African American art and African sculptures and poems that speak to her essence.

Within these walls, she meets with students of diverse racial/ethnic heritages for mentoring, academic sessions, research tasks, as well as friendship. Griffin, Pifer, Humphrey, and Hazelwood (2011) conducted in-depth interviews with 28 Black professors affiliated with two public research universities and found that a small number of faculty responded to climate hostility and racism with physical departure from the institution. However, most faculty engaged in other forms of departure including departmental departure (invisibility), self-definition, and service engagement.

Both Jones and Humphreys describe incidents that speak to institutional resistance to their achieving promotion and tenure. Griffin et al. (2011) also reported that the tenure review period was most likely high risk in the faculty college life cycle for increased racist maneuvers and undermining actions. The chair's unilateral decision to recruit undergraduates to vote on Dr. Humphrey's promotion, with full awareness that she had encountered numerous microaggressions in the form of name calling, yelling, confrontation about grades, and refusal to complete assignments, was designed to prevent her from obtaining promotion.

Fortunately, supportive faculty colleagues, the university union leader, and the grievance committee helped her design an effective defense. Likewise, weeks before his full-professor review, Dr. Jones was verbally humiliated in the midst of student and faculty observers by a White female chairperson over a minor incident. It is quite possible that she was attempting to elicit from him the stereotypical *angry Black man behavior* (Wingfield 2007), which would affirm that he was unworthy for promotion to full professor. Gendered racism leads to similarities in experiences for males and females, but differences as well.

The use of Black misandry (i.e., an exaggerated pathological aversion toward Black men created and reinforced in societal, institutional, and individual ideologies, practices, and behaviors) seemed to influence Dr. Jones's encounters with the White female chairperson who accused him of bullying, even though she initiated the confrontation (Smith, Yosso, and Solorzano 2007).

Dr. Jones and Dr. Humphreys also shared feelings of powerlessness when they learned that student grades were changed without their approval. However, inconsistent with the *modern mammy* and *angry Black man* stereotypes, both took a stance and challenged these actions. In the case of Dr. Humphreys, the student's grade was changed to its original incarnation, and the student was required to stay longer at the institution. Dr. Jones pursued a grievance that resulted in more specific university policy for all university faculty. Sue et al. (2008) would refer to these instances as indications of microvalidation—the most abhorrent category of microaggression.

Dr. Humphreys no longer takes phone calls from students and only responds to e-mails with copies to the dean and associate dean for adequate documentation. Hendrix (1998) found that students use more stringent criteria to judge the credibility of Black faculty, which can lead to subtle and direct challenges to their course standards and expectations. However, Dr. Humphreys has an unspoken line about how much *challenging* can occur before it becomes abusive. As a result, she has made a decision to have disruptive and belligerent students removed by university security when she initially feels threatened or disrespected.

According to McGowan (2000), three patterns can account for Black female faculty classroom interactions with White students: evaluations of teaching effectiveness, challenges to authority, and student lack of respect. These findings are also supported by Harlow's (2003) research, which shows that students tend to question both the authority and competency of African American female faculty and students' stereotypes of African American female faculty (e.g., Bavishi, Hebl, and Madera 2010).

Dr. Jones has aligned with another African American female colleague on his campus, and Dr. Humphreys has found support with another African American male colleague in her college who shares similar worldviews and values about teaching, research, and service. Although the contextual and structural issues have not changed for either professor, their micro-experiences are less psychoemotionally harmful because they have defined personal and career boundaries. They no longer look to White faculty for support, praise, or self-definition, but seek career guidance and support for African-heritage societies and organizations.

They also make time to focus on their personal lives and to carve out interests beyond the institutional environment. They are aware of the dynamics of racism and sexism and are better able to make decisions to protect themselves in the world of White academia, where nothing is really as it seems.

IMPLICATIONS AND SUGGESTIONS FOR GRADUATE
STUDENTS WITH PROFESSORATE ASPIRATIONS

Pertinent to preparation for the world of the academy is recognition of the importance of research, service, and teaching as the primary evaluative criteria for most university campuses; although the weighting of each will vary according to the type of institution. It is important to *cultivate an interest in inquiry and to demonstrate this interest by conducting empirical research studies and presenting research* at relevant conferences and organizations affiliated with your discipline (e.g., anthropology and kinesiology).

Aligning with instructors early on in your academic training who can mentor your publishing objectives is central. *Immersion in both qualitative and quantitative research methods and statistical programming* will provide a strong foundation for this research requirement. During graduate school, *establish working alliances and interdisciplinary research interests with other African American students and students of color.* You should also begin to conduct a self-assessment to discover exactly what is required for your growth and development.

Accept a position in a cultural environment that offers opportunities to establish social support and meet your needs. The climate surrounding the institution is just as important as the university campus. High levels of racism, prejudice, and small minority populations can influence personal or life satisfaction, which easily generalizes to work satisfaction. It is best not to expect colleagues (sometimes of the same race/ethnicity) to assist you with the development of such relations. In some instances, others may actually resent your efforts to attract research funding or to publish more or in more highly rated journals.

Do not anticipate that people of color or African Americans will necessarily offer support, but be receptive if they do, and remember to honor the norms and standards of the culture in which you were socialized in interactions with members of your racial/ethnic group (e.g., respect of elders). Unfortunately, internalized racism impacts people of color just as racism influences the attitudes of Whites, so do not become alarmed if you encounter such attitudes. Make certain to *serve in departmental, university, and regional and national service capacitie*s to show adequate service and to join professional organizations specific to your discipline. *Give your best for each class*, and remember that even your absolute best may receive complaints and low student ratings. In these instances, document your efforts, develop thorough course syllabi, and improve what you can, and then accept what cannot or should not be changed.

Finally, if circumstances become unmanageable or simply uncomfortable you will have to *decide whether to stay or leave.* However, the longer you remain in a department at a particular institution, the more difficult it becomes to start over again. You should continue to conduct this self-assessment throughout the first years to gauge your satisfaction with the position relative to your lifestyle and expectations. Sleeping too long can lead to growth or to stagnation. Inevitably, it will be your choice.

The cautionary tales that we have just offered about the experiences of people of color in White academic settings can be repeated by hundreds of scholars. Lena Wright Myers (2002) reported that women of color are often singled out for a bitter type of racist behavior that others do not experience, but suggested it mirrored a level of racism experienced by all scholars of color.

Similarly, Thomas and Hollenshead (2001) indicated that African American and other faculty of color at research universities experience a lack of respect and recognition, feel pressured to change their research agenda (especially when focusing on issues of race and/or gender) and found non-supportive colleagues and a lack of collegiality. The situations are different as well as the individuals, but the message is the same: *White schools remain the preserves of White privilege.*

FINAL THOUGHTS

In the final chapter of *Alice in Wonderland*, titled "Alice's Evidence," when her sister brushes the leaves from her face, Alice wakes to realize that her memories are merely remnants of a confusing dream. Interestingly, her awareness started when she took a risk during a debate with a character in the dream (i.e., the Queen) and actually *named* characters in the Queen's court for what they really were (i.e., a deck of cards) which further enhanced her consciousness. At that point, Alice recognized that Wonderland was unreal and simply an illusion, which accounted for her inability to make sense of the diverse characters and situations that she had encountered earlier.

There were no absolute truths, and outcomes depended upon a complex and unpredictable set of influences (e.g., who made the rules). Like Alice, Dr. Humphreys and Dr. Jones have been aroused from a dream state because they have finally acknowledged the absurdity of their environments. Ironically, sleeping for a lengthy period has liberated them to assist others who decide to follow the rabbit down this same hole.

REFERENCES

Astin, Helen S., Anthony L. Antonio, Christine M. Cress, and Alexander W. Astin. 1997. *Race and Ethnicity in the American Professorate, 1995–1996.* Los Angeles: University of California, Higher Education Research Institute.

Bavishi, Anish, Michelle R. Hebl, and Juan M. Madera. 2010. "The Effect of Professor Ethnicity and Gender on Student Evaluations: Judged before Met." *Journal of Diversity in Higher Education* 3(4):245–56.

Bell, Derrick. 1992. *Faces at the Bottom of the Well: The Permanence of Racism.* New York: Basic Books.

Carrol, Lewis, John Tenniel, and Peter Hung. 2009. *Alice's Adventures in Wonderland: With Through the Looking-Glass* (Oxford World's Classics). Oxford: Oxford University Press.

Delgado, Richard, ed. 1995. *Critical Race Theory: The Cutting Edge.* Philadelphia: Temple University Press.

Fenelon, James. 2003. "Race, Research and Tenure: Institutional Credibility and the Incorporation of African, Latino, and American Indian Faculty." *Journal of Black Studies* 34(1):87–100.

Fries, Christopher J., and James R. McNinch. 2003. "Signed Versus Unsigned Student Evaluations of Teaching: A Comparison." *Teaching Sociology* 31:333–44.

Griffin, Kimberly, Meghan A. Pifer, Jordan R. Humphrey, and Ashley M. Hazelwood. 2011. "(Re)Defining Departure: Exploring Black Professors' Experiences with and Responses to Racism and Racial Climate." *American Journal of Education* 117:495–526.

Hammermesh, Daniel S., and Amy Parker. 2005. "Beauty in the Classroom: Instructors' Pulchritude and Putative Pedagogical Productivity." *Economics of Education Review* 24(4):369–76.

Harlow, Roxanna. 2003. "'Race Doesn't Matter But . . .': The Effect of Race on Professor Experiences and Emotion Management in the Undergraduate College Classroom." *Social Psychology Quarterly* 66:348–63.

Harris, Shanette M., and Michael T. Nettles. 1996. "Ensuring Campus Climates that Embrace Diversity." Pp. 330–371 in *Educating a New Majority: Transforming America's Educational System for Diversity*, edited by L. I. Rendon and R. O. Hope. San Francisco: Jossey-Bass.

Henderson, Tammy L., Andrea G. Hunter, and Gladys J. Hildreth. 2010. "Outsiders within the Academy: Strategies for Resistance and Mentoring African American Women." *Michigan Family Review* 14(1):28–41.

Hendrix, Katherine Grace. 1998. "Student Perceptions of the Influence of Race on Professor Credibility." *Journal of Black Studies* 28(6):738–63.

Johnsrud, Linda K., and Kathleen C. Sadao. 1998. "The Common Experience of 'Otherness': Ethnic and Racial Minority Faculty." *Review of Higher Education* 21(4):315–42.

Ladson-Billings, G. 1998. "Just What Is Critical Race Theory and What Is It Doing in a Nice Field Like Education?" *Qualitative Studies in Education* 11(1):7–24.

Leik, Robert K., and Alexandra R. Goulding. 2000. "Threats to Academic Identity and Commitment for Faculty and Color." *Advances in Life Course Research* 5:143–57.

McGowan, Juanita M. 2000. "Multicultural Teaching: African American Faculty Classroom Teaching Experiences in Predominantly White Colleges and Universities." *Multicultural Education* 8(2):19–22.

McKay, N. Y. 1997. "A Troubled Peace: Black Women in the Halls of the White Academy." Pp. 11–22 in *Black Women in the Academy: Promises and Perils,* edited by Lois Benjamin. Miami: University Press of Florida.

Menges, Robert J., and William H. Exum. 1983. "Barriers to the Progress of Women and Minority Faculty." *Journal of Higher Education* 54(2):123–44.

National Center for Educational Statistics. 2008. *Digest of Educational Statistics 2007.* Washington, DC: U.S. Department of Education.

Pierce, C. 1970. "Offensive Mechanisms." Pp. 265–82 in *The Black Seventies,* edited by F. Barbour. Boston: Porter Sargent.

Pittman, Chavella T. 2010. "Race and Gender Oppression in the Classroom: The Experiences of Women Faculty of Color with White Male Students." *Teaching Sociology* 38(3):183–96.

Rose, Harold M. 1966. "An Appraisal of the Negro Educator's Situation in the Academic Marketplace." *Journal of Negro Education* 35(1):18–26.

Ryu, Mikyung. 2008. *Minorities in Higher Education 2008: Twenty-Third Status Report.* Washington, DC: American Council on Education.

Seo, Byung-In, and Dawn Hinton. 2009. "How They See Us, How We See Them: Two Women of Color in Higher Education." *Race, Gender & Class* 16:203–17.

Stake, Robert E. 1995. *The Art of Case Study Research.* Thousand Oaks, California: Sage Publications.

Stanley, Christine A. 2006. "Coloring the Academic Landscape: Faculty of Color Breaking the Silence in Predominantly White Colleges and Universities." *American Educational Research Journal* 43:701–36.

Sue, Derald Wing, Christina M. Capodlupo, Kevin L. Nadal, and Gina C. Torino. 2008. "Racial Microaggressions and the Power to Define Reality." *American Psychologist*: 277–79.

Sue, Derald Wing, Christina M. Capodilupo, Gina C. Torino, Jennifer M. Bucceri, Aisha M. B. Holder, Kevin L. Nadal, and Esquilin, M. 2007. "Racial Microaggressions in Everyday Life." *American Psychologist* 62(4):271–86.

Sue, Derald Wing, and Madonna G. Constantine. 2007. "Racial Microaggressions as Instigators of Difficult Dialogues on Race: Implications for Student Affairs Educators and Students." *The College Student Affairs Journal* 26(2):136–43.

Sue, Derald Wing, David P. Rivera, Nicole L. Watkins, Rachel H. Kim, Kim Suah, and Chantea D. 2011. "Racial Dialogues: Challenges Faculty of Color Face in the Classroom." *Cultural Diversity and Ethnic Minority Psychology* 17(3):331–40.

Tate, William F. 1997. "Critical Race Theory and Education: History, Theory and Implications." *Review of Research in Education* 22:197–247.

Turner, Caroline, Sotello Viernes, Juan Carlos González, and J. Luke Wood. 2008. "Faculty of Color in Academe: What 20 Years of Literature Tells Us." *Journal of Diversity in Higher Education* 1(3):139–68.

Wingfield, Adlar Harvey. 2007. "The Modern Mammy and the Angry Black Man: African American Professionals' Experiences with Gendered Racism in the Workplace." *Race, Gender & Class* 14(1/2):196–212.

Wright Myers, Lena. 2002. "A Broken Silence: Voices of African American Women in the Academy." Westpost, CT: Bergin & Garvey.

Yin, Robert K. 1994. *Case Study Research: Design and Methods.* Thousand Oaks, CA: Sage.

IV

Survival Techniques in Academia

Chapter Ten

We Are All Huskies

Constructing a Collective Memory After the Tragedy at Northern Illinois University

Bobbi A. Knapp

Valentine's Day, February 14, 2008, is a day that will forever be marked in the history of Northern Illinois University (NIU). It was on this otherwise ordinary day that former NIU student Steven Kazmierczak entered into Cole Hall, a large lecture hall, and proceeded to shoot 54 rounds of bullets into the auditorium. In a shooting frenzy that lasted just over two minutes, Kazmierczak killed five students and wounded 18 others before turning the gun on himself. Unfortunately, tragic scenes such as this are becoming more commonplace and have affected thousands of people at various educational institutions throughout the United States.

Coming to terms with what happened on campus was a process of synthesizing information from the media, official word from the university, and stories from people who were on campus that day or knew people who had witnessed what happened. It is safe to say that many people were in a state of shock. The preverbal "I can't believe it happened here" and "It is just so surreal" were common statements. This violent act was outside our understanding of what living, working, and learning on a college campus entailed.

Of all days for such a tragedy to occur, perhaps, Valentine's Day is one of the most meaningful. Normative understanding of Valentine's Day ignores its bloody past. The Catholic Church acknowledges a few saints named Valentine, all of whom were martyred. One legend has it that Valentine performed marriages that were outlawed by Roman emperor Claudius. When the emperor found out about the marriages Claudius ordered Valentine to be put to death. The origins of Valentine's Day speak to our collective and, thus, selective memory as a society in that we have *forgotten* about the death of a saint in our desire to celebrate a day of love.

This chapter explores how the Northern Illinois University community began its own process of constructing a collective memory after the shooting on Valentine's Day 2008. For many members of the NIU community, it became apparent that the university community was in the process of strategically developing a collective memory of the university after this horrific event. This chapter also examines the discourses used to form a collective memory of Northern Illinois University as it moved forward after this tragedy.

UNFURLING THE CONCEPT OF COLLECTIVE MEMORY

Memory is an important locus of study for scholars across various disciplines such as history, cultural studies, and sociology (Winter 2006). Some scholars suggest that the prominence of memory in research is unique to modernity—a time in which academics are encouraged to see memory as a social construct rather than just relinquish it to the categories of private and personal (Bartelson 2006). Commonly, *memory* is thought of as how we remember things from the past. But the concept dealt with in this chapter is that of collective memory, "widely shared perceptions of the past" (Bell 2006, 2).

These communal memories work to create and maintain social cohesion, which in turn generates social identity. Bell (2006) notes that "memory plays a major role in determining the dynamics of individual and collective identity formation, which in turn shapes both perceptions and political action" (29). This sense of belonging often creates allegiance to what Anderson has referred to as an *imagined community* (Anderson 1991). Yet one should not think of collective memory as being uncontested. It is indeed within these moments of conflict and points of omission that underlying power dynamics are momentarily exposed and reproduced.

At such a point, it is important to delineate the concepts of memory and history. Unlike history, which attempts to reflect the past, collective memory is concerned with how the past is remembered (Assmann 1997). Not to suggest that memory is not vital to the construction of history, but instead history acts as a reminder that memory is selective. "The ethics of memory includes within it an ethics of forgetting. Memory is not always beneficial; it can be counter-productive. It can obstruct the potential from moving forward, for envisioning alternative futures" (Bell 2006: 24). Such omissions can provide much insight into often deeply entrenched lines of power.

Times of trauma can be especially upsetting to the maintenance of collective identities. It is said that trauma occurs "when there is a break, a displacement or disorganization in the orderly, taken-for-granted universe" (Sztompka 2000, 457). NIU student Dan Sweeney was quoted as saying, "It was just surreal. Even when the first shot was fired I couldn't believe it was happening. It didn't seem to register with anyone" (Noel, Kimberly, and Mitchum 2008, 1).

This break from the norm is also noted in the memorial issue of *Northern Now*, a magazine marketed to alumni, which states, "On February 14 students in geology class, taking notes and thinking about their plans for Thursday night, came face-to-face with madness. Eighteen were wounded and five did not survive" (Malone 2008, 1). Bell (2006, 6) notes that "as identities are challenged, undermined and possibly shattered, so memories are drawn on and reshaped to defend unity and coherence, to shore up a sense of self and community." Such identity work through the development of collective memory is, thus, common in mass tragedies.

Broadcasting tragedies across the nation creates a *prosthetic memory*, which results in far extending social solidarity (Landsberg 2004). At the memorial service, President Peters stated, "The enormous outpouring of love we have experienced this past week reminds us that this community . . . this state . . . this nation . . . and this world are connected to each other in fundamental and unchanging ways" (Peters 2008c, 8). The role of the media was also acknowledged by a writer of the student newspaper who noted that "much of how people remember NIU will depend on what they read, see or hear in the media" (Bruce 2008, 5).

President Peters made it clear that he did not want this tragedy to define the university. Peters ends a letter he sent out to students, faculty, and staff with, "The eyes of the world are focused on Northern Illinois University. Let us continue to show the world that a single act of violence does not define us and will not keep us from being the individuals or the university community that I know we can be" (J. G. Peters, personal communication, February 16, 2008). This is particularly important, as Bell (2006) notes, because traumas often play an important role in future perceptions and actions.

Peters attempts to direct future perceptions in a favorable course with the following quote, which adorns the back cover of the special memorial issue of *Northern Now*, "We will not allow ourselves to be defined by this tragedy. Forever changed, yes—but not shackled to fear. May we use this moment to draw closer together—to lift up all who struggle and to re-enter the light of a new day. And always forward, together forward" (Peters 2008c, 8). The phrase "forward, together forward" comes from the university's fight song.

METHODOLOGY

In an attempt to highlight the ways in which a collective memory was constructed around this event, this chapter examines sources closely linked to the university and surrounding community. In the months following the shooting, information was collected from personal communications sent from President John Peters to faculty, staff, and students, the university's website, the alumni magazine, the student newspaper the *Northern Star*, DeKalb's *Daily Chronicle,* and the *Chicago Tribune.*

A textual analysis was used in the gathering of data from the various sources. Of particular interest was the discourse of family and community, as they seemed to inundate the communications sent out by the university administration. Data were compiled, data that seemed to support this newfound sense of family and community as well as data that highlight some of the internal conflicts. This chapter shows the process that one university went through to form a collective memory of itself and *its people* after a mass killing on campus. It is a narrative that hopefully no reader has to personally experience.

CONSTRUCTING A COLLECTIVE MEMORY AT NORTHERN ILLINOIS UNIVERSITY

Community was central to the collective-memory work at NIU. In a letter in the student newspaper the first day back to classes Peters (2008a, 1) wrote, "We have all experienced something profound, something extraordinary, something heartbreaking, and we have experienced it together. We all are hurting. We all are longing for normalcy. We all will take care of each other." The memorial service was described as having an overwhelming theme of unity running through it (Thomas 2008a). Bell (2006) notes that such focus on community and unity often occurs after experiences of trauma.

Within this construction of community, one can see the symbiotic relationship of remembering and forgetting (Bell 2006). Zehfuss (2006, 228) notes that "forgetting is not simply the opposite of remembering. Remembering is structurally dependent on forgetting, is always already marked by forgetting." The act of forgetting in the memory process is a part of creating a selective memory (Young 1993; Nathan 2003; Meskell 2006). As NIU began the process of building a collective memory of the university after the tragedy, parts of its history were incorporated into its new identity while others were, for the most part, omitted.

The following historical reference appears in the memorial issue of *Northern Now*:

> In 1895 . . . Governor John Peter Altgeld set out the core values of the school
> that was to become Northern Illinois University. "Above all things," he said,
> "we want this institution to stand on the basic principle that all people are born
> equal, and that only industry, intelligence, and effort shall lead to preferment."
> (Malone 2008, 1)

This historic description of NIU as a place where all people are equal is a key layer in the formation of a collective memory that views the NIU community as one united family, but what was left out of the discussion of community is the racially charged threat that was found scrawled on a bathroom wall in December 2007 (just two months before the shooting). The threat, found in a women's bathroom on campus, referenced the Virginia Tech shootings and included a racial slur to "tell those n*****s to go home" (WBBM 2007, 7). The campus was shut down the first day of finals in response.

Following the threat, a number of editorials in the school newspaper touched upon the racial tension on campus. The administration put together a campus-climate survey giving students, faculty, and staff an opportunity to express their feelings about student life at NIU (Stone 2008). Immediately after the shooting, people questioned if there was any connection to the earlier threat. As soon as Peters dismissed any connections, the talk of the December threat and the racial aspects of it were no longer publicly discussed.

The idea of community, who belongs and who doesn't, was a point of contestation. After the tragedy, there were two points of conflict in the development of a community identity. The first involves the shooter. Numerous memorials were erected on campus after the shooting. The three most controversial memorials included a row of crosses by King Memorial Commons, wood cutouts of huskies outside of Cole Hall, and crosses outside the Lutheran Campus Ministries. What made these memorials controversial was that they memorialized not only the five NIU students killed but also Kazmierczak, who killed himself at the end of his rampage.

The small crosses were placed on the mound on February 15 by Greg Zanis. Within a day of being driven into the ground, one of the crosses was removed and placed at another site, while the names of the five victims were written on the remaining crosses. Young (1993, 6) suggests that "by creating common spaces for memory, monuments propagate the illusion of common memory"; notably, this space becoming one of the main places people left flowers and other symbols of their grief. Many students probably did not realize that there had once been six crosses here as the sixth cross was removed before students came back for classes.

Husky cutouts were placed outside of Cole Hall on February 21. Bianca McGraw, a graduate student at NIU, created the installation. McGraw said, "I chose to do Huskies because of their communal connection with the university and the DeKalb community" (Tschirhart 2008b, 5). McGraw noted the Huskie figures were a response to the symbolism of the crosses as Christian icons, a religion not all community members share. When asked about why she decided to include six cutouts, she said, "He [Kazmierczak] was just as much a Huskie as the rest of us. Many of us choose the wrong path and I think he can be seen as a stray" (Tschirhart 2008a, 5).

In an editorial, one student writes, "Six crosses and six Huskies is not right. We lost five Huskies that day, not six" (Cannon 2008, 6). A makeshift sign placed near the Huskies, in large black and red letters, reads, "Together We Will Prevail." In smaller letters on the bottom left portion of the poster board it reads, "Once a Huskie always a Huskie!!" It is unknown if the creator meant this as a comment about Kazmierczak and his time enrolled at NIU or perhaps as a reference to his or her own status as an alumni.

Most controversy was reserved for the large crosses that adorned the lawn of the Lutheran Campus Ministries building. Pastor Diane Dardon states that the decision to place six crosses outside the ministry was influenced by the 33 crosses that Virginia Tech had put up after the tragedy on that campus not a year before (Thomas 2008b). She states, "Six are dead. Six families are grieving. Six children of God are gone" (Thomas 2008b, 1).

The editorials about the six crosses extended well over a month after the shooting, with the final editorial on the topic being published in the March 26 issue of the *Northern Star*. The arguments took both sides, but the majority of those who wrote in lined up with the belief that there should not be six crosses. Those supporting the display of six crosses noted that the crosses are symbols of lives lost and they were not intended to honor anyone (Altergott 2008)—an acknowledgment of those that love Stephen and the difficulties they are going through (Jensen 2008) and symbolic of Kazmierczak's role as a victim (Aguirre 2008).

The arguments against having six crosses included the idea that people need to heal before they are able to forgive (Cannon 2008); it is a way of publicly honoring a murderer (Kammes 2008); and "placing a cross, representing a killer, with five other crosses, representing those killed, diminishes the respect those who died have earned" (LaLonde 2008, 6). Sometime between the night of March 16 and the morning of March 17, 2008, one of the crosses in front of the ministry was removed and burned on the main thoroughfare of campus (Feldheim 2008). A new cross was put up to replace the one that was taken.

The heralded concept of community started to unravel around the decision of what to do with Cole Hall, the building in which the shooting took place. On February 27, two days after classes resumed, Governor Blagojevich and NIU president Peters announced a plan to demolish Cole Hall and spend $40 million to erect a new building on campus that would act as a memorial facility.

The *Chicago Tribune* dedicated a full page to the decision. Letter writers attempted to establish their place in the community and, thus, their right to have their voices heard on this decision. One person writes, "Speaking as a parent of a student who was in the classroom during the shooting, I am all for tearing that building down" (Linda 2008, 13). Others started with "as a former student" (Buban 2008, 13), "I am a December 2007 graduate" (Zentefis 2008, 13), and "I am a student at Northern Illinois University" (Kinnally 2008, 13).

Due to the financial costs involved, the dialogue about Cole Hall extended beyond the NIU campus. One writer notes, "You don't squander $40 million to erase a memory that can't be erased" (Chapman 2008, 13). The right of people outside of the university campus to have a say in what is done to Cole Hall was normalized through commentary found in the *Chicago Tribune* that states, "Hundreds of readers responded to that editorial [asking if Cole Hall should be torn down] and the overwhelming majority said the building should be saved" (*Chicago Tribune* 2008, 12).

The demand for voices to be heard emerged on campus as well. This seemingly unilateral decision to raze Cole Hall "made many on campus flinch. Disbelief at being left out of the process was palpable" (Meagher 2008, 6). Iiona Meagher writes, "While best intentions may be at heart, neglecting to tap into the feelings of those most affected—NIU's faculty and student body—is problematic. Their opinions must be better addressed if we are to continue moving Forward, Together Forward" (2008, 6). The theme of community that had been strung together by the administration was looking as if it might unravel.

On the afternoon of March 4, 2008, President Peters sent out an e-mail to all students and colleagues regarding the future of Cole Hall:

> Our family has been injured, and we turn inward to comfort each other and gather strength for the journey ahead. The tremendous response from across our campus and the overwhelming appreciation we have gained for each other is testament to the strong sense of community that defines NIU. (Peters 2008b, 1)

He notes that "we have family business to attend to" (Peters, 2008b: 1). Peters (2008b, 2) concludes, "We must engage in a campus-wide discussion about the future of Cole Hall. Our answer should represent a consensus opinion formulated by all members of our campus community." This contrasts with his earlier statement in the *Chicago Tribune*, which said that he "made the decision that we had to raze that, we had to demolish that building and replace it with something fitting, something fitting our needs and as a memorial" (Chapman 2008, 13).

In his letter to NIU students and faculty, Peters (2008b) notes that he came to that decision not on his own but after talking with students, parents, faculty, and alumni. This comment along with his statement that "ultimately, our decisions on an appropriate memorial, reassignment of classroom spaces and the future of Cole Hall must address both the emotional and practical considerations we face as an injured but united campus community" (Peters

2008b, 2), work to reestablish the importance of community at the university after the tragedy.

FINAL THOUGHTS

A March 31, 2008, article noted that NIU is still pondering its potential place in history (Bruce 2008). The executive director of the local historical society said, "How NIU moves forward will be part of how history remembers NIU" (Bruce 2008, 5). President Peters seemed to be very aware of this fact. Before the moment of silence that took place in the King Commons one week after the shooting, Peters closed his speech with, "So I call on each of you to *remember* [italics mine] and love" (Gross 2008, 5). What *exactly* we were to remember is unclear.

Zehfuss (2006, 228) argues that "forgetting is obscured by an understanding of memory that renders it as telling the truth about the past. Such an understanding plays on the power of the 'we remember.'" A student who attended the moment of silence seemed to have remembered it *correctly* when she says, "We're a family. We are one Huskie family, period" (Irizarry 2008, 5). All of which is a reminder of how the collective memory of Northern Illinois University, as it comes out of this tragedy, is constructed.

We hope to never again experience such a tragedy. Yet such senseless violence does happen and, with that understanding, we need to be prepared. All faculty members should be familiar with their university's procedures for gunmen on campus. The presented case study gives insight into the issues one university faced coming out of such a tragedy. Although it most likely does not represent what every educational institution that has experienced shootings on campus went through, it does provide the reader with a starting point for understanding if you find yourself in a similar situation.

REFERENCES

Aguirre, Christine M. 2008. "Cole Hall Shooter Was a Victim Too." [Letter to the editor]. *Northern Star* 6, February 29.

Altergott, Christina. 2008. "Six Crosses Symbolize All Lives Lost Feb. 14." [Letter to the editor]. *Northern Star*, 6, February 29.

Anderson, Benedict. 1991. *Imagined Communities: Reflections on the Origin and Spread of Nationalism*. New York: Verso.

Assmann, Jan. 1997. *Moses the Egyptian: The Memory of Egypt in Western Monotheism*. Cambridge, MA: Harvard University Press.

Bartelson, Jens. 2006. "We Could Remember It for You Wholesale: Myths, Monuments and the Constitution of National Memories." In *Memory, Trauma and World Politics*, edited by Duncan Bell, 33–53. London: Palgrave Macmillan.

Bell, Duncan. 2006. "Introduction: Memory, Trauma and World Politics." In *Memory, Trauma and World Politics*, edited by Duncan Bell, 1–29. London: Palgrave Macmillan.

Bruce, Giles. 2008. "Pondering NIU's Potential Place in History." *Northern Star*, 5, March 31.

Buban, Mike. 2008. "Flashback." [Commentary]. *Chicago Tribune*, Section 1:13, February 29.

Cannon, Ashley. 2008. "Five Crosses Should Be Displayed, Not Six." [Letter to the editor]. *Northern Star*, 6, February 29.

Chapman, Steve. 2008. "Don't Capitulate to Tragedy." [Commentary]. *Chicago Tribune*, 13, March 2.

Chicago Tribune. 2008. "Time Heals . . . Not Bulldozers." *Chicago Tribune*, 12, February 29.

Feldheim, Benji. 2008. "NIU Memorial Cross Burned Outside Church." *Daily Chronicle*, A3, March 20.

Gross, Ben. 2008. "One Week Later." *Northern Star*, 5, February 25.

"The History of Valentine's Day" (n.d.). Accessed October 14, 2009. http://www.history.com/content/valentine/history-of-valentine-s-day.

Huyssen, Andreas. 1995. *Twilight Memories: Making Time in a Culture of Amnesia*. New York: Routledge.

Irizarry, Herminia. 2008. "NIU Mourns with Silence." *Northern Star*, 5, February 25.

Jensen, Sean. 2008. "A Secular Perspective on Sixth Cross." [Letter to the editor]. *Northern Star*, 6, March 5.

Kammes, Jeremiah. 2008. "Cole Hall Shooter Does Not Deserve a Cross." [Letter to the editor]. *Northern Star*, 6, March 3.

Kinnally, Calan Patrick. 2008. "Student's View." [Commentary]. *Chicago Tribune*, Section 1:13, February 29.

LaLonde, Paul. 2008. "Kazmierczak Should Not Have a Cross." [Letter to the editor]. *Northern Star*, 6, March 19.

Landsberg, Alison. 2004. *Prosthetic Memory: The Transformation of American Remembrance in an Age of Mass Culture*. New York: Columbia University Press.

Linda. 2008. "A Parent's Desire." [Commentary]. *Chicago Tribune*, Section 1:13, February 29.

Malone, Michael P. 2008. "Memorial Issue." *Northern Now* [memorial issue]:1, Spring.

Meagher, Ilona. 2008. "Students, Faculty Should Have Say on Cole. *Northern Star*, 6, March 4.

Meskell, Lynn. 2006. "Trauma Culture: Remembering and Forgetting in the New South Africa." In *Memory, Trauma and World Politics*, edited by Duncan Bell, 157–75. London: Palgrave Macmillan.

Nathan, Daniel. 2003. *Saying It's So: A Cultural History of the Black Sox Scandal*. Urbana: University of Illinois Press.

Noel, Josh, James Kimberly, and Robert Mitchum. 2008. "I Was Prepared for That to Be My Last Moment." *Chicago Tribune*, Section 1:1 and 9, February 15.

Peters, John G. 2008a. A Letter from President Peters: Resolve to Move Forward. *Northern Star*. February 25. http://northernstar.info/campus/a-letter-from-president-peters-resolve-to-move-forward/article_9daa71db-23bc-5bab-b69e-90209faa3739.html.

Peters, John G. 2008b. Forward Together Forward. Northern Illinois University, March 4.http://www.niu.edu/peters/messages/colehall_update.shtml.

Peters, John G. 2008c, Spring. "Presidential Speech at the Memorial Service." *Northern Now* [memorial issue]:8, Winter.

Stone, Dan. 2008. "University Council Addresses Campus Climate Surveys as Method in Strategic Planning." *Northern Star*, January 31. http://www.northernstar.info/articl/print/1978/.

Sztompka, Piotr. 2000. "Cultural Trauma." *European Journal of Social Theory* 3, 449–67.

Thomas, David. 2008a. "NIU Family Grieves Together at Memorial Service." *Northern Star*, 3, February 25.

Thomas, David. 2008b. "NIU, Lutheran Campus Ministry Discuss Future of Memorial Displays." *Northern Star*, 1, March 6.

Tschirhart, James. 2008a. "Regional History Center to Preserve Makeshift Memorials." *Northern Star*, 1, March 6.

Tschirhart, James. 2008b. "Artist: Huskie Cutouts 'Communal Memorials.'" *Northern Star*, 5, March 25.

WBBM. 2007. "Students Glad NIU Officials Took Threat Seriously." December 10. http://www.wbbm780.com/pages/1310930.php.

Winter, Jay. 2006. "Notes on the Memory Boom: War, Remembrance and the Uses of the Past." In *Memory, Trauma and World Politics*, edited by Duncan Bell, 54–73. London: Palgrave Macmillan.

Young, James E. 1993. *The Texture of Memory: Holocaust Memorials and Meaning*. New Haven, CT: Yale University Press.

Zehfuss, Maja. 2006. "Remembering to Forget/Forgetting to Remember." In *Memory, Trauma and World Politics*, edited by Duncan Bell, 213–30. London: Palgrave Macmillan.

Zentefis, Angela. 2008. "2007 Grad Speaks." [Commentary]. *Chicago Tribune*, Section 1:13, February 29.

Chapter Eleven

Horror Stories from the Hallowed Halls of Academia

How Six Women Lived to Tell the Tale

Claire H. Procopio, Helen Tate, Kristina Horn Sheeler, Krista Hoffmann-Longtin, Sarah Feldner, and Karrin Vasby Anderson

This chapter could easily be titled "The Girlfriends' Guide to Surviving Academic Horror Stories." The *Girlfriends' Guide* to anything is something of an inside joke with the women whose experiences are highlighted herein. They first met in graduate school and have been turning to each other ever since to help process and respond to the many strange encounters life in the academic world produces.

Soon after leaving graduate school, the subjects of this chapter realized how valuable they found one another's perspectives in tough times and began to share what they learned about the rules of the academic game with others at conferences and in publications. This chapter is offered in the hopes that their collective challenges and strategies to overcome those obstacles may help you face down whatever horror is lurking in your campus corridors.

Taking advice from strangers is probably a bad idea in the horror genre, so background information on the women is offered. The subjects have worked at institutions across the United States from community colleges to research-one universities and served in roles from staff to faculty to associate vice presidents. They have different professional goals and diverse family situations. They are the same, however, in a shared commitment to participating in a network that supports one another.

Many studies have pointed out the value of personal networks to student success in the academy (Eby et al. 2008; Eggens, Werf, and Bosker 2008; Power et al. 2011) and especially to the importance of social support for minority student success (Bhopal 2010; Baker 2013).

Few studies, however, have considered the importance of these kinds of networks to faculty, staff, and administrator success. Instead, research into employee turnover in higher education has focused on variables like gender (Clark and Corcoran 1986; Rausch et al. 1989), wage equity (Hagedorn 1996; Johnsrud, Heck, and Rosser 2000), job stress (Barnes, Agago, and Coombs 1998), faculty productivity (McGee and Ford 1987), disciplinary affiliation (Xu 2008), and collegial relations (Manger and Eikeland 1990).

Lack of research into how support networks might improve employees' circumstances in the academy is unfortunate because harassment in higher education is all too common. Defining workplace harassment as "psychological terror in working life that involves hostile and unethical communication," Rosa Velez (2013, 16) points to global survey data that indicate up to 36% of faculty members and 68% of all employees in higher education have experienced workplace harassment. Jo (2008, 572–73) found poor treatment from an immediate manager was the number-one reason women reported voluntarily leaving midlevel academic administrator posts.

Moreover, lack of strategies for dealing with academic horror stories is expensive. Jo (2008) reports that turnover in the professoriate ranks costs universities millions of dollars annually.

Arguably, the non-monetary costs of faculty turnover are worse. Nagowski (2006, 69) states, "Associated costs of faculty turnover include disruptions and the loss of continuity in teaching and research programs, in graduate and undergraduate advising, and in departmental and institutional governance and cohesiveness." Personal costs to the individuals involved in unhappy academic situations are another significant consideration.

Trouble in the academy is encountered at some point in everyone's career. Each of the accounts offered herein includes its own tale of horror and survival. Know that these horrific events are often more about the way academia functions than they are about your personal survival strategy. In what follows, you will hear separate accounts that describe not just horrors that have been encountered, but how being consciously embedded in a network of professionals facing the same challenges can help to ward off some scares.

Specifically, in this chapter, you are treated to two pieces of girlfriends' advice on surviving and thriving: 1) how to use your experiences in a support network to become more strategic in fighting Freddie, Jason, or Michael and 2) how to build a network to sustain you before your career is killed off like a character in *Scream*.

THE SECRET LIVES OF ADMINISTRATORS: YOU'RE NOT CRAZY, THEY REALLY ARE OUT TO GET YOU

Many who seek careers in higher education imagined some extension of their graduate school life—the life of the mind! The endless graduate seminar with interesting colleagues, thought-provoking conversation and edifying, transformative moments in the classroom.

Hopefully you are laughing now; if not, you may soon be crying. A career in higher education has its advantages, but anyone looking for "edutopia" is going to be sorely disappointed. Indeed, "the governance structure and the hierarchical organization [of higher education] may serve as an incubator for the establishment or maintenance of a bully culture" (Twale and De Luca 2008, 17–18).

The imposition of a corporate culture (Washburn 2005) coupled with reduced state funding (*Chronicle of Higher Education* 2014) compounds the risk for an uncivil culture where self-governing faculty compete for scarce resources (Twale and De Luca 2008) and, once tenured, are often guaranteed life-long employment. It is the perfect storm for workplace politics. Having a support network outside your campus can mean survival. For those in administrative roles or campus leadership positions, this is especially true.

Those in leadership roles are inevitably caught up in campus politics. As any department chair can tell you, as soon as you become chair, you find out information about your colleagues that you may wish you didn't know, and you also get a perspective of the institution you didn't have before. You are responsible for implementing administrative initiatives and expected to advance your department's interests to administration.

Being caught in the middle can be isolating. If you are going to be in any administrative role, you are going to need an external support network to process what you are experiencing. And while friends and family can often provide support, if they do not work in higher education, it can all seem a bit mystifying to them. In their worlds, these people would just be fired! The girlfriend support network of the subjects in this chapter provides that safe place not only to vent but to process, to regroup, and to gain confidence in their ability to handle the challenges of administrative life.

Cindy's path into higher education administration was augured early in her career. She defended her dissertation in the same semester that she became the interim department chair of a small department at a private liberal arts college. Cindy served as chair for eight years, and while her major department was doing well, her institution was suffering from decreased enrollment and deferred maintenance.

The economic downturn of 2008 was the institution's breaking point—the college restructured from 15 academic departments to five divisions. Cindy was asked to head one of the divisions, and soon thereafter, the division heads were given their first assignment—reduce the faculty and staff by 10%.

The deliberations were confidential and painful. Cindy wanted to tell her colleagues what was going on. She wanted to process her thinking with others, and she wanted to plead her case more broadly and seek support for ways that she could advocate for her new program areas. She couldn't do any of these on her own campus, making her external support network, aka the girlfriends, even more important to her sanity.

In the end, her division took half of the total faculty cuts. For Cindy, it was heartbreaking. She did have a few victories in the deliberations, but compared to the losses, they were small and, due to the confidentiality of the process, no one outside of the committee would ever know what she did to advocate for her programs. They would only see what was lost. Cindy's girlfriends provided a sounding board to process all that was happening and gave her support and encouragement through some incredibly painful times.

After implementing the cuts, Cindy began to heal wounds, regroup, and move forward. She was successful in earning the trust of new faculty colleagues, and they developed a sense of community as a new unit. She was less prepared for rebuilding trust and confidence in the provost and other division heads. Their relationships deteriorated over the next year until they completely unraveled during an external program review.

Cindy's program was scheduled for an external review and, as coincidence would have it, one of her girlfriends was on the national association's program review task force. Cindy brought her in to review the program, and she offered valuable feedback about their strengths, weaknesses, and areas of opportunity. In addition, she identified some political trouble areas that Cindy did not see coming. During the on-site visit, Cindy's girlfriend had some unusual conversations with members of the administration leadership and was able to warn her of pitfalls ahead.

In the months that followed, Cindy came to see what her girlfriend recognized much more clearly as the political tension and conflict increased. Having a girlfriend who knew the inside players at her institution, knew of her faculty's support, and had seen evidence of her accomplishments was incredibly affirming during a very difficult time for Cindy. She needed to be able to talk through these difficulties with someone who really knew the circumstances on her campus but who was not on her campus. Cindy was fortunate to have a savvy, insightful cheerleader in her girlfriend—someone who could remind her of her strengths and give her the courage to do what she needed to do.

Administrators often become isolated, and not being able to talk through issues can leave one feeling unsure. What the girlfriend network gave Cindy, as an administrator, was a sounding board for the issues she faced, affirmation of her abilities and confidence to handle the challenges.

Anyone seriously considering administrative work should cultivate an external network. It is not a question of whether you will need it, but when. While Cindy's network has been within her discipline, for an administrator, it's not a necessity. What is important in the small world of higher education is a trusted network external to one's campus. Finally, waiting to cultivate that network until you need it is too late. Begin to build it before you need it.

Even before the jump to administration, faculty members face the professional challenge of staying current in their fields and contributing to their disciplines. Newly minted faculty face pressure to publish or perish at a time when they are experiencing upheaval in other areas: starting a new job, moving to a new city, maybe starting a family, and leaving familiar surroundings to start in a new department. Below, two examples are offered to explain how this situation can be a horror and how it can be overcome.

WRITING ALONE CAN BE SCARY: DON'T DO IT WITHOUT YOUR GIRLFRIENDS

Doctoral-granting programs in the United States make up a small minority of possible institutions in which one may find employment after completing the PhD. Whereas the research focus of a PhD-granting institution may be intense, the majority of job seekers do not land that type of position; many are not even seeking it. However, research productivity is an expectation of most tenure-track positions. As a result, keeping your research moving forward with a heavy teaching load is a challenge many scholars face.

Further exacerbating the problem is the growing acknowledgment that graduate programs do very little "to prepare their students to teach" (Bok 2013). New assistant professors may neglect their research as they take on daily teaching and service responsibilities, as these duties have built-in accountability and research does not.

Kerry Ann Rockquemore (2014) writes about the "trap of over-functioning on teaching and service while under-functioning on research and writing." To avoid experiencing the last-minute horror of trying to complete research in the time that is left after teaching, service, family, and a little sleep, Mary and Janice developed their own survival network to manage the chaos.

Mary and Janice published their first essay on the importance of female support networks in the academy in the early 2000s (Anderson et al. 2004). They introduced themselves and the challenges they faced, being relatively new to academia. Their essay focused on how their network helped them find their identities within academia.

As they reflect now, at midcareer, they can see how their network helped them thrive in their choices; for Mary and Janice, that meant building a strong research agenda. They were able to survive and thrive as researchers by 1) coauthoring with each other, 2) broadening their network, and 3) utilizing their network(s) to build publication, conference, and speaking opportunities.

Strategic Coauthoring

As new assistant professors in departments with high teaching expectations and graduate programs, Mary and Janice recognized the importance of timely and consistent publication; something they could accomplish working together. They published their first book by combining data from their dissertations. Because their new institutions had the same research expectations for tenure and promotion, they had a shared vision in terms of the publishers to which they wanted to submit the manuscript and the deadline for the project's completion.

The book made a strong impact on their tenure and promotion cases. Since then, Mary and Janice have published two additional research articles and one university-press book. They have both published single-authored chapters and brought each other in on other projects as well, including invited lectures, grants, conference papers, and panels.

The book project grew out of necessity but has grown into an enjoyable collaboration that has spanned nearly 10 years and now includes connections that extend to graduate students and research colleagues across the country. Along the way, they have not only coauthored but also served as reader, editor, and reviewer for one another as well as research mentor for each other's graduate students.

Of course, coauthorship can quickly turn into its own horror story if care is not taken to develop relationships that make sense personally and professionally. Mary and Janice recommend considering the following issues before cultivating or committing to a research partnership:

- Professional rank: Coauthoring with a more experienced scholar can be a great way to jump-start your research program, but if you appear as *junior* author too often, your own research abilities may be questioned. If, however, you and your research partner are of similar rank, alternate author order regularly and also publish independently; the coauthored pieces will augment rather than detract from your scholarly reputation.
- Program of research: Coauthoring works best when it's not forced. When you share a research interest, methodological approach, and/or writing style, collaborative pieces can come together seamlessly. Coauthoring may also be a good strategy for scholars whose research approaches are different but complementary. Either way, the research should take prior-

ity. Working with friends can be fun, but its sustainable long term only when it produces a mutually beneficial program of research.

• Personal style: Although the product of a program of research is public, the process can be highly personal. Each scholar has her or his own strategies for choosing projects, staying on schedule, and responding to feedback. Sharing this process with a collaborator allows opportunities for mutual encouragement, but it also leaves each individual vulnerable as a writing partner edits one's carefully constructed prose, takes the project in an unexpected direction, and/or pushes (or fails to meet) agreed upon timelines.

If you have established a successful research partnership, the benefits may prompt you to use the skills you have cultivated to broaden your scholarly network.

Broadening the Network

Mary and Janice's initial network has broadened to include a writing accountability group at home and research groups developed at professional conferences. The initial goal of the local writing group was to provide a safe space where individuals from different departments could discuss research goals and challenges and offer support while moving forward on research. The group meets weekly over lunch or coffee.

During their meetings, each member shares her goals for the week, accomplishments from the previous week, challenges in meeting the previous week's goals, and ways to move forward. It has become a weekly accounting intimately focused on daily writing in the same ways that the authors may traditionally think about being accountable to their students or service contributions on a daily or weekly basis.

One of them has benefitted from a research group started while in graduate school, almost serendipitously, while attending a preconference seminar. Members of the preconference discovered so many productive connections in their research interests and areas of expertise that they collaborated on an edited book. A listserv was created to facilitate the book process, and it remains active ten years after the book's publication. Members still use it routinely to plan conference submissions, collaborate on articles and book chapters, distribute calls for research, and announce new publications.

CAPITALIZING ON THE NETWORK

In academia, productivity begets opportunity. If you are networked with other publishing scholars, you are more likely to be invited to contribute to special journal issues, serve on editorial boards, present at specialty conferences, and review books. Active professional networks can also facilitate speaking opportunities at other institutions, and members of these networks may assign one another's scholarship to their students.

This, of course, can be both a blessing and a curse. If your networks are closely related to your program of research, the opportunities that present themselves are likely to be valuable. If, however, a network you have joined pulls you away from your area of specialization or tempts you to place your research in a publication tier or type not valued by your institution, then those opportunities can become liabilities. Early in Mary's and Janice's careers, they had to work diligently to choose projects that fit their skills, schedule, and professional priorities.

At this point in their careers, one way that their network sustains them is by bringing others into their circle and creating opportunities for their success, thereby sustaining their own. Mary and Janice have mentored graduate students who became writing partners and conference collaborators. Colleagues at other institutions look closely when their students apply for positions at their schools. Their friends have listened to and shared their perspectives with younger scholars struggling with professional challenges that their advisors and colleagues may be ill equipped to help them navigate.

Additionally, some of their networking has moved to social media where academics of all rank mingle freely. For example, communication scholars on Twitter use the #TeamRhetoric hashtag, which allows Mary and Janice to share links, make announcements, and digitally gather to discuss events like the presidential debates, the state of the union address, and political conventions. Colleagues who are also friends can use Facebook to share articles, promote one another's publications, and maintain relationships despite the constant demands on their time.

Because academic publishing is often presented as a solitary activity, scholars sometimes overlook the ways in which networking can support publication. When it comes to scholarly productivity, however, trying to go it alone can be the ultimate horror story.

Support networks are important to overcoming the routine difficulties any academic will face, but they are perhaps even more important when you enter the land of the truly bizarre horror. The next tale looks at the importance of being firmly embedded in a network of supportive colleagues when the world turns upside down.

ESCAPING WHEN YOU FIND YOURSELF THROUGH THE LOOKING GLASS

"But I don't want to go among mad people," Alice remarked.
"Oh, you can't help that," said the Cat: "We're all mad here."—Lewis Carroll

Lori has worked in higher education long enough now to know the usual downsides associated with the job—shrinking budgets, a cantankerous colleague or two, and the occasional disgruntled student. But her first job held horrors way beyond the usual.

She had just finished her PhD and was expecting her first child when she and her husband secured jobs and moved back to their home state. Lori's timing happened to coincide with her state's launching of its first ever community college (CC) system. She took a job at one of the new CCs four months before it opened its doors for the first time. Built for 500 students, 1,800 showed up that first semester. It was exciting but, like the family moving to the tranquil little town in a horror film, Lori should have heard the dissonant music playing on the soundtrack.

Lori began to suspect things were strange when the chancellor spent their first faculty meeting talking about how to position the blinds in their offices; he wanted them to look uniform from outside. Did he not have any news more relevant to faculty? It quickly became clear to Lori that the new administration was in over its head. Their super-secret accreditation documents were never seen by faculty, and their accrediting agency rejected them. Shortly after this event, the chancellor called Lori into his office to ask if she would spy on other faculty and report on who had been going to see state legislators about his poor management techniques. A few weeks later, he was fired.

Lori thought, "At least we'll get some competent leadership now." What her institution got instead was a revolving door of interim appointments, with each stranger than the last.

The college went through six chancellors in five years. One chancellor read their tenure documents aloud to them and insisted on his interpretation that the school didn't offer tenure (it did). Another appointed all faculty to the *bomb squad* to check classrooms for bombs and signal the *all clear* in response to their many bomb threats. A third ignored the chairperson of the accreditation team's exit report to tell Lori she thought he enjoyed the sandwiches they'd ordered for lunch.

Lori insisted that she could elaborate also on the three fired faculty senate presidents in the same five years, the multiple lawsuits, and the mass exodus of talented colleagues. However, she chose to emphasize the idea that the reader is best served by gaining a picture of a college that felt very much *through the looking glass* to those of trying to teach their classes and help students who needed a path into higher education. It was the support of colleagues on her campus that helped Lori survive; it was the support of the girlfriends that helped her escape.

Community colleges can sometimes promote disciplinary isolation. Faculty teach five or six classes and serve on committees. The workload keeps

one very busy—often too busy (and too underfunded) for attending professional conferences in one's field. You may be the only faculty member in
your area of concentration. Lack of colleagues with your background can
contribute to your disciplinary knowledge *going cold*. You aren't discussing
new publications, and your focus on freshman and sophomore courses means
you aren't reading them for class.

Add to that context the horrors in senior leadership Lori's school experienced. Getting stuck in that rotten situation or leaving the academy was a real
possibility for her. It was Lori's contact with her discipline-based network of
girlfriends that kept her publishing, attending conferences, and positioning
herself for the jump to a different university that she eventually made. In
Lori's horror story, there was more than safety in numbers, there was a path
out of wonderland.

Having a support network proved remarkably helpful as the girlfriends
tackled the daily requirements of work in academia like dealing with budget
cuts, meeting publication goals, and surviving difficult administrators. A
support network can also provide . . . well . . . support. The next two accounts
explore an all-too-common demon in higher education—the fear that you
don't belong—and how you can use your network to affirm your role as
protagonist of your higher-education adventure.

YOU CAN'T GET THERE FROM HERE: HORROR TALES FROM THE NONTRADITIONAL CAREER PATH

When Debra took a job as a contract faculty member nearly twelve years ago,
she told herself it would be just for a few years—until she chose the right
PhD program. She was teaching full time and enjoying settling in a new city.
Her wonderful new colleagues provided her with a readymade professional
and social community.

Debra kept herself busy while telling herself she'd go back to get the PhD
when the time was right, when she was ready, when her partner finished his
degree, and when she found the right program. Each year she'd attend her
primary professional conference, and her network of colleagues would ask
about her plans to start a PhD program. Debra had her ready answer. After
all, she had been telling herself this narrative for many years.

Narratives of Constraint

Years after entering the profession, Debra read O'Meara, Terosky, and Neumann's (2008) "Faculty Careers and Work Lives", a study that focuses on
how faculty careers are structured through language. O'Meara and colleagues (2008, 18) analyzed nearly 1,000 books and articles on faculty and
the academic environment over the past 20 years, to conclude that faculty

often focus on *narratives of constraint.* The language academics use emphasizes "'just making it,' 'treading water,' 'dodging bullets' or barely 'staying alive'" (2008, 2).

During her time as a lecturer, Debra rarely felt the impact of this narrative. She had girlfriends who believed her contributions were valuable. She felt successful in her role, and, luckily, her department leadership was supportive of her exploration of new opportunities.

Debra took on special responsibilities as a basic-course director, lead academic advisor, and internship coordinator. She also worked with colleagues to write a grant proposal to incorporate service learning and civic engagement into the curriculum and eventually accepted a position working with her office of community engagement. Opportunities for growth were less available in Debra's new position, however, and she knew that she needed a change.

Narratives of Growth

She finally began that PhD she'd always talked about, but it was tough. Debra loved working on community engagement, but she wasn't teaching, and though classified as faculty, had no faculty privilege—and it was odd to be a student again. Debra was frustrated when her single, traditional-age classmates said, "I'm so busy with my assistantship and class," while she was working full time, managing her family, and taking classes at night. She felt old and out of touch with her classmates.

When Debra had crises of faith, she knew she could rely on her girlfriends and network to affirm her by asking questions: Are you doing work you enjoy? Are the questions you're asking answerable in the literature of that discipline? and Do you feel like your colleagues support you?

O'Meara and colleagues (2008, 18) contend that the alternative to the narrative of constraint is the *narrative of growth.* These stories focus on the relationships built through one's work, opportunities to make positive change, and feeling a sense of agency in their institution(s). At their core, faculty members want to "pursue their scholarly passions and find personal and professional meaning" (20). Ultimately, this was the narrative that most resonated with Debra. Even though she didn't follow the traditional path, she chose positions and colleagues in the academy that still allowed her to pursue the work she loved.

The (Non)traditional Path

As Debra completes the doctoral degree, she is keenly aware of the changing face of the faculty in the United States. The more conferences she attends and research she conducts the more she understands that her path is not nearly as nontraditional as previously imagined. The realities of the job market are such that many current PhD students will not pursue traditional faculty jobs. According to data from the NSF 2012 Survey of Earned Doctorates, nearly half of all PhD earners were planning to work outside of higher education.

Yet the culture of PhD graduate programs often makes it hard for individuals to explore alternative paths. When students enter doctoral programs, June (2011, A16) explains, "Their professors and many of their peers expect them to become professors—cut from the same cloth as their graduate advisors." Again, a supportive network becomes critical to success. Debra was surrounded by colleagues and friends who supported her decision on the timeline she needed. No one in her network considered her career path a *consolation prize*, even though there were times she felt that way herself. After all, these narratives are strong and persuasive.

In her third role at her institution, Debra is a director in a faculty development office where her primary research interest is the socialization and organizational identities of faculty members. Her nontraditional path through the academy has been supported by her network as a story of growth rather than constraint. One's networks become powerful resources for telling one's career stories. By focusing on growth, the stories of seemingly nontraditional career paths can become a positive and affirming construction rather than a denial of the realities of academic life.

Sometimes it does not matter what path one takes through the academy. One can still feel like an interloper. Like something out of *Invasion of the Body Snatchers*, we know we look like professors on the outside but we fear that we are really impostors soon to be discovered.

HAVE I WANDERED INTO A DEEP, DARK FOREST WHERE I DON'T BELONG?: OVERCOMING IMPOSTOR SYNDROME

As Alice looks back on her path to tenure, she recognizes that her horror came from her own conjuring of feelings of fear, suspense, and panic. To be sure, the tenure-track system, in many ways, is designed to invoke the palpable fear that drives any good horror story. Her story is less about the fear that comes from facing an ax-wielding madman and more like an anxiety-filled rollercoaster ride with many twists and turns and unexpected drops, but also fulfilling escalations.

Alice was trained in a traditional PhD program and surrounded with a tribe of direct peers who were in the same life stage as she and who shared interests in many of the same intellectual questions that she did. Her first faculty appointment found her at a midsize university with a strong focus on research and an equally strong focus on high-quality teaching. In Alice's on-campus interview, she met all of her future colleagues, and they knew that she respected their work and the legacy they built. Alice felt privileged to have landed among such established scholars. And she was.

She never lost her appreciation for working within a department of good scholars. But once Alice left the safe cocoon of graduate school and entered this forest of giants without her direct peers, she felt the downside to landing such a nice position.

Alice was the only assistant professor among the big names at her institution. All three professors in her department were well-known in their respective disciplines, and the colleague closest to her in age and experience was seven years her senior, and a superstar to boot. A feeling of intimidation and an incredible case of imposter syndrome became the antagonist in Alice's horror story.

A recent commentary in *The Chronicle of Higher Education* (Leonard 2014) contends that imposter syndrome is simply a part of the academy. Leonard argues, "It is impossible to talk about impostor syndrome in universal ways. Impostor syndrome is not just about feeling out of place or unworthy—it is a symptom of a culture that falsely defines success and worthiness through the myth of meritocracy."

Alice couldn't put her finger on any specific intimidating behaviors of her colleagues; yet she was haunted. "How could I possibly measure up to them?" she often said to herself. In her first three years, she remained the only assistant professor and was constantly engaged in impression management on a grand scale. Her colleagues chose her because they felt that she was up to the task. Nevertheless, she was never truly convinced that this was indeed the case.

Like all new faculty, Alice was trying to find her place—how to fit her teaching into the new university culture, how to navigate the dynamics of faculty politics, and how to create a new life in a new city as a new assistant professor. One would think she could ask her new colleagues for advice, but Alice always felt that her questions were those to which she should already know the answers.

Alice was simultaneously trying to learn the ropes and engage in impression management. How could her colleagues—the very people who would be evaluating her third-year review and promotion and tenure dossiers—see her as competent and capable if she admitted she was scared and confused? Her girlfriends created a safe space where she did not feel that she had to pretend that she had everything figured out. On the day Alice gave her first midterm for a new course and only two students had enough time to finish, she did not go across the hall to find out what she should do. She went to her keyboard and started an online discussion with her support network.

The beauty of a diverse network of colleagues is that each person has already seen a great deal. Many have tools in their toolboxes that they are willing to share. Time and time again, Alice returned to her network as a sounding board—to vent and get support, but more importantly to problem solve.

In many ways, it was her network (i.e., her girlfriends) that helped her realize she was not crazy and was not experiencing anything different from her peers. That network helped her to move beyond feelings of intimidation and insecurity to a place where she was doing the job they knew she could do. Alice gained confidence through the support of her girlfriends. With that new sense of confidence, she moved beyond panic to realize her new institution could be an academic home for her.

Once the forest was no longer so dark and scary, Alice was able to become more actively engaged in navigating the politics of her institution. Boice's (2000) research on new faculty confirms this experience. He urges early-career faculty to get engaged in their campus community as a way to learn norms and build relationships of trust. Having conquered her imposter syndrome Alice came to realize what she cared about, what she believed in, and how her work reflected those values and has built a comfortable academic home.

HOW TO BUILD YOUR NETWORK

Clearly, the subjects in this chapter have found considerable help facing professional challenges by participating in self-aware support networks. Research suggests academic support networks offer personal support, a forum for academic discussion, and a way to benchmark progress: network cohesion is heightened by physical presence, shared experiences, and a sense of common purpose (Pilbeam, Lloyd-Jones, and Denyer 2013).

Faced with horrors in the hallowed halls, anyone can apply a similar strategy to craft their own self-aware support network—find some like-minded colleagues and do things with them. The network identified in this chapter began in graduate school, where friendships and time are abundant. The subjects had little sense then that they were building professional connections that would last a lifetime. If you are fortunate enough to still be in school, start making friends now where physical presence and shared experiences are an easy part of your network cohesion.

If, however, you are already working, it can be harder to build your network, but that doesn't mean you shouldn't do it. Two of the *girlfriends* have built separate networks of colleagues on their own campuses, and they meet regularly to cheer on one another's writing efforts. Don't feel as though you have to stay within the confines of your own department or even your own campus.

Find people with similar research interests at conferences or on committees, and invite them to start up an academic support group. Schedule regular meetings as you would with any committee assignment. Have a task to accomplish. For example, hold one another accountable for how many pages you've each written in a two-week period—that sense of common purpose increases the odds the network will cohere. Meet someplace fun—the campus coffee shop works for one such group. If you make an effort to show interest in each other, you will find that conversation covers the task goals of the group quickly and grows to include other topics.

If you're forced to work at a distance, use social media to stay in touch. Online tools can be an excellent way to touch base with your network, but look for ways to increase network cohesion through seeing each other face-to-face when possible. Professional conferences can be excellent places to reconnect annually with your network. Even if the members of your support network are in different fields, look for common-topic conferences (e.g., assessment and pedagogy) that might offer a reason for you to reconnect face-to-face on a regular basis.

Perhaps what has been less clear from these tales of survival is that the groups work because all members contribute. The temptation in reading a chapter on how to survive horror stories in the academy is simply looking for "what's in it for me?" That's not a bad impulse; it's just not enough.

Ironically, to benefit from a support network one must first be willing to give to it. Trust and genuine concern for others is, after all, the cornerstone of a real support network. If you cannot contribute to it, you cannot benefit from it. The more you deposit in the network the more dividends you will actually have to collect when you need to make a support withdrawal.

Finally, and perhaps most importantly, you need to view your participation in any support network as a tool for advocating for the improved circumstances of others beyond the network. The women in this network, for example, present a mentoring panel each year at their national conference. Most attendees are young women, the next generation of female scholars. The subjects in this chapter have had countless conversations with younger professionals about thriving in the academy. Advocating for fewer horror stories in the first place helps to create more humane workplaces for us all. What better way to turn your horror story into an adventure tale?

REFERENCES

Anderson, Karrin Vasby, Sarah L. Bonewits, Kelly Carter McDorman, Jennifer Burek Pierce, Claire H. Procopio, Kristina Horn Sheeler, and Helen Tate. 2004. "Voices about Choices: The Role of Female Networks in Affirming Life Choices in the Academy." *Women's Studies in Communication* 27(1):88–110.

Baker, Christina N. 2013. "Social Support and Success in Higher Education: The Influence of On-Campus Support on African American and Latino College Students." *Urban Review*, 45(5):632–50.

Barnes, Laura, Menna O. Agago, and William T. Coombs. 1998. "Effects of Job-Related Stress on Faculty Intention to Leave Academia." *Research in Higher Education*, 39(4):457–69.

Bhopal, Kalwant. 2010. *Asian Women in Higher Education: Shared Communities.* Staffordshire: UK: Trentham Books.

Boice, Robert. 2000. *Advice for New Faculty Members: Nihil Nimus.* Needham Heights, MA: Allyn & Bacon.

Bok, Derek. 2013. "The Authors Must Prepare Ph.D. Students for the Complicated Art of Teaching." *The Chronicle of Higher Education*, November 11. Retrieved March 3, 2014 (http://chronicle.com/article/The authors-Must-Prepare-PhD-Students/142893/).

Carroll, Lewis. 2005. *Alice's Adventures in Wonderland.* San Diego: ICON Group International. Retrieved March 22, 2014 (http://eds.a.ebscohost.com.ezproxy.selu.edu/eds/ebookviewer/ebook/bmxlYmtfXzE0OTIxMV9fQU41?sid=98d153a6-94c5-4ce6-807b-adf-ce6d10fac@sessionmgr4001&vid=1&format=EB&rid=1).

Chronicle of Higher Education. "25 Years of Declining State Support for Public Colleges." Washington DC: CHE. Retrieved March 7, 2014 (http://chronicle.com/article/25-Years-of-Declining-State/144973/).

Clark, Shirley M., and Mary Corcoran. 1986. "Perspectives on the Professional Socialization of Women Faculty: A Case of Accumulative Disadvantage." *Journal of Higher Education* 57(1):20–43.

Eby, Lillian T., Tammy D. Allen, Sarah C. Evans, Thomas Ng, and David L. DuBois. 2008. "Does Mentoring Matter? A Multidisciplinary Meta-Analysis Comparing Mentored and Non-Mentored Individuals." *Journal of Vocational Behavior* 72(2):254–67.

Eggens, Lilian, M. P. C. van der Werf, and R. J. Bosker. 2008. "The Influence of Personal Networks and Social Support on Study Attainment of Students in University Education." *Higher Education* 55(5):553–73.

Hagedorn, Linda Serra. 1996. "Wage Equity and Female Faculty Job Satisfaction: The Role of Wage Differentials in a Job Satisfaction Causal Model." *Research in Higher Education* 37(5):569–98.

Jo, Victoria. 2008. "Voluntary Turnover and Women Administrators in Higher Education." *Higher Education* 56(5):565–82.

Johnsrud, Linda K., Ronald H. Heck, and Vicki J. Rosser. 2000. "Morale Matters: Administrators and Their Intent to Leave." *The Journal of Higher Education* 71(1):34–59.

June, Audrey Williams. 2011. "More Universities Break the Taboo and Talk to Ph.D.'s About Jobs Outside Academe." *The Chronicle of Higher Education*, November 6. Retrieved March 11, 2014 (http://chronicle.com/article/More-Universities-Break-the/129647/).

Leonard, David J. 2014. "Impostor Syndrome: Academic Identity under Siege?" *The Chronicle of Higher Education Blogs: The Conversation*, February 5. Retrieved March 18, 2014 (http://chronicle.com/blogs/conversation/2014/02/05/impostor-syndrome-academic-identity-under-siege/).

Manger, Terje, and Ole-Johan Eikeland. 1990. "Factors Predicting Staff's Intention to Leave the University." *Higher Education* 59(19):281–91.

McGee, Gail W., and Robert C. Ford. 1987. "Faculty Research Productivity and Intention to Change Positions." *The Review of Higher Education* 11(1):1–16.

Nagowski, Matthew P. 2006. "Associate Professor Turnover at America's Public and Private Institutions of Higher Education." *American Economist* 50(1):69–79.

National Science Foundation, National Center for Science and Engineering Statistics. 2012. *Doctorate Recipients from U.S. Universities: 2012.* Special Report NSF 14-305. Arlington, VA. Retrieved March 11, 2014 (http://www.nsf.gov/statistics/sed/2012/).

O'Meara, KerryAnn, Aimee LaPointe Terosky, and Anna Neumann. 2008. "Faculty Careers and Work Lives: A Professional Growth Perspective." *ASHE Higher Education Report* 34(3):1–221.

Pilbeam, Colin, Gaynor Lloyd-Jones, and David Denyer. 2013. "Leveraging Value in Doctoral Student Networks through Social Capital." *Studies in Higher Education* 38(10), 1472–89.

Power, Ronika K., Beverley B. Miles, Alyce Peruzzi, and Angela Voerman. 2011. "Building Bridges: A Practical Guide to Developing and Implementing a Subject-Specific Peer-to-Peer

Academic Mentoring Program for First-Year Higher Education Students." *Asian Social Science* 7(11):75–80.

Rausch, Dianne K., Bonnie P. Ortiz, Robin A. Douthitt, and L. L. Reed. 1989. "The Academic Revolving Door: Why Do Women Get Caught?" *CUPA Journal* 40:1–16.

Rockquemore, Kerry Ann. 2014. "Thriving Amidst Academic Chaos." *National Center for Faculty Development and Diversity*, January 8. Retrieved March 3, 2014 (http://www.facultydiversity.org/news/news.asp?id=153201&hhSearch-Terms=%22teaching+and+trap%22).

Rosa Vélez, Mariam Ludum. 2013. "Workplace Harassment in Higher Education." *Leadership: Magazine for Managers* 31:16–17.

Twale, Darla J., and Barbara M. De Luca. 2008. *Faculty Incivility: The Rise of the Academic Bully Culture and What to Do About It*. San Francisco: Jossey-Bass.

Washburn, Jennifer. 2005. *University Inc.: The Corporate Corruption of Higher Education*. New York: Basic Books.

Xu, Yonghong Jade. 2008. "Faculty Turnover: Discipline-Specific Attention Is Warranted." *Research in Higher Education* 49(1):40–61.

Chapter Twelve

Turning Nightmares into Victories

Handling Promotion and Tenure Horrors

Lin Huff-Corzine and Melvin Rogers

Nightmares, that is, frightening dreams, experiences, or situations that produce intense feelings of anxiety, fear, or terror (Macmillan 1979, 684), best describes the effect of living through the horror that some faculty encounter as they approach promotion, but even more so as they are considered for tenure. Faculty applying for promotion and tenure want to be successful; they want to be victorious. Being promoted to associate professor with tenure is less about the monetary benefit of a promotion than it is about self-esteem and being recognized by one's colleagues as worthy to hold the position.

Faculty being reviewed for promotion and tenure are putting their life's work under a microscope for their academic superiors to scrutinize, deliberate, and decide whether they think the individual's record is sufficient to continue on an academic career path at their institution. This is a process that even the most outstanding young faculty may find nearly takes their breath away as if the evil nightmare spirit that was thought to suffocate sleeping people is still alive and well.

In this chapter, the details of three real-life cases of promotion and tenure nightmarish horrors are presented with suggestions for how the faculty member may be able to handle some of the terror faced along the road to tenure and/or promotion as well as how she or he may look to administrators who support fair practice that may also be codified in the university's policies.

The first scenario presents a case focusing on department collegiality, the second on publishing and teaching issues, and the third on required overcommitment. Each story is followed by the outcome and takeaway lessons. The final section centers on the importance of a *clean* system of promotion and tenure—one with clear guidelines and expectations, not only for the faculty member under review but also for the faculty reviewers.

CASE 1: DR. DEAD MEAT

It was the early 1990s, and the good Dr. Dead Meat was to come up for promotion and tenure the next year. She knew from the way one of the two full professors in the department acted that he was not particularly fond of her, but she also knew that she was doing a good job. She was publishing on a regular basis, the students liked her, and she had increased the number of majors from 27 to nearly 200 in her specialty—which the department needed to stay on good terms about with the dean.

Then one afternoon, her world seemed to fall apart. Two of her friends, one a tenure-track assistant professor and the second a full professor, in the department called her aside to talk. Apparently, during a dinner with a job candidate, the less-than-nice full professor explained to the attendees that he would see that she would become "dead meat." When one of the dinner group pointed out that she published well and that students really liked her the full professor said that he really didn't care and when pushed for his reasoning for wanting to grind her into "dead meat," he stated, "Because she doesn't vote like I do."

So what is she to do? If faced with a full professor who makes threats, does she become Dr. Dead Meat?

Actually, there are a number of possible alternatives. To begin, Dr. Dead Meat should reread the department promotion and tenure guidelines, assuming such a document exists. If it exists and spells out the expectations for promotion and tenure and does not refer to voting in line with one's senior colleagues, which would be highly unlikely, that will be one point in her favor. In this particular case, the promotion and tenure guidelines included nothing about voting in line with senior colleagues, of course, but it also was less than clear about what was expected to be awarded tenure.

One colleague explained to her that the tenured faculty usually "give tenure to people they like" and commented that "one time we gave tenure to 'Dr. Deadbeat' because we liked his wife. That was sure a mistake." Statements like this one should be entered into a journal that the young woman, or anyone facing a similar nightmarish situation, needs to keep.

The journal can be kept in a hard copy format or on a computer, whichever way the person is more comfortable writing out the information. However, the journal entries need to be kept private, so never use the e-mail system, especially university-connected ones, to record incidents. The entries should include data such as the date and time of any related event, name(s) of individual(s) making statement(s), other people who heard the comment(s), a description of exactly what happened, and the date and time of the journal entry. Entries should be made as soon after the incident as possible so that details are recalled more accurately and completely.

Dr. Dead Meat's next move should be to set up an appointment with the department chair to report the statements made about her tenure application and how another faculty member explained the *unethical* decision-making processes sometimes used when making tenure and promotion decisions.

In this case, the assistant professor in question requested that the full professor, who had proclaimed that he would see that she was "dead meat," be removed from the process—that is, that he would not be allowed to participate in any personnel issues having to do with her evaluations, promotion, or tenure. The little salt cross-placed outside of his office to purify the area didn't hurt either.

In this case, the department chair was hesitant to exclude the full professor from the review process, so her next stop was the dean's office where she made the dean aware of the situation. He was a reasonable fellow and agreed to disregard any input the full professor may offer in regard to her promotion and tenure.

Another option would be to explore your discipline's regional- and national-level policy documents regarding ethics and collegiality. Regional and national sociology associations normally have policies on ethical conduct in research, teaching, and service (e.g., Mid-South Sociological Association's [MSSA] and American Sociological Association's [ASA] Codes of Ethics) (MSSA 2014; ASA 2008). Such standards are used by the membership to guide appropriate behavior at conferences, but they can also be applied more broadly to ethical behavior among colleagues at their colleges and universities.

Case 1: Dr. Dead Meat's Outcome

Because the full professor's behavior was so inappropriate, it was relatively easy to convince persons higher in the academic hierarchy to ignore his input related to the assistant professor's evaluations, especially those completed as part of the promotion and tenure process. Dr. Dead Meat was granted a promotion and tenure in spite of the evil attempts on the part of the full professor to influence his *friends* on the department- and college-level promotion and tenure committees.

She was victorious, but that triumph did not come without nightmares along the way. In fact, if someone who knew her well examined her publication record, it would be clear that the threats made by the evil professor influenced her (in)ability to publish at the same rate over the year following his attacks on her professional career.

Case 1: Dr. Dead Meat's Take-Aways

- Face the issues, the nightmares, head-on. Bring the inappropriate behavior to the attention of colleagues in the department.
- Use the hierarchical system at your institution of higher education to take control of the situation. Go to the department chair, the dean and Academic Affairs, if necessary.
- Use the ethical-standards documents available from your regional and/or national associations.
- Keep up your academic performance.
- Keep a journal where incidents of unethical conduct and statements are recorded.

CASE 1A: DR. DEAD MEAT—BACK-ON-TRACK—OR SO SHE THINKS

As time passed, Dr. Dead Meat flourished as a tenured associate professor, but in an effort to reduce the travel and semi-separate lives she and her spouse lived, they sought jobs closer together. When the opportunity arose, they decided to take it. The new university that hired her spouse as a department chair and made her an offer at the associate-professor level refused to hire her with tenure. She decided that having the family together was worth the chance and the extra work it would take to apply for tenure during the second academic year as her contract specified; therefore, she accepted the offer.

With the right to return to her first position with tenure at the former school in her back pocket, so to speak, off she went to the new university. What she didn't know was that a couple of people in the new department didn't want her spouse as chair. Their angle to force him out was to block her tenure.

While she was preparing the tenure documentation, periodic comments were made that caused her some concern. On one such occasion, while she was preparing the tenure file, one of the persons hoping to remove her spouse from the chairship passed by her office and snidely asked, "Are you having fun yet? I just want to know if you're having fun."

Thankfully, she had received information about how these faculty members were working against her prior to that incident. Of course, she had learned from her prior experience and had not only her written comments in her journal but also the informant's written statement. Later in the process, a faculty member from another department, who was serving on the college promotion and tenure committee, shared what he saw as unethical behavior on that committee with the dean and then informed the provost about the situation.

Case 1a: Dr. Back-on-Track's Outcome

Again, she received tenure but not without being subjected to some bumps, emotional bruises, and bullying along the way. What she had hoped would be a transfer to a more collegial department was not to be.

Just because you deserve a promotion or tenure doesn't mean it will be forthcoming. The newly tenured Dr. Back-on-Track survived this bump and the provost, who interviewed everyone, said he couldn't figure out why she wasn't hired with tenure.

Case 1a: Dr. Back-on-Track's Take-Aways

- Universities are not always the friendly, collegial, low-stress institutions of higher education that many students and the general public alike visualize.
- Don't expect that academe will provide you with a safe environment or one where you will be treated fairly. Expect that you will need to stand up for yourself some time along the path to promotion and/or tenure. A recent study of higher education employees found that 62% of those surveyed either witnessed or were the target of bullying during the previous eighteen months (Hollis 2012).
- As suggested in the Dr. Dead Meat scenario as well as in the sexual harassment literature, if you begin to perceive that you are being bullied, keep a journal documenting each time an act of bullying occurs.
- Perhaps more important, know that you are not alone. Literally thousands of faculty and staff who work in academe are bullied each year and many continuously for years. What this means is that there is a problem, a disastrous problem for many in our own disciplines, that allows and even actively hides the demeaning and hostile treatment to which some faculty and staff are subjected.
- If you are bullied, don't hide it. You aren't the problem; the bully is the problem.

CASE 1B: DR. BACK-ON-TRACK BECOMES DR. WANT-A-PROMOTION (WAP) — ARE YOU KIDDING?

Sometimes a faculty member must continue working in a department where the bully is also located. That was the case for Dr. WAP as she was advised to postpone going up for a promotion to full professor until either the bullies left the department or the department, which comprised two disciplines, split into separate units. She did as her department chair advised. She waited.

Case 1b: Dr. Want-a-Promotion's Outcome

As soon as the department split, Dr. WAP went up for promotion and was advanced to full professor.

Case 1b: Dr. Want-a-Promotion's Take-Aways

- Assuming that you have a record that is deserving of a promotion, the correct path may be to wait, even though it means that your income will be lower. No promotion means no pay increase.
- On the other hand, the correct path may be to go up for promotion, even when advised that the timing isn't right.
- Women are more likely than men to take the advice of the chair when instructed to wait to go up for a promotion. Women are also less likely than men to be promoted to full professor. Perhaps taking advice from the chair and other colleagues means fewer promotions to full professor for women. Perhaps there is a causal relationship between taking advice and fewer promotions for women in academe.
- Whatever the case may be, within reason, each faculty member must make their own choice about the timing of their promotion application.

CASE 2: DR. RESEARCH—YOU PUBLISH WHERE?

At his third year review, Dr. Research was admonished for publishing in the *wrong* places and for teaching some of his courses in African American studies. According to Dr. Research, he was told that articles needed to be published in peer-reviewed journals to count toward tenure and promotion—but which peer-reviewed journals had not been clarified. However, when Dr. Research placed some of his work in certain peer-reviewed journals (e.g., *Journal of Black Studies*) he was told that journals such as this one were too easy to publish in so they would not fully count.

In addition, he was admonished for teaching in African American studies. Although he had been approached to teach in the multidisciplinary program by the director, and he had received approval to do so from the department chair, he was told that he didn't teach enough in the discipline for which he had been hired.

It was difficult, but Dr. Research survived the third year, which his department viewed as the pivotal year for tenure-track faculty. But when it was time to go up for promotion and tenure, he was again met with roadblocks.

His dedication to the discipline and his publication record were again being questioned.

The department expected a certain number of peer-reviewed articles, and the number of publications Dr. Research had was right on the border—the border that could end in promotion and tenure or not. Most upsetting was the fact that he had been *advised* to withdraw two papers from journals where he had sent them for review so they could be resubmitted to other journals the chair thought would be more *appropriate* places for them to appear.

This advice on the part of the chair was especially upsetting because the department guidelines allowed for papers to count toward publication when they were submitted to a journal, a practice we do not support, as well as when they were accepted for publication or when they were actually published. By talking Dr. Research into withdrawing two papers from journals, the chair had in effect reduced the number of Dr. Research's publications. Of course this slowed the publishing process and meant the number of publications Dr. Research had when going up for tenure and promotion would more likely be viewed as inadequate.

Another problem he faced during the tenure and promotion process concerned a grant he had received. Dr. Research had been advised by an associate dean to set up a small business and to run the grant through that entity rather than pay large indirect costs by going through the Office of Research. When his tenure and promotion file reached the provost, his grant work was checked by the Office of Research. This exposed the unethical way the grant had bypassed the university and the provost now wanted to see him gone as well. Clearly, this faculty member was in deep trouble.

Case 2: Dr. Research's Outcome—You Publish Where?

Because one assistant dean was known to help faculty find assistance with promotion and tenure issues by listening and then reaching out to an administrator in Academic Affairs, Dr. Research made his way to this empathic administrator. Their meetings began during his third year review and continued through the tenure process. Dr. Research listened closely to the advice he received and translated the advice into behavior that led to a successful tenure and promotion outcome.

Specifically, the first meetings between the struggling faculty member and the administrator were set up to discuss how to handle the third year review. The administrator advised him to know the department promotion and tenure guidelines by heart and to get all interpretations of the guidelines in writing.

In this case, if the department refused to count the teaching he did in African American Studies or the papers he published in journals such as *Journal of Black Studies* he needed to realign his work and work products to fit within the departmental expectations—at least until he received tenure. This was hard advice for Dr. Research to hear but he understood that it could mean the difference between success and failure when applying for promotion and tenure.

The bad advice to withdraw papers from journals just before going up for tenure and promotion was another issue. Clearly, Dr. Research had been bullied into doing something that could lead to having too few publications to meet the department guidelines for tenure and promotion—a situation that had to be remedied as soon as possible.

In one case he was able to explain that the paper should remain in the review process, but it was too late to salvage the second one at the journal from which it had been withdrawn. He quickly submitted it elsewhere, however, and the number of publications he had in his file when it went outside the department for review met the department guidelines.

When the provost found the unethical grant behavior Dr. Research had been a part of, it was truly luck that was on his side. The same administrator who had assisted him through the early stages of the promotion and tenure process had also been privy to a conversation at a department party at which a full professor, who worked on the same grant, was bragging about how she, a full professor, along with the associate dean had pulled off the grant in such a way that it circumvented the Office of Research and set up the assistant professor as the CEO of a so-called company.

Once this information was passed on to the provost, he focused his anger on the more experienced full professors but still sternly advised the assistant professor about moral and ethical issues involved in grant writing and administration.

Case 2: Dr. Research's Take-Aways

- When something doesn't feel right, it probably isn't. During his third-year review, Dr. Research felt that he was being treated unfairly. The messages he received were mixed. Yes, teach in African American studies, but you aren't teaching enough within the department. Yes, publish in peer-reviewed journals, but not in *certain* peer-reviewed journals.
- Understand that sometimes good things come to people who are willing to wait. If you find that your department does not value publications placed in certain journals or that the number of publications expected makes it next to impossible to publish qualitative pieces, you have two choices. You can look for another school that holds the type and/or topics of your work in higher esteem than where you are currently employed, or you can change your targeted journals or type of methodology until you obtain tenure.

- Never, never, never agree to withdraw papers that have been submitted to peer-reviewed journals just because someone, even if it is your chair, tells you to do so.
- Keep in contact with people that will work as your advocates—faculty and administrators who want to see your path end in victory.

CASE 3: DR. YEAH SAYER—SERVICE OVERLOAD

Dr. Yeah Sayer started working in her department as an instructor because she had not yet completed her dissertation. Accepting an instructor position at most schools of higher education means that the employee teaches more courses than tenure-earning or tenured faculty, and it certainly meant that in Dr. Yeah Sayer's department. The contract read that once she completed her dissertation, which she was to do within the first year of employment, she would be moved to a tenure-track position. Still, as she was trying to complete her dissertation, Dr. Yeah Sayer was also required to teach four large classes each semester.

Within the first few months, Dr. Yeah Sayer was also asked to take over the undergraduate program in her area, which came with the advising responsibility for approximately 200 majors. Knowing that there would be no chance of a tenure-track position unless she did the extra work, Dr. Yeah Sayer agreed to temporarily accept the added tasks. A course reduction, you ask? No. Sorry. You are needed in the classroom. A pay increase, you ask? Sorry, but the budget does not allow for a pay increase. So, Dr. Yeah Sayer had the work added to her list of responsibilities without compensation.

At the beginning of her second year at the university, Dr. Yeah Sayer completed her dissertation and was moved to a tenure-track position with a three-course teaching load. Instead of receiving a reduced service load like other tenure-track faculty, however, Dr. Yeah Sayer was applauded for the excellent work she had done with the program and was asked to lead the program review and assessment required by her regional accrediting body. She's the only one with the in-depth knowledge needed to complete this review, she's told.

Dr. Yeah Sayer explains her dilemma to the department chair, noting that she needs time to do research and publish. In addition, now that Dr. Yeah Sayer has received an evaluation, she understands that service does not count for very much when it comes to the evaluation of her work overall. Again, Dr. Yeah Sayer takes on the assignment but does so with some hesitancy. By the end of the second year, Dr. Yeah Sayer has served the department well, but has no publications. She struggles through the third year, her second on a tenure-track line, but the more she tries to get in some research time the more her service obligations block the time to do so.

During the third year, Dr. Yeah Sayer's department completes an in-depth pre-tenure review. At this stage in the process, the tenured faculty expect to see a minimum of three to five publications or the equivalent in peer-reviewed journals. Dr. Yeah Sayer had managed to eke out one publication during her first two years, which is far below what is expected. She became desperate. With the service load she had been assigned, Dr. Yeah Sayer could not see how she would be able to obtain tenure.

Case 3: Dr. Yeah Sayer's Outcome

Dr. Yeah Sayer was in a difficult position, and she knew it. She also knew that others on tenure-track lines in her department were not required to accept the same heavy service load that she had been assigned. In fact, it was as if she had been coerced into taking on much too much service. The department benefited, but she alone lost the time and energy to publish—the most important task required to successfully apply for and be granted tenure.

In her desperation, Dr. Yeah Sayer contacted the well-known assistant dean. She was literally in tears as she told her story. Once they spoke, the unofficial faculty advisor set up a meeting between a spokesperson and advocate for faculty from upper-level administration. Following that meeting, and with Dr. Yeah Sayer's consent, the administrator explained the situation as she saw it to the department chair.

This faculty member was being treated differently from others in the department who were at a similar stage in their careers. This meant that the collective-bargaining agreement, which had been negotiated between the faculty and the university board of trustees, was being violated. Faculty, it reads, are to have equal opportunity to obtain tenure and promotion. The repercussions of singling out an untenured faculty member to assume service duties beyond the norm in the department also meant that she would have a legitimate case against the university if she did not receive tenure.

Dr. Yeah Sayer received an immediate reduction in her duties to bring them in line with other tenure-track faculty. Though it was not easy to make up for lost time to do her research she did obtain tenure. She also learned how to be a Nay Sayer, which can be extremely difficult for young faculty who want to do the right thing for the department and the students that they teach.

Case 3: Dr. Yeah Sayer's Take-Aways

- From the administrative angle, department chairs need to be aware of the amount of time various tasks take and be sure that assignments among tenure-track faculty, in particular, are generally equal. In Dr. Yeah Sayer's case, the chair needed to even out assignments given to the tenure-track faculty so that all had an equal chance of obtaining tenure and a promotion to associate professor. More senior faculty need to be assigned the work of directing programs, completing assessments, and preparing documents for regional or national program reviews.

- Dr. Yeah Sayer, on the other hand, needed to learn that it is acceptable to discuss an assignment that seems out of line with others in similar positions. She is not required to simply accept any assignment offered when she knows that it puts her at a disadvantage.
- Although she was able to find her way to victory by going to empathetic administrators, if the faculty are unionized, faculty can also go to the union leadership or grievance representative for assistance.

ADMINISTRATIVE RESPONSE: DR. P&T CLEANS UP THE SYSTEM

Thus far, the individual horror stories of promotion and tenure have ended with recommendations for what the faculty member can do when dealing with the nightmares some faculty endure when applying for promotion and/ or tenure. Suggestions such as the ones included here are important because they encourage faculty to stand up for themselves and to look for assistance from someone who can offer an unbiased review of the situation.

In the cases presented, some administrators from departments across campus would introduce themselves to new faculty and offer to answer questions or provide assistance as needed. If the situation could be handled within the department, a positive step had been made at the lowest level of organization. If no satisfactory results were achieved in the department, it went to the college and occasionally on to academic affairs where the faculty's situation was handled head-on. In some cases, the situation was solved face-to-face at the department or college level, but at other times department, college, or university policies or regulations held the answers.

Faculty members often overlook the importance of documents that outline their expected performance even within their department, let alone policies at the college or university levels. Such was the case for Dr. Yeah Sayer's problem with her assignment. The department guidelines and the collective bargaining agreement (yes, they're union) clearly say that faculty must be given *equal opportunity* for success. But as we will show, these documents also regulate the process of tenure and promotion, and the insistence that they be followed by college- and university-level administrators can mean the difference between a nightmare and a victory.

As much as many faculty members may be looking for flexibility and may have even chosen academic careers because they tend to lack rigidity, when applying for promotion and tenure it is structure that's important. A clean, clear structure reduces the nightmares associated with the year-long process of promotion and tenure review.

Although Dr. WAP's bid for promotion and tenure ended in victory, she considered it a success riddled with flaws. Thus, when she secured a position that allowed her to *clean up* the system of promotion and tenure, she studied what needed to be done and then undertook the three- to four-year process to make it happen. To the administrator who cares, however, the development of policies and procedures is worth it.

To begin, each department was required to prepare a promotion and tenure document that, as clearly as possible, spelled out what a faculty member needed to accomplish to secure tenure and promotion to both associate professor and full professor. Some were better than others, of course, but that is why the review process didn't stop with the department chair.

The college dean and academic affairs personnel also had to review and work with the departments' personnel committees to approve each department document. Some are still better than others, but all department promotion and tenure guidelines are now reviewed at least every five years by all supervisory levels at the university. Following the hierarchy, once the department reviewed the guidelines, each college was required to prepare promotion and tenure policies that were also reviewed at the university level.

To keep young faculty informed about their progress toward tenure and promotion, meaningful cumulative progress evaluations (CPEs) were developed. Unlike faculty annual evaluations, CPEs require the tenure-earning faculty to prepare a file beginning in their second year of employment that outlines their successes in teaching, research, and service. CPE files are then reviewed by the tenured faculty, the department chair, and the dean.

At each level of the review process, the files are rated as *above expectation*, *at expectation*, or *below expectation*. Written reasoning that follows the departmental promotion and tenure guidelines must be provided for the rating chosen. Each year thereafter until they are going up for promotion and tenure, faculty add to the CPE file, which is reviewed and rated at the three levels noted above so that by the time they apply for tenure and promotion, there are no surprises.

Believing that fairness is fundamental to just decision making, Dr. P&T worked with the faculty senate to reformulate the university-level promotion and tenure regulations to reflect her basic philosophical dedication to fairness (UCF-3.011 Tenure 2011). Having watched the system of promotion and tenure, as well as working with people facing nightmare situations, there were certain structural changes that she knew had to be enacted.

Not everyone in every department can be held to the same standards. Some departments have heavier teaching loads, while others are more research oriented. Faculty in some disciplines can obtain large grants relatively frequently, while others may never have the opportunity to seek external funding. Thus, the promotion and tenure regulations must allow sufficient flexibility in the interpretation of the standards so that faculty in all disciplines can reasonably expect to fulfill the requirements.

Because Dr. P&T had witnessed a narrow definition of teaching, which was primarily restricted to classroom or online instruction, she ensured that teaching activities also included curriculum development, development of innovative course methodologies, publishing teaching-related articles, and so on.

Dr. P&T had noticed structural deficiencies in the promotion and tenure process that could lead to failure for a faculty member to receive promotion and/or tenure, but that could also lead to lost grievances and/or lawsuits on the part of the university. Thus, the way external reviewers are chosen is spelled out very clearly, as is the process each committee is expected to use when completing their review of tenure and promotion files.

The result is that half of the external reviewers are chosen by the faculty member, while the other half are nominated by the tenured faculty in consultation with the department chair. And each committee is expected to be "professional and discriminating in its decision making and will make its review based on consideration of the facts and supportive evidence contained in the candidate's application" (UCF-3.011 Tenure 2011, 6). Committee members were no longer expected to endorse, or not endorse, faculty candidates for tenure or promotion. The results of their reviews are to be evidence driven, not based on friendships.

A final major change that became university policy relates to Dr. Dead Meat's horror story, the first case of this chapter. Basically, committee members must not participate in the voting on an application if there is a conflict of interest or if there is a reasonable risk that personal factors may impair the reviewer's objectivity regarding an individual applicant (UCF-3.017 Promotion of Tenured and Tenure-Earning Faculty 2011, 5).

This addition may well be the one most important change Dr. P&T was able to enact. Faculty who cannot vote objectively—that is, based on the facts contained in the applicant's file—cannot vote.

The first time this section was used by a faculty member applying for promotion came almost immediately after it was put in place. Dr. Lab, who applied for promotion, had had major disagreements about lab equipment and publication rights with Dr. D., whose spouse was a leading figure on the department promotion committee.

When Dr. Lab brought this conflict forward to Dr. P&T, it was decided that there was sufficient evidence of a conflict to require Dr. D.'s spouse to recuse himself from the committee. He did so, rather reluctantly, but he did. That helped clean up the promotion process, the primary goal for adding such wording in the first place.

FINAL THOUGHTS

In summary, individual assertiveness, empathetic supporters, and structural changes can make a positive difference for individuals going through the process of review for promotion and/or tenure. This is a win-win situation for the faculty and the university.

The faculty are likely to have fewer nightmares and more victories, while the university can be expected to endure fewer lost grievances and lawsuits as well as greater productivity from the faculty. In fact, while some universities suffer several lost lawsuits each year, others with sound policies, such as the ones presented here, are much less vulnerable because their systems are structured to support fairness, a fairness based on evidence-based research.

REFERENCES

American Sociological Association Code of Ethics and Policies and Procedures of the ASA Committee on Professional Ethics. (2008). Retrieved on April 21, 2014, from the ASA website. http://www.asanet.org/images/asa/docs/pdf/CodeofEthics.pdf

Hollis, L. P. (2012). *Bully in the Ivory Tower.* Patricia Berkley, LLC.UCF-3.011 Tenure. (2011). Retrieved on April 29, 2014, from the University of Central Florida Regulations website. http://www.regulations.ucf.edu/~regs/pdf/notices/Reg3.011TenureJan11.pdf

Mid-South Sociological Association (MSSA). (2014). Committee on Professional Ethics. Retrieved on April 21, 2014, from the MSSA website. http://www.midsouthsoc.org/soc/wp-content/uploads/2010/12/MSSA-Code-of-Ethics.pdf

UCF-3.017 Promotion of Tenured and Tenure-Earning Faculty. (2011). Retrieved on April 29, 2014, from the University of Central Florida Regulations website. http://www.regulations.ucf.edu/~regs/pdf/notices/Reg3.017Promotion_Jan11.pdf.

Index

academic freedom: in discipline of sociology, 91; and program review, 61, 62; standardization as threat to, 61

accommodation, resistance with, 9

acculturation, 24–27; assimilation strategy of, 24, 25, 27, 28; bi-dimensional model of, 25; external constraints on, 25; integration strategy of, 25, 27, 28; linear model of, 24; marginalization strategy of, 25, 27, 28; opportunistic assimilation in, 28–29; as psychological journey, 31; separation strategy of, 25, 27

acculturative stress, in international students, 24–27

Achor, Shirley, 9

active listening, in job interviews, 44

adjunct positions, 35

administrators, support networks for, 155–157

advertisements, job, 92

affirmative action, in California, 90

African American(s), historical exclusion of, 3, 4, 108

African American faculty, 123–137; Critical Race Theory and, 127; microaggressions against, 124–127; at public New England university, experiences of, 128–135; at small liberal arts college, experiences of, 111; student evaluations of, 125, 126, 135;

suggestions for graduate students from, 136–137; themes in experiences of, 124–126

African American women faculty: discrimination in hiring of, 90; microaggressions against, 125–126; student reception of, 90–91, 125–126, 131–132, 135

AJS. See American Journal of Sociology

Alice's Adventures in Wonderland (Carroll), 123, 137, 160

allocentric personality, 28

Almaguer, Tomas, 5

American Journal of Sociology (AJS), 80, 82–84

American Sociological Association (ASA): Guides to Graduate Departments, 81; job interviews at annual meetings of, 39; journal of, 82; on women in sociology, 90

American Sociological Review (ASR), 80, 82–84

Anderson, Benedict, 144

annual meetings, job interviews at, 38–39

application packets, job, 37–38, 93

ASA. *See* American Sociological Association

Asia, international students from, 18

Asian faculty, 125

ASR. See American Sociological Review

About the Editors

Earl Wright II, a native of Memphis, Tennessee, is professor of Africana studies at the University of Cincinnati. For nearly twenty years, Earl has engaged in research on the sociological significance of the W. E. B. Du Bois–led Atlanta Sociological Laboratory, the moniker bestowed on scholars engaged in sociological inquiry at Atlanta University between 1895 and 1917. His groundbreaking research on the school, *The First American School of Sociology: W. E. B. Du Bois and the Atlanta Sociological Laboratory*, challenges many of the accepted dogmas in American sociological history and has led to numerous revisions of the history of the discipline. Additionally, he has authored seventeen peer-reviewed journal articles and four books.

Thomas C. Calhoun is associate vice resident for academic and student affairs and professor of sociology at Jackson State University. Prior to coming to Jackson State University, he served as associate provost for academic affairs and chairperson of the Department of Sociology at Southern Illinois University at Carbondale. He has served previously as president of the Association of Black Sociologist, Association of Social and Behavioral Scientist, Mid-South Sociological Association, and the North Central Sociological Association. He has published extensively in the area of deviance. He is the recipient of the Aida Tomeh Outstanding Teaching Award and the 2016 J. Milton Yinger Distinguished Career Award from the North Central Sociological Association, the A. Wade Smith Outstanding Teaching Award, and the James E. Blackwell Distinguished Career Award from the Association of Black Sociologists. He received his BA in sociology from Texas Wesleyan College, MA in sociology from Texas Tech University, and the PhD in sociology from the University of Kentucky.

About the Contributors

Karrin Vasby Anderson is professor of Communication Studies at Colorado State University, where she teaches courses in rhetoric, political communication, and gender and communication. She is coauthor of two books: *Woman President: Confronting Postfeminist Political Culture* and *Governing Codes: Gender, Metaphor, and Political Identity*. Dr. Anderson is a recipient of the National Communication Association's James A. Winans and Herbert A. Wichelns Memorial Award for Distinguished Scholarship in Rhetoric and Public Address, the Outstanding Book Award from the Organization for the Study of Communication, Language, and Gender, the Michael Pfau Outstanding Article Award in Political Communication from NCA's Political Communication Division, the Organization for Research on Women and Communication's Feminist Scholarship Award, and the Carrie Chapman Catt Prize for Research on Women in Politics.

Donald Cunnigen is a specialist in race relations, social movements, and social inequality. His particular expertise is in the area of White southern liberalism and the American civil rights movement. As a cum laude graduate of Tougaloo College in Mississippi with a double major in sociology-anthropology and Afro-American studies, he earned an MA in sociology from the University of New Hampshire and an AM in sociology from Harvard University. He also holds a PhD from Harvard. Cunnigen is a native southerner who has devoted his scholarly attention to the social changes that reshaped the region. Presently, he is working on a volume titled, *Race in the Age of Obama*. In addition to race relations, social movements, and social inequality, he has conducted research and published in the area of sociology of education, especially examining the experiences of people of color in institutions of higher learning and the role played by scholars in African American colleges.

Breanne Fahs is associate professor of women and gender studies at Arizona State University, where she specializes in studying women's sexuality, critical embodiment studies, radical feminism, and political activism. She has published widely in feminist, social science, and humanities journals and has authored four books: *Performing Sex*, *The Moral Panics of Sexuality* (with Mary L. Dudy and Sarah Stage, 2013), *Valerie Solanas* (2014), and *Out for Blood* (2016). She is the director of the Feminist Research on Gender and Sexuality Group at Arizona State University, and she also works as a private-practice clinical psychologist specializing in sexuality, couples work, and trauma recovery.

Sarah Bonewits Feldner (PhD, Purdue University 2002) is associate professor in communication studies at Marquette Communication. Her research focuses on rhetorical approaches to organizations with a particular emphasis on the organizational identity, legitimacy, and corporate social responsibility. Recent publications appear in the *International Journal of Strategic Communication* and *Management Communication Quarterly.*

Elena Gheorghiu is an international student and PhD candidate (ABD) in international conflict management at Kennesaw State University. She completed her bachelor's degree in environmental economics and a graduate certificate in pedagogy at the Academy of Economic Studies, Bucharest Romania. She also has a master's degree in urban and rural planning and development from the University of Bucharest, Romania. Elena's research focuses on intercultural dynamics engendered by the globalization process, including multicultural organizational conflict, teamwork diversity, and immigrants' quality of life. She is currently teaching courses in introduction to sociology and research methods at Kennesaw State University. She loves dogs and all outdoor activities and for now, she is taking care of her fish, Oberon.

Hamon Ha-am is the pseudonym for a professor in the social sciences, working at a small liberal arts college in the American South.

Shanette Harris focuses on the psychology of diversity and multiculturalism, including race/ethnicity, gender, social class, and sexual orientation. Current research relates to eating disorders and disturbances, violence as a health issue, and cultural variation in health behavior. Most recent projects examine sociocultural-ecological correlates of eating behavior among African American females and cultural moderators of the race/ethnicity-personality hardiness relationship.

Thomas Hochschild's primary teaching and research interests include urban sociology, community, community service, social psychology, deviance, and social stratification. While he enjoys doing research and has published several papers in peer-reviewed journals, his primary passion is teaching. What he enjoys most about teaching is helping students find a sociological issue that moves them personally, and then working with them to develop the analytical and research skills to more fully understand and address the issue. To that end, he believes it is important to engage students with out-of-classroom activities whenever possible. For example, he often provides service-learning opportunities so that students can learn and reflect on sociological issues while providing service to the community. Through in-class instruction and experiential learning, these students acquire the theoretical knowledge, methodological proficiency, cultural competency, and leadership skills essential to become effective agents for positive social change.

Krista Hoffmann-Longtin, PhD, is assistant professor of communication studies at Indiana University Purdue University, Indianapolis (IUPUI), and assistant dean for faculty affairs and professional development for the Indiana University School of Medicine. Her research focuses on faculty development, organizational/professional identity, and strategic communication in academic health settings. Using applied improvisational theater techniques, Krista works with faculty across the IU system to more effectively communicate their research to students and the lay public. She holds a BA in Telecommunications from Ball State University, an MA in Communication from Purdue University, and a PhD in Education Leadership and Policy Studies from Indiana University.

Lin Huff-Corzine, who holds the rank of full professor and serves her department as the undergraduate program director, earned her PhD in sociology at Washington University in St. Louis and her BA from the University of Nebraska, Lincoln, where she graduated Phi Beta Kappa with majors in sociology and women's studies. Prior to that, she earned a diploma in nursing from Blessing Hospital in Quincy, Illinois, and primarily worked in psychiatric nursing, which culminated in an appointment to head nurse of a 50-bed closed acute-care psychiatric unit in the St. Louis area. Lin's research focuses on violent crime, particularly mass murder and more recently human trafficking, but she also has papers on topics such as the effects of drug transportation routes on homicide and robbery, firearm lethality, risk factors associated with assaults on police officers, the spatial distribution of sexual assaults, and the impact of subcultural experiences on lethal violence rates. Professor Huff-Corzine coauthored *The Currents of Lethal Violence*, a monograph, and has published in numerous journals including, but not limited to, *Criminolo-*

gy, *Homicide Studies, Violence and Victims, Victims and Offenders,* the *Journal of Child Sexual Assault, Deviant Behavior, Justice Research and Policy,* and the *Journal of Contemporary Criminal Justice.*

Bobbi Knapp is currently associate professor in the Department of Kinesiology at Southern Illinois University with cross-appointments in sociology and women, gender and sexuality studies. Trained as a sport sociologist, Knapp was working as a lecturer at Northern Illinois University at the time of the shootings on February 14, 2008, the experience that was the impetus for her chapter. In addition to the construction of collective memory around tragedies, Knapp is also interested in the role that sport often takes in the aftermath of such events. Most of Knapp's presented and published work focuses on the ways in which ideal femininity and hegemonic masculinity are reinforced and resisted within different sporting environments. Her research on women's tackle football and CrossFit are some of the foundational pieces on those subjects in the field of sport sociology.

Malintzin is the pseudonym for a professor in the social sciences, working at a small liberal arts college in the American South.

Joe Michalski is a scientist teaching in the Department of Sociology at King's University College at the University of Western Ontario. He earned his PhD in 1993 in sociology from the University of Virginia, where he studied primarily under Murray Milner Jr. and Donald Black. Dr. Michalski then spent most of the 1990s at the University of Toronto engaged in program-evaluation research after helping launch the Centre for Applied Social Research. These days as a tenured professor, Dr. Michalski focuses his sociological energies primarily on the pursuit of *pure sociology*: the scientific study of social life without reference to individual psychology, motivations, or "human nature."

Carolyn Cummings Perrucci is professor and director of undergraduate studies in Sociology at Purdue University, where she has served as department head and has taught and conducted research in the areas of gender, work, and family. She has coauthored or coedited five books and over 60 book chapters and articles in the leading journals in sociology and related disciplines. Her coauthored book, *Plant Closings: International Contexts and Social Costs,* won the Outstanding Scholarly Achievement Award of the North Central Sociological Association (NCSA). She has served as elected vice president and president of the NCSA; elected vice president, member of the board of directors, and chair of the Division of Youth, Aging and the Life Course of the Society for the Study of Social Problems; and elected member of the governing council and chair of the section on sex and gender of the

American Sociological Association. She received the 2014 Distinguished Woman Scholar Award at Purdue.

Robert Perrucci is professor of sociology at Purdue University. His research has been funded by the National Science Foundation, National Institute of Mental Health, and the Alfred P. Sloan Foundation. He has authored/edited 19 books and has published over 90 book chapters and articles in leading journals in sociology in the areas of work and organizations, and inequality and political economy. He is a former editor of *The American Sociologist, Social Problems, and Contemporary Sociology* and has held elected positions as president of the Society for the Study of Social Problems and the North Central Sociological Association, and chair of the Organizations and Occupations section of the American Sociological Association.

Claire Procopio is associate professor in communication and the Elizabeth Weeks Jones Endowed Professor in the Humanities at Southeastern Louisiana University. She has over 20 years' experience in higher education teaching and administration, having served in various posts including accreditation steering committee director for her campus, undergraduate coordinator, major field assessment chairperson, and institutional effectiveness director. She currently teaches organizational communication and has won numerous teaching awards including Baton Rouge Community College's *Best of the Best* award. She is a past president of the Louisiana Communication Association and active in the National Communication Association serving on the Learning Outcomes in Communication taskforce in 2014 and 2015 and speaking to attendees of NCA's job fair on Interviewing with Insight in 2015. Her recent publications appear in *Communication Education* and *Academic Leadership.*

Melvin Rogers earned his master's degree in public administration/urban studies from the University of Nebraska, Omaha, and entered the corporate world where he served as the human resource supervisor with Rockwell Space Company and marketing in training specialist for Chrysler Corporation and worked in labor relations with Ford Motor Company. In 1996, Mr. Rogers joined the faculty at the University of Central Florida, where he served two years as the master's program and internship coordinator for the Department of Public Administration. In addition, Melvin was the faculty advisor for Phi Alpha Alpha. He was recognized for his outstanding teaching with the 1999 Excellence in Undergraduate Teaching Award. His professional memberships include the American Society of Public Administrators (ASPA) and the National Society of Personnel Administrators (NSPA). In addition, he has worked on behalf of the community by serving for four years on the City of Orlando-Human Relations Board.

Kristina Horn Sheeler (PhD Indiana University, 2000) is professor of communication studies and associate dean for academic programs in the Indiana University School of Liberal Arts at Indiana University-Purdue University Indianapolis (IUPUI). She teaches undergraduate and graduate courses in gender and political rhetoric and has taught in the Czech Republic, Poland, and Macedonia. Her research focuses on gender and political communication, studying the ways that political candidate identity is contested and constructed in popular media. Her most recent book, *Woman President: Confronting Postfeminist Political Culture* (2013) coauthored with Karrin Vasby Anderson, assesses the debilitating frames through which the 2008 candidacies of Hillary Clinton and Sarah Palin were presented to the public. *Woman President* won the Organization for the Study of Communication, Language, and Gender's 2014 Outstanding Book Award and the National Communication Association's 2014 Winans-Wichelns Memorial Award for Distinguished Scholarship in Rhetoric and Public Address.

Brian J. Smith is professor of sociology and internship coordinator in the Social & Criminal Justice program at Central Michigan University. His teaching and research interests include social inequalities and criminal justice, corrections, youth and education, and juvenile delinquency/justice. Prior to entering academia, he worked at a residential treatment center for emotionally disturbed youth and at a community corrections agency for adult parolees and probationers.

Deborah L. Smith is professor of teacher education at Saginaw Valley State University. She received an MDE improving teacher quality grant in 2009 and again in 2015. Her teaching is focused on literacy, where she draws upon her eight years of experience in the classroom as a middle-level language arts and high school English as a Second Language (ESL) teacher. Her research focuses on diversity and urban school turnover, disciplinary literacy, and improving teaching through best practice. Dr. Smith has had moments of distress and success in academia and hopes that the chapter on paperwork, meetings, and program review helps others to meet the challenge of teaching in the 21st century.

Cristina S. Stephens is an international faculty native of Romania. She earned her undergraduate degree from the Academy of Economic Studies, Bucharest, Romania, a graduate certificate in social policy from the University of Oxford, England, where she attended as a Soros-Chevening scholar, and a PhD in sociology from Georgia State University. Prior to joining Kennesaw State University in 2009, she worked as a research analyst for the American Cancer Society in Atlanta where she conducted research on the quality of life of cancer survivors. Her research interests lie in the areas of immigration, acculturation, multicultural health behavior and quality of life. She teaches a variety of sociology courses, but she particularly enjoys social theory courses where she has the chance to introduce sociology majors to her favorite social thinker, Alexis de Tocqueville. Dr. Stephens lives with her husband, her two elementary school children, and intransigently no pets, in Roswell, Georgia. During her free time, she enjoys a bit of gardening.

Mangala Subramaniam is associate professor in the Department of Sociology at Purdue University. Her research is in the broad areas of gender (and intersections with caste, race, and class) and social movements. She has recently authored/coauthored articles in journals such as *Contemporary Perspectives in Family Research, Current Sociology, International Sociology,* and *Research in Social Movements, Conflicts, and Change.* Her current research projects focus on violence against women and the law, gender and social impacts of institutional arrangements for improved seed technologies, and the role of community organizations for HIV prevention in India (https:// web.ics.purdue.edu/~msubrama). She has an interest in the sociology of knowledge as it relates to knowledge production and dissemination within the discipline. She has served as secretary/treasurer of the American Sociological Association's Sex & Gender section and has been elected treasurer (2016–2017) of Sociologists for Women in Society.

Helen Tate is associate vice president for academic affairs and professor of communication at Georgia Southwestern State University. She has 16 years' experience in higher education administration, serving as department chair and division head at Columbia College (South Carolina) before accepting her current position. Dr. Tate was recognized as a South Carolina Governor's Distinguished Professor and is the recipient of several teaching awards, including the Faculty Excellence and Students' Choice Awards. She earned her PhD in speech communication from Indiana University and her MA and BA in speech communication from Idaho State University. Her research focus is the rhetorical construction of feminist identity, but she spends most her time on student-support initiatives. She is active in the National Communication Association, serving as chair/program planner for the Women's Caucus, 2010. She was raised out west, but currently resides in the peaceful community of Americus, Georgia.

Alma L. Zaragoza-Petty was born and raised in Los Angeles, California. She is a first-generation high school and college graduate. Currently finishing up her doctoral work at UC Irvine in education policy and social contexts, she is a professional counselor who has worked with youth of color through college outreach efforts in urban high schools for over 10 years. She is a Eugen Cota-Robles and College Board Professional Fellow and was recently a Ford Foundation Dissertation Alternate. As part of her personal commitment to fostering equity, she has served as a mentor through various programs at her university. Current inequities in educational opportunities for low-income youth and youth of color continue to shape her academic research and professional commitments. She plans to continue her research as a professor upon completing her degree.

CPSIA information can be obtained at www.ICGtesting.com
Printed in the USA
BVOW08s1215140916

461704BV00018B/5/P